THE AUDACIOUS RACONTEUR

THE AUDACIOUS RACONTEUR

SOVEREIGNTY AND STORYTELLING IN COLONIAL INDIA

LEELA PRASAD

CORNELL UNIVERSITY PRESS

Ithaca and London

Publication of this open monograph was the result of Duke University's participation in TOME (Toward an Open Monograph Ecosystem), a collaboration of the Association of American Universities, the Association of University Presses, and the Association of Research Libraries. TOME aims to expand the reach of long-form humanities and social science scholarship including digital scholarship. Additionally, the program looks to ensure the sustainability of university press monograph publishing by supporting the highest quality scholarship and promoting a new ecology of scholarly publishing in which authors' institutions bear the publication costs. Funding from Duke University Libraries made it possible to open this publication to the world. Learn more at the TOME website, available at: openmonographs.org.

First published 2020 by Cornell University Press

Library of Congress Cataloging-in-Publication Data

Names: Prasad, Leela, author.
Title: The audacious raconteur : sovereignty and storytelling in colonial India / Leela Prasad.
Description: Ithaca [New York] : Cornell University Press, 2020. | Includes bibliographical references and index.
Identifiers: LCCN 2020005702 (print) | LCCN 2020005703 (ebook) | ISBN 9781501752278 (paperback) | ISBN 9781501752285 (pdf) | ISBN 9781501752292 (epub)
Subjects: LCSH: Literature and society—India—History—19th century. | Literature and society—India—History—20th century. | Storytelling—Political aspects—India. | Politics and literature—India—History—19th century. | Politics and literature—India—History—20th century. | Imperialism in literature. | India—Intellectual life—19th century. | India—Intellectual life—20th century.
Classification: LCC DS428. P73 2020 (print) | LCC DS428 (ebook) | DDC 809/.8954—dc23
LC record available at https://lccn.loc.gov/2020005702
LC ebook record available at https://lccn.loc.gov/2020005703

CONTENTS

MAPS

ACKNOWLEDGMENTS

There are now many overgrown trails along the twenty-five years of the meandering research for this book, which began when I was a graduate student at the University of Pennsylvania. I start by thanking the late Roger D. Abrahams, who insisted that I convert the term paper I wrote for his course into a book proposal. As will be apparent, I have many libraries and archives across continents to thank. In India, I thank the Tamil Nadu state archives, Connemara Public Library, the Theosophical Society, the Madras Literary Society, and the Roja Muthiah Library, all in Chennai; Sabarmati Ashram Library in Ahmedabad; State Central Library, City Central Library, and Osmania University's library in Hyderabad; and the Maharashtra State Archives in Pune. In the UK, my thanks to the University of Reading's Archive of British Publishing and Printing, the John Murray Archive (now held by the National Library of Scotland), the India Office Records at the British Library, University College London Archives and Special Collections, and the archives of the Royal Anthropological Society, the Folklore Society, and the Inner Temple. A very special thanks to the staff at the University of Witwatersrand Historical Papers Research Archive, Johannesburg, who scanned and sent overnight letters from Bartle Frere's family correspondence. My gratitude to Linda Purnell of Duke University's interlibrary loans department for her tireless efforts to procure rare copies of books from elusive holdings. I thank the following institutions for supporting my research through grants and awards: the American Academy of Religion, the American Philosophical Society, Duke University's Trinity College of Arts and Sciences, the Josiah Charles Trent Memorial Foundation, and the North Carolina Center for South Asian Studies.

Following up on nearly every personal name or location mentioned in the prefaces of the works of the scholars I discuss in this book, I visited many homes in India—often on false trails—in search of biographical details. Sometimes my searches took me to dilapidated or re-utilized former colonial buildings and sites. The chapters will evoke the ambience of these searches, the serendipities of my discoveries, and above all, the friendships with the families of three of the authors. I rediscovered Pandit S. M. Natesa Sastri through his grandson Gopalakrishnan, who translated Natesa Sastri's novel *Dinadayalu* for me. It was a translation that made me think, rather fundamentally, about how the semantics of translation stretches into the past, or at least into what the past offers to the present. Getting to know Mr. Gopalakrishnan over nearly twenty years brought with it the joy of spending time with his wife, Anandha, and their creative son Chandrachoodan, aka Chandru or Shyam. I thank Dr. Babu and Mr. Karan Kumar, who showed me the threads leading back to their great-grandfathers P. V. Ramaswami Raju and M. N. Venkataswami, respectively—and to the rich conversations with Mr. Sundaresan and Mr. Lakshman Rao that shape the understandings I propose in this book.

One of the greatest sources of pleasure and surprise was the help I received from friends old and new, who threw themselves into the enigmatic searches for biographical traces, out of curiosity, love of history, and indeed, in some cases, old ties. I recount the stories and outcomes of such collaborations in individual chapters but record my thanks here to Trevor Martin and Vincent Pinto in Pune, Harshawardhan Nimkhedkar in Nagpur, and (then) army major Ravi Choudhary in Hyderabad. I am indebted to the late Mr. S. Muthaiah, who published my queries to him in his columns in the national daily *The Hindu*; it is because of his gesture that my book stepped out of the archives into the living spaces of the families of Pandit Natesa Sastri and P. V. Ramaswami Raju. In the same vein, I offer my thanks to Narendra Luther, who published my query about M. N. Venkataswami in his column in the Hyderabad-based newspaper the *Deccan Chronicle*.

At Duke, Larissa Carneiro helped translate nineteenth-century burial records in Portuguese that I got from churches in Pune, and David Morgan pointed me to Victorian postmortem photography. To both of them, my deep thanks. My students Zaid Adhami, Yael Lazar, Seth Ligo, Alex McKinley, Sungjin Im, Mani Rao, and Yasmine Singh provided laughter, assistance, and ideas—and love in their inimitable ways. Carter Higgins, visiting fellow at Duke, helped me at the proverbial eleventh hour. For instilling confidence in my belief that Anna de Souza, whose life was virtually irretrievable outside of a colonial record, could still be known alternatively through a "sense reading" of her life, my gratitude to V. Narayana Rao. I am indebted to miriam cooke, Bruce Lawrence, Ebrahim Moosa, and Mani Rao for their thorough, brilliant, and timely comments on drafts. I thank Ebrahim especially for the liberty I could take in sounding out ideas and snatches of rough writing for immediate opinions; it is a rare privilege. I am grateful to Ann Grodzins Gold, Brian Hatcher, and Ajay Skaria for their transformative feedback on the entire manuscript. In Jim Lance at Cornell University Press,

I have the pleasure of an editor who "got it" from the get-go; to Jim and to his colleagues Amanda Heller, Clare Jones, and Mary Kate Murphy, my sincere thanks. Some of the research and ideas I articulate in chapter 2 of this book are derived in part from "Nameless in History: When the Imperial English Become the Subjects of Hindu Narrative," in *South Asian History and Culture* 8, no. 4 (2018): 448–60, © Taylor & Francis, available online: www. tandfonline/com/10.1080/19472498.2017.1371504.

While writing this book, I stumbled through a period of intense and sudden personal loss, and I am enormously grateful to friends who supported me beyond measure over that time: Maya Aripirala, Marc Brettler, miriam cooke, Joyce Flueckiger, Asma Khan, Ranjana Khanna, Jyotsna Kasturi, Sumana Kasturi, Bruce Lawrence, Uma Magal, Sangeetha Motkar, Ebrahim Moosa, Kirin Narayan, Aparna Rayaprol, Karin Shapiro, Deepshikha Singh, and Kena Wani.

The warm and steady support of my brother Chandramouli and my sisters-in-law Indira and Vijaya makes all my ventures possible, no less this one. To Shankar, my brother, who insightfully read every draft of every chapter, a reading that also understood, and hummed with, the loss of our father, a Shakespeare scholar and my best critic, "I can no other answer make but thanks, And thanks; and ever thanks." To Prasad, my husband, my tenth muse, "ten times more in worth than those old nine." Thank you, forever.

I completed this book because of the daily encouragement from my mother, Srimathi, a schoolteacher with an insatiable love for reading and a great skill with languages. She passed away when the book was about four pages short of being done. I had held a ticket to Hyderabad in my hands, and she had sent her suitcase over to my house in anticipation of my arrival. If this book breathes something of the imminent and the immanent, ascribe it to the same winter of 2018 in which I went on to lose another parental figure, my father-in-law, C. S. Rao, who was also awaiting the completion of this book.

I dedicate this book to my parents, Srimathi Nagarajan and S. Nagarajan, and to my daughters, Anandini and Akshayini.

THE AUDACIOUS RACONTEUR

Introduction
"That Acre of Ground"

Can a subject be sovereign in conditions of hegemony? Can forces of hegemony and empire suffocate creativity? This book is about "that acre of ground" over which empire could not have jurisdiction, that ground which cannot be taken from us, not even by the most empowered oppressor. The phrase is Caribbean writer George Lamming's, who uses it to evoke the location within him that remains ever generative through displacements.[1] I call on that phrase for the specific resonance it has with this book on the figure of the audacious raconteur in colonial India, a figure who not only flourished in colonial India but also can be found thriving in any time or place where there is systematized oppression or othering. In an interview with the anthropologist (and fellow West Indian) David Scott, Lamming elaborates on that acre of ground: "It is inexhaustible, and the one thing that one could not bear to lose and go on breathing would be that acre—that is to be held on to. And that is what I mean, too, when I say that no limitation of sovereignty in the political sense can alter that, because that acre is also itself a component of the imagination."[2]

The Backstory

In 1617 Thomas Roe, an emissary of King James 1 of England, stepped into the resplendent court of the Mughal emperor Jahangir in Delhi. He

1

had come to plead on behalf of a chartered joint-stock English company, the East India Company, for permission to trade. The Company had already been trading in India since 1611 out of the port town of Masulipatnam (now Machilipatnam) on the southeastern coast of India. On this coastline, known as the Coromandel Coast, which bustled with spice and textile markets, the English vied with French and Dutch traders. The Company had also been trading on the west coast of India out of Surat (in modern Gujarat). These settlements, however, were small; the British, fully aware of the potential of trading with India, wanted to expand their base. Roe knew, as did the English Parliament, that he had stepped into the court of the richest empire in the world; India at that time commanded about 25 percent of the world's GDP in contrast to Britain's 2 percent. Jahangir, for his part, saw an opportunity to curb Portuguese power on the western coast of his empire and so gave Roe his permission to set up trading posts in Surat and, shortly afterwards, in Hugli (in Bengal) on the eastern coast. The goods traded and the trading routes tell another sordid story. For instance, saltpeter used in gunpowder went to England; opium, which the Company grew in India, went east to China to pay for Chinese tea and porcelain.[3] Jahangir's permission changed India's destiny forever. As Mughal power began to wane in the late seventeenth century, the Company built up its own armies, at first with the declared intent to protect its warehouses ("factories"), and then to expand its zones of trade. By 1700 the Company had engaged in military conflict with the Mughal ruler and had established fortified settlements in the key ports of Madras, Calcutta, and Bombay. These settlements would later become capital cities of the "presidencies," the political zones of British India.

Over the next two centuries, the Company grew rapidly, often exploiting tensions between competing powers—the Mughals, the Marathas, the nawabs of Awadh and Bengal, and the French in India. The year 1764 was especially pivotal. In the battle of Buxar, Company officer Robert Clive defeated the combined forces of the weakened Mughals, and the Mughal emperor was forced to grant the Company the *diwani*, the right to collect tax from the provinces of Bengal, Bihar, and Orissa. The nawab of Bengal, who controlled these extraordinarily wealthy provinces, remained the administrative head, but the Company appointed itself his "revenue minister." Brazen looting, territorial expansion, and overseas deposits rather than local investment fueled the Company's growth. Rampant corruption raked in fortunes for the Company's officers, who became known as "nabobs"; from just the spoils of wars, Clive transferred hundreds of millions of pounds to the Company and himself made millions of pounds. Stories of the rapacity of Company officers reached the English public, and the Company's directors, in response to

MAP 1. India with presidencies, 1880
Source: Map by Bill Nelson. Based on information from G. U. Pope, *Text-book of Indian History* (London: W. H. Allen & Co., 1880).

public opinion, appointed in 1772 a "governor-general" who would oversee the governance of its Indian territories. The gleam of personal wealth was no less a reason for this shift in administration. This new system of governors-general and its official infrastructure sanctioned a rule of bloody conquest. Princely territories were ruthlessly annexed, draconian laws were drawn up, and India's wealth was steadily siphoned off. After the Indian Uprising of 1857–58, when the Company received its first jolt, direct "Crown rule" replaced Company rule. India became the most prized of Britain's colonies.[4]

Mapping India

Indeed, by the 1880s, the British had come to believe that their empire was at its summit. Most of India had been colonized and surveyed.[5] Beyond the northern rim of India, the sacred and ancient Himalayan peak Chomolungma, also known as Sagarmatha, had been measured and renamed Mount Everest after an Englishman.[6] Imperial and provincial gazetteers and census handbooks described and catalogued nearly every corner and community. Ancient Sanskrit and Pali texts were translated into English. Languages and laws were codified. Those who advocated for European knowledge as the best means to educate Indians triumphantly imagined that Indian universities and colleges had successfully produced a surplus of brown clerks, the cogs of the wheels of a colonial administration. The field of anthropology began to conceive itself as a "science" and a "discipline," and professional societies such as the Royal Anthropological Institute (1871) and the Folk-Lore Society (1878) now stamped as bona fide the collection and publication of knowledge about Indian culture.[7]

Despite all this mapping, renaming, and claiming, where in the cavernous hollow of empire could one find everyday India? This question became peculiarly urgent to the missions of the empire and the Church of England. It also created a lucrative marketplace for Indian exotica. Stories, songs, and proverbs recorded from the "lips of natives" promised to reveal a quotidian India different from the India of maps and ancient texts and political conquests. A pioneer in this quest was Mary Frere, daughter of the governor of Bombay Presidency, who asked her Indian ayah, Anna Liberata de Souza, to tell stories while they traveled together through south India. She sent the first few stories to her sister in England, her letters transmitting an India animated by princesses, cobras, jungles, and more. Recording more stories, she published *Old Deccan Days, or, Hindoo Fairy Legends Current in Southern India* in 1868, and enlivened the collection by including Anna's life story. "Will no one go to the diggings?" Frere asked, echoing an antiquarian interest.[8] Frere seems to have appealed to a motley group of British colonial administrators, their daughters and wives, and Christian missionaries, who began to publish "Indian folklore."[9]

And so there emerged, between 1865 and 1930, a staggering number of collections of Indian lore from presses in London, Calcutta, Bombay, and Madras (today Kolkata, Mumbai, and Chennai). But this world of fascinating stories is also haunted. It is haunted by the footnoted voices of barely acknowledged storytellers and assistants, by coercive collecting methods, by disparaging commentary, and by drastic alterations to texts.[10] Captain Richard C. Temple, for example, "induced" stories, to use his word, by heavily doping the bards who fill his three-volume *Legends of the Punjab*, while Flora Annie Steel called Indian narrators "wild beasts" who were prone to "stampede."[11] The story of a text called *Qanoon-e-Islam, or, Customs of the Moosulmans* illustrates how texts were distorted. As Sylvia Vatuk shows, this text was written in Hyderabad in the Deccan by a scholar and Unani physician, Ja'far

Sharif, at the behest of Gerhard Herklots, a British army surgeon. Originally published in 1832, Sharif's *Qanoon-e-Islam* was a descriptive account of the customs and practices of Muslims of the Deccan. Herklots translated and annotated Sharif's text for English audiences. In 1863, when Higginbothams of Madras republished it, it was massively generalized and called a standard text of "Indo-Mahomedan" practices. And in 1921 the administrator William Crooke completely altered the original and published it as *Islam in India*, a "new" text that was far removed from Sharif's *Qanoon-e-Islam*.[12]

Lines of transmission of stories within British publishing circuits resulted in heavily doctored texts. British authors borrowed Indian cultural material from one another through published and unpublished sources. The preface of W. H. D Rouse's volume *The Talking Thrush and Other Tales from India* (1922) tells us that the stories were part of a larger ethnological survey undertaken by Crooke in the (then) Northwest Provinces and Avadh:

> Some [stories] were recorded by the collector from the lips of the jungle-folk of Mirzapur; others by [Crooke's] native assistant, Pandit Ramgharib Chaube. Besides these, a large number were received from all parts of the Provinces in response to a circular issued by Mr. J. C. Nesfield, the Director of Public Instruction, to all teachers of village schools. . . . In the re-telling, for which Mr. Rouse is responsible, a number of changes have been made.[13]

Finally, the word "collection" itself was an open category that froze contemporary lived traditions into the tenets of ancient texts. Many "collectors" collated stories from well-known written corpuses without consulting living oral sources at all.[14] The missionary Charles E. Gover compiled and translated Tamil, Telugu, Kannada, and Malayalam songs from various textual sources (about which he is vague), calling his collection *The Folk-songs of Southern India* (1871). The orientalist Forster Arbuthnot, writing under the disingenuous pseudonym "Anaryan," compiled stories from a variety of Sanskrit collections, drawing mostly on the translations of other well-known orientalist scholars like William Jones, H. T. Colebrooke, Henry H. Wilson, and Max Muller. Extended extracts from Vatsyayana's Kama Sutra (second or third century CE) are seamlessly used in the introduction and the conclusion to illustrate the *contemporary* "social domestic economy of the Hindoos."[15]

My Search

About twenty-five years ago, I chanced upon Mary Frere's *Old Deccan Days* in a library in the American Midwest. Its many voices gripped me, enticing me to the field of colonial folklore collection and ethnography. The tracks in this field led me through libraries and archives and gravesites and abandoned buildings across India, England, and America. I sifted through thousands of pages of correspondence in publishers' archives, manuscripts of collections, minutes of professional societies, letters, photographs, and miscellaneous lists from colonial India and many standalone Indian publications. In the Folklore Society's archives in University College London, for instance, I read a manuscript titled "A Folktale of Kumaon" in the calligraphic handwriting of Pandit Bhagwan Das Sharma, who had written down the story when he stopped at a stage bungalow near the village of Bans in the foothills of the Himalayas.[16] In the University of Reading's publisher archives, I read the exasperated letters that Dwijendra Nath Neogi wrote to Macmillan protesting the miscalculation of royalties on his books *Sacred Tales of India* (1916) and *True Tales of Indian Life* (1917).[17] The faces and voices of Indian authorship began to intrigue me.

Of course, ethnography in colonial India was not just a British enterprise. It is true, as I have noted, that many Indians—bards, servants, clerks, *munshis* (interpreter or secretary), pandits, and general village folk—appear namelessly or facelessly as "old native storytellers" in the margins and footnotes of British-authored collections. But Indian scholars, writers, schoolteachers, and lawyers also published independent collections of stories, monographs on customs and traditions, and translations and adaptations of Sanskrit and regional literatures. Some Indian-authored collections ostensibly reflect little difference in tone and method from British-authored collections. For instance, the Reverend Lal Behari Day, in his *Folk-Tales of Bengal* (1883), says:

> After a great deal of search, I found my Gammer Grethel—though not half so old as the Frau Viehmännin of Hesse-Cassel—in the person of a Bengali Christian woman, who, when a little girl and living in her heathen home, had heard many stories from her old grandmother. She was a good story-teller, but her stock was not large; and after I had heard ten from her I had to look about for fresh sources. An old Brahman told me two stories; an old barber, three; an old servant of mine told me two; and the rest I heard from another old Brahman.[18]

Other collectors like Ganeshji Jethabhai, a lawyer from the peninsula of Kathiawar (in modern Gujarat), extracted and polished ninety-four stories from unspecified "local chronicles" and published this collection in Gujarati in 1885 for school use. He had the book translated into English in 1903 as *Indian Folklore*; the book promptly drew strong negative remarks from British reviewers for its "unscientific" methods.[19] Under the same title, Ram Satya

Mukharji, a government official in Tamluk (Bengal), published stories in 1904 that he remembered from his childhood.[20] Some other collectors had a literary bent. For instance, Shovona Devi, Rabindranath Tagore's niece, published twenty-eight stories in her collection *The Orient Pearls: Indian Folklore* (1915). These stories exude the aura of Tagore's short stories about Bengali rural life, but they also reflect Shovona Devi's upbringing in an upper-class English-educated Hindu household, which employed long-term domestic caretakers who told her stories.

But it is a different kind of Indian presence that I write about in this book. This remarkable presence, which has altogether escaped notice, is not of an Indian narrating stories in confined and controlled spaces, or of an Indian writing in conformity to European norms. On the contrary, the Indian figure I discovered is a zesty raconteur in the public square, full of life, audaciously challenging the ideological bulwark of colonialism. I use the word "raconteur" to recognize the art of narration that storytellers in colonial India consciously commanded. The "audacious raconteur" is also a riposte to the pejorative colonial construct of "old native storyteller." I argue that even the most hegemonic circumstances cannot suppress the "audacious raconteur," a skilled narrator who sometimes uses the idioms of the dominant to point to a narrative space that, while seeming to be entwined with the dominant, in fact remains sovereign and beyond subjugation.

The Raconteurs

Four raconteurs from southern India anchor the argument of this book: Anna Liberata de Souza, an ayah who narrated stories to the English daughter of the governor of Bombay; P. V. Ramaswami Raju, a London-trained, Madras-based Indian lawyer and literary scholar who published stories and plays in English, Tamil, and Sanskrit; M. N. Venkataswami, a librarian in the Muslim state of Hyderabad who wrote exclusively in English about his community's stories and traditions; and S. M. Natesa Sastri, an epigraphist employed by the British government of India, a prolific writer in many genres.

To begin with, the unexplored archive of these raconteurs tells us that their awareness of colonial history, English social etiquette, or Western narrative genres enables them to challenge concepts and conceits central to colonial rule and rhetoric—Western modernity, history, science, and native knowledge. At times they used the very language, genres, and Enlightenment paradigms of the West to re-present concepts of religion, culture, and history through their experiential understandings of those concepts.

To this extent we can say that the archive is ironic: it embraces norms of colonial knowledge production while modifying or flouting them. The English language itself becomes a tool for play and for protest, not insignificant considering that by the 1880s, English had become established in India as a powerful language of education, public discourse, societal class, and literary exposition. Here we might say is the reverse of the colonial mimicry that the literary critic Homi Bhabha posits. Bhabha argues that the colonizer and colonial discourse operate through a "metonymy of presence," by which the colonizer refigures the colonized as "almost the same but not white" or "almost but not quite." This almost-ness, however, reveals the ambivalence of colonial discourse because this discourse must concede that what is also present in colonial subjection is the "menace" posed by the colonized.[21] In relation to Bhabha's argument, the "not quite" space is the very space through which the raconteurs of this book demonstrate their sovereignty. Anglophonic terms and technologies camouflage a mastery over Indian ways of knowing, creating, remembering, and being; they take us past the menacing subject to the unsubjugable person—whose sovereignty over the territory of self, culture, and art is unassailable. I elaborate on this idea of sovereignty later in this introduction.

This archive of the raconteurs brings to mind James Scott's analysis of power-stratified interactions, in which the "hidden transcript" is "a critique of power spoken behind the back of the dominant" by the subordinated group.[22] Scott contrasts hidden transcripts with the "public transcript," the openly visible interaction between a dominating group and the subordinated one. In public transcripts, the speech and bodily gestures of the subordinated acquiesce to the discourse of power. Hidden transcripts are to be found off-stage in everyday performative arts such as jokes and rumors, gossip and gestures and stories that generally veil authorship and identification. Behind this veil, the subordinated individual drops acquiescence and replaces it with disobedient critique and perhaps even talk of rebellion. Brian Hatcher tells the story of how the nineteenth-century Bengali social reformer and scholar Ishvarchandra Vidyasagar responded to an English school principal who had put his feet on the desk while conversing with Vidyasagar. When the Englishman visited, Vidyasagar reciprocated with the same gesture by placing his shoe-clad feet on the desk. When reprimanded by a supervising Englishman, he feigned surprise. After all, he said, this was etiquette he had learned from the English themselves. This rejoinder, Hatcher points out, drawing on Scott, is "a kind of pantomime that enacts a form of insubordination."[23]

The raconteurs in this book, however, do not rely on "hidden transcripts." Their voices are bold and articulate. They speak in public and quasi-public spaces—in mainstream publications, governors' mansions, and public service commission hearings. And they field the risks and pay the price of offending an aggressive regime. In these overt settings, they critique the grand claims of colonial policy, interrogate imperial self-aggrandizements, overturn reigning scholarly methods, and refuse denigrating constructs of culture and person. Life would have been far better without colonialism. This outspokenness is achieved through a rambunctious creativity that challenges the fictions of the empire. Lamming understands the nuanced dialectic between the so-called public and the private:

> That is when you come to public affairs, about how decisions are going to be made, according to the constraints of resources, constraints of resources which are in conflict with unlimited expectations or the expressions of a limited expectation brought about by the uncritical and sometimes irresponsible promises made by people who are shaping the society, you realize that there is a limited sovereignty there, but a limited sovereignty acknowledged in the public domain does not necessarily demand a limited sovereignty in the power of the self to perceive why you have to limit that sovereignty. In other words, there is a sovereignty that remains intact in spite of the limitations which you must concede about another kind of sovereignty in the public domain. This is an unending process of thinking of how one has always to rework the ways in which one claims and exercises the power and the authority of an individual and subjective perspective.[24]

The genius of the raconteur's creativity is that it performs a critique of power without the raconteur declaring an intent to be audacious. Our reading strategies, grounded in their narrations, however, help us discern their audacity. This book begins with the story of Anna Liberata de Souza, the narrator of the stories in Mary Frere's Old Deccan Days (1868). Anna's life story is known only through "The Narrator's Narrative," which Frere provides in the highly successful book. I was forced to revisit my earlier favorable interpretation of this book after I stumbled on an extraordinary passage in a colonial memoir by an English botanist who described Anna's pitiful economic state a decade after Old Deccan Days had been published. I adapt Michael Polanyi's theory of meaning-making and rely on intuition and cultural commonality to engage in a "sense reading" of the very same manuscript materials. Sensing Anna, I find she was subaltern only in her economic situation. In voice and in spirit, she was creative and bold: she conveyed to Mary, the daughter of the powerful governor of Bombay Presidency, how she believed the British had failed in India—in education, in economics, and in understanding India's vibrant oral culture. In fact, it emerges that Anna de Souza was a prescient critic of the modernity promised by colonialism. A sense reading also holds up the bleak reality that colonial anthropology, with its pretensions to contextualization, ignored the personhood of storytellers. Was "culture," the ostensible raison d'être of colonial anthropology, itself constructed from a fundamental absence of the living person who animates it? A sense reading of Frere's manuscript suggests that the answer is yes.

The Madras-based lawyer P. V. Ramaswami Raju (1852–1897), the second raconteur in this book, challenged the view of the English that India lacked historical consciousness. Coming from a Telugu-speaking family of a land-owning caste, he trained as a barrister in London and taught Telugu and Tamil at University College London. A prolific writer, he published plays, essays on religious subjects, fables in English, and social drama and comedies in Tamil and Telugu. For empire-conscious Victorian audiences, Ramaswami Raju's plays seem to offer classic oriental settings with quasi-historical British and Indian characters and plots. Yet, in a masterly way, through wit and irony, these plays construct characterizations that deflate imperial personae and conceits, as exemplified by his 1876 play *Lord Likely*. Across his writings, we see Ramaswami Raju using what I describe as a double register, a literary strategy that enables him to speak simultaneously in two voices across cultures and sometimes languages, producing meanings that ripple in counter-flowing directions. His dramatic poem in Sanskrit, *Srimat Rajangala Mahodyanam*, a fictional account of the "rise of the English race and its empire," deftly contains the history of the English within a Hindu cosmos and telos where the progenitor of the English falls from the heaven of Indra, the Hindu king of gods, to his ruin. This artistic move effectively punctures the grandiose idea of "English history," showing it as valued only by British imperial historians.

If the notion of English history falls apart through Ramaswami Raju's writings, the imperial bastion of the scientific method is challenged in the writings of M. N. Venkataswami (1865–1931), who came from the Telugu-speaking caste of Medaras (bamboo weavers) who had settled in Nagpur in central India. Fascinated by an autographed copy of Venkataswami's biography of his father, which I chanced upon in a used book store in London, I procured the lone extant copies of his other writings, all self-published, from various libraries. Reading these self-published books, I realized that I was in the presence of a writer who adopted the scientific method endorsed by colonial anthropology and folklore, but in every way possible he went against its sacrosanct ideal of objectivity. Nineteenth-century Europe, as we know well today, embraced the idea that truth could be secured through

the scientific method, a method based on experiment, evidence, and classi-
fication. The method flourished in overseas anthropology, where it abetted
racist theories of civilizational progress and the violence that accompanied
the implementation of these theories. And so the colonial anthropology
of stories was more like the archaeology of living communities than like
rigorous science. It was in his writings, all of which were in English, that
Venkataswami exuberantly restored the "subject" to the science of anthropology. Undeterred by his class, caste, and race, he titled many of his books
after members of his family; he used new photographic technology to alter
family photographs and to provide startling illustrations for his fairy stories;
and he used oral stories to counter the so-called objective accounts of imperial historians. I trace how Venkataswami vivifies the human subject in *The
Story of Bobbili* and in his biography of his father, *Life of M. Nagloo*. He pow-
erfully asserts—through techniques that I collectively term the "subjective
lens"—that at the heart of anthropology and history is not some rarefied
notion of objectivity but prismatic subjective truths that come from everyday experience.

Without the "native scholar," the shelves of oriental and folklore scholarship would have been empty, and colonial governance would not have com-
prehended Indian texts and practices. Colonial discourse regarded the native
scholar, not unlike the native storyteller, as a repository of vernacular knowledge adept in indigenous languages (and sometimes an accomplished translator), with access to esoteric materials and communities. But this discourse
did not recognize the native scholar as a sophisticated analyst. Analysis was,
by and large, assumed to be the prerogative of the European patron. This
subordinated perception in the discourse limited the salary and professional
recognition for native scholars employed in the colonial government. For
these scholars, government employment also meant obeying service rules
and not criticizing the colonial government or its officials. Yet the astounding
range of writings of the government-employed Tamil Brahman scholar Pandit S.
M. Natesa Sastri (1859–1906), who was hailed as a native scholar, shows that
despite all the attempts of the colonial government to subordinate Indian
scholars, it could never rein in their creative selves. I show that Natesa Sastri's
facets as a prolific epigraphist, folklorist, and novelist make him a kaleidoscopic
author who could contest political power through the power of his imagination.
When we see how Adeline Georgiana Kingscote, a racist penny novelist (who
had lived in India as the wife of a British colonel), plagiarized and published
Natesa Sastri's stories and then gratuitously named him a mere co-collector,
the veil of collaboration falls. The irony of the construct of "native scholar"
is exposed. But kaleidoscopic authorship offers more than a critique of the

idea of "native scholar"; it also allows us to see how justice can be achieved through narrative. Natesa Sastri's outspoken criticism of discrimination in colonial service resulted in his being denied deserved promotions and salaries commensurate with his experience and erudition. He sets right this wrong in his autobiographical novel *Dinadayalu*, which illustrates the poetics of Indian storytelling entangled in empire. The play of self across Natesa Sastri's writings—his vivid descriptions, remembrances, interpretations, and insider critiques—dismantles imperial exclusiveness in the arts of recollection and record.

Sovereignty

Audacious narration indicates and generates sovereign spaces. The sovereignty of raconteurs, however, is not the Hobbesian sovereignty that measures the state's exercise of absolute territorial authority over a body politic. Nor is it the same as the concept that Michel Foucault and Giorgio Agamben discuss. State sovereignty, Foucault argues, expresses itself in the surveillance and bio-discipline of human bodies. Agamben's sovereign state can be brutal. It carves out a "state of exception"; it transgresses, even transcends law and determines who has the right to possess rights.[25] The state structures that these thinkers critique are driven by a conceptualization that likens the sovereign to an omnipotent (Christian) god and the state to an unassailable panoptic authority. In the contexts of both precolonial and colonial India, such a view already runs into problems. Numerous studies of land and rulership in precolonial South Asia show that grammars of sovereignty were textured and context sensitive. Sometimes sovereignty was shared or brokered among many unequal centers of power around a major ruler, sometimes multiple rulers: in the late sixteenth and seventeenth centuries, the kings of Vijayanagara shared political power with a large number of local chiefs and administrative power with merchants who collected taxes on their behalf.[26] When the thirteenth-century king of the Kakatiya kingdom (today in Telangana) presented ritual insignia to a powerful subordinate to "share the substance of his sovereignty,"[27] he was engaging in the customary practice of displaying and distributing sovereignty through ritual and aesthetic idioms. In early Hindu political theology, sovereignty is shared by deities and rulers: if the deity was the timeless sovereign, the ruler was the temporal potentate. In other political theologies, deified sovereignty comes from the deity's fluid power to bless on the one hand and to harm on the other, creating relations of power that vary across thresholds of life.[28] Then there are monasteries, themselves empowered by landholdings and shastric knowledge, which often mediate divine and human power relations and transactions. In Sufi imagination, sovereignty is explored as a power that flows between the Almighty, the beloved, and the exalted saint, a dynamic that allows for the teasing out of human predicaments and for the fashioning of the self.[29] The oral traditions of the Meo Muslim community from Rajasthan record perspectives that counter centuries of oppressive regimes and state-sanctioned histories that portray the Meo as criminals. Through epics and ballads in the Mewati language, Meos create and claim a cultural sovereignty for themselves that sustains their ethnic identity and inspires their resistance to hegemonic power.[30] Thus India, indeed all of South Asia, was always a field of multiple, linked, competing, and fragmented political and ritual sovereignties.

The nineteenth century spawned a new complexity in imaginings of sovereignty as the colonial government began to propagate the idea of the British monarch as a benevolent supreme ruler for the colony. The idea could not hold on to its monolithic grandiosity. Milinda Banerjee shows how in Bengal and in the princely states of Cooch Behar and Tripura, hybrid sovereign figures emerged in response to the colonial assumption of absolute power. These figures, who ranged from princely elites and Hindu and Muslim nationalists to martial peasants, drew on models of "divine, human, and messianic kingship" available in European, Christian, Indic, and Islamic registers to assert countervailing power and authority.[31] Banerjee's work reinforces the point that European models of sovereignty, with their own political and symbolic machinery, could never be merely replicated or sustained in the colonial state. Nor were these models invariably considered desirable. The goal of the Gandhian *satyagrahi* (the truth-striving warrior), as Ajay Skaria shows, is to "refuse both subordination to and exercise of sovereign power," a sovereign power that is organized on the Enlightenment principle of autonomy.[32] Aided by other means, the colonial state made a directed effort to claim and consolidate sovereignty over India after the shocks of the 1857–58 Uprising. It began to map and measure land, native bodies, and customs and practices, and in so doing become an empire of knowledge—what Nicholas Dirks calls an "ethnographic state."[33]

Yet audacious narrations command an epistemic sovereignty, which shows that the "ethnographic state" could not become sovereign. If part of the empire's claim to power lies in its pretense to omniscience, audacious raconteurs—who own and control indigenous narrative space—challenge this power, even revoke it. Their narrations index spaces that the colonizer is unable to usurp. The raconteurs demonstrate that colonial knowledge about India was hollow because it tried to erase what could not be erased: an ethos of oral culture, ties of kinship, and varieties of past-consciousness; in short, the everydayness of everyday life. Their sovereignty does not arise from a Kantian moral autonomy that is propelled by a free and rational will and by self-legislation.[34] It comes instead from the sharing of an ethical space of being and belonging. In the midst of everyday life and its relationships, accountable to love and other emotions, guided by this—and otherworldly beings like gods and fairies—audacious raconteurs are *symbiotically sovereign*. As we remember with Lamming "that acre of ground," the notion of an atomistic Kantian sovereignty itself stands questioned.

The web of interconnections is contextual and particular to each raconteur. Anna Liberata de Souza's epistemic sovereignty derives from her clarity about what mattered to her (her children, her parents, her grandmother, her oral stories)—and what mattered was something that the modernity of colonialism could not give or take away. Ramaswami Raju's lotus-like sovereignty stems from a faith—in Hindu spirituality and, more important, in transnational human values—that allows him to stand outside the colonial episteme and critique it. M. N. Venkataswami's subjective lens displays a sovereignty of stance which insists that relationships, not vacant objectivity, make history, stories and songs, and even business tangible. Finally, Natesa Sastri's kaleidoscopic authorial self, which makes him sovereign in colonial disciplines, is inspired, and complicated, by his loyalty to his family, and by his passion for Tamil landscapes of history and culture. These symbiotic connections and callings make sovereignty, as Banerjee puts it, "something which everyone can aspire for."[35]

Ethnographic Turns

The figure of the audacious raconteur does not merely hover in an archive. It suffuses everyday life. This book, which began in a geographically scattered colonial-era archive, took a serendipitous ethnographic turn that brought me back to contemporary India. Never have I conducted ethnographic research that was this tantalizing. Deliberate searches, a haphazard pursuit of gut feelings and stray leads, fortuitous meetings with total strangers who shared an interest in the colonial past are all part of the research for this book. Through shoe leather and sheer luck, I discovered, over years, the families of Ramaswami Raju and Natesa Sastri in Chennai and M. N. Venkataswami in Hyderabad. Most families did not have copies of all the books written by their author ancestors. As I began to interact with these families, writings from a hundred years ago came alive in fresh ways for the families and for me. I learned how the autobiographical overtones in Natesa Sastri's novel resonated in his grandson's life, how Ramaswami Raju's dramatic poem was inspired by his mystical experience, and how Venkataswami's mother, long dead, is even today a living presence that appears to help the family in times of need.

As I recount in the pages of this book the journey of my search for living families and material traces, a meta-commentary on ethnography as a form of narrative ethics unfolds, and unfolds in a different manner with each raconteur. Narrative ethics holds that ethical deliberation is a narrative endeavor, one that allows us to explore human predicaments through reflection, recollection, and retelling. Linguistically and culturally mediated and conditioned, interwoven with material things, narrative always expresses a relation to something larger than itself. Some themes especially illustrate the "narrative ethics" in this book. First, although I most explicitly develop a "sense reading" of Anna Liberata de Souza in order to discover the terms on which she may have understood herself and negotiated the colonial world she lived in, sense reading informs my interpretation of *all* the raconteurs in this book. Indeed, as research encounters gaps and silences or ambivalences, the hypothetical or the intuitive assumes greater ethical significance in one's method; the turn to "sensing" possible readings is inevitable and calls for an acknowledgment of limitations, chance, and failure in the research process. Second, when research occurs over a long stretch of time, as it did for this book, one sees things differently, hears new inflections, and asks fresh questions. This book narrates the arc of this change. Third, drawn as I have been into the narrative worlds of "my" raconteurs, I agree with Adam Newton, who observes that "one faces a text as one might face a person, having to confront the claims raised by that very immediacy, immediacy of contact, not of meaning."[36] Working between the vivacious voices of an archive and the aspirations of living persons, however, I have had to ask: What would a face-to-face connection really mean in this context where texts intersect with lives? What exchanges invisibly occur as descendants and I co-construct stories of their ancestors, some privy to them, some privy to me? As I reconnected with the physical sites in Pune where I had grown up, Anna de Souza's story started to acquire a material immediacy in my own imagination, and I began to understand the palpable ways in which everyday artifacts and acts triggered self-recognition in descendants. The archive that I had constructed itself became a living, enduring presence, a presence that leads me to believe that the audacious raconteur is a necessary ethical and artistic figure in human experience.

Chapter 1

The Ruse of Colonial Modernity

Anna Liberata de Souza

I was sure that Gandhiji's ghost was stirring the overturned steel cup under our fingers. It had arrived in the Ouija board that my older brother, a friend, and I, the youngest, had made. We knew it back then as "planchette," the newest occult rage among children living on the university campus in Ganeshkhind in Poona (Pune). Our collective age no more than thirty, we sat hushed and excited while Gandhiji, summoned by me, jerkily moved across the board answering our questions, choosing between yes, no, maybe, or enigmatic silence. The summer heat had raised our anxiety about forthcoming results on recent exams, and evidently only Gandhiji could tell us the truth, even if it was in Marathi, a language he had not known in his lifetime.

Every raspy movement of the cup, manipulated by our fingers, echoed in the stable whose mud floors were caked and cracked. The stables, several of them, were among the derelict outbuildings of the large estate attached to the bungalow we lived in. It had once been the palatial home of a British officer. Such lime-washed bungalows, complete with stables, servants' quarters, storehouses, and landscaped garden spaces, speckled the campus of the University of Poona (now called Savitribai Phule Pune University), which had once been the site of the bloody battle of Khadki in 1817 between the Marathas and the colonial British. These houses had been converted into faculty and administrative staff quarters, often too large for their modern, modest occupants. Each bungalow had a tiny kitchen and a tinier storeroom that were dark and airless. These unventilated rooms were originally intended for the Indian cook and the ayah of the colonial British household; domestic manuals of the time warned a novice English wife in India, "The kitchen is a black hole, the pantry a sink."[1]

The Ghosts of Ganeshkhind

On this campus, in such a bungalow, my childhood unfolded in the 1970s. The abundant giant trees—pipal and banyan, neem and tamarind—and the abandoned outbuildings created an ideal setting for a rich supply of stories and encounters with ghosts and their doings. So we needed no persuasion to believe that swirling inside the overturned glass, predicting that we would all pass our exams, was Gandhiji's spirit.

The colonial past lived here. The aged trees and structures all seemed to exhale 150 years of irreconcilable history. Half a kilometer away from my home was a low-lying rambling park with scattered old graves and stone benches, all under a canopy of trees, flanked by well-maintained tar roads. I had heard from a trustworthy source that here, a British memsahib dressed in white had fallen off her horse and died. Her white ghost roamed the grounds each night, looking for her saddle and hat. In later years I recalled this specter as symbolic of the empress perennially searching for her lost throne and crown. I have often wondered if ghost stories about colonial India were a masterly way for formerly colonized people to assert justice, poetic and otherwise.

Another few hundred feet away, beyond a small hill, was a majestic Italian-Gothic building with Romanesque arches and a central tower surrounded by lavish well-maintained lawns. I knew this structure as "Main Building," home of the administrative offices of the University of Poona. In the evenings, after the offices closed for the day and watchmen became more lenient, the lawns were taken over by scampering children and cooing lovers. Long after the secret summonings of spirits in my childhood, I was to discover another presence in Main Building whose elusive truth would haunt me for decades. This presence was of an Indian ayah who had told vivid stories in the living quarters of Main Building when it was a stately residence one hundred years before I played on those lawns.

This haunting began in earnest in 1989, when Main Building suddenly reappeared before me in the American Midwest. In a less frequented aisle of a university library, I had just picked up a yellowing copy of a book, attracted by its maroon cover, which bore a thumb-sized image of a golden Ganesha

FIGURE 1. Main Building, University of Poona (Savitribai Phule Pune University). Photograph by Akshayini Leela-Prasad, February 2020.

FIGURE 2. Government House, Poona, circa 1875. Unknown photographer.

who was wearing a British crown. As I leafed through the first pages of *Old Deccan Days; or, Hindoo Fairy Legends, Current in Southern India*, published in 1868, I was startled to see a hand-drawn picture that looked like Main Building, captioned "Government House." At the bottom of the page, a line read, "Anna Liberata de Souza died at Government House, Gunish Khind, near Poona, after a short illness, on 14th August, 1887." Although the line itself referred to Government House in Poona, the picture depicted Government House in Parel, Bombay. Main Building, I soon learned, had at one time been called Government House, its construction commissioned in 1864 by Bartle Frere, the governor of Bombay from 1862 to 1867. British governors of the Bombay Presidency made Government House in Poona their monsoon residence from 1866, spending the rest of the year in Government House in Parel, Bombay (Mumbai).[2]

Anna Liberata de Souza: The First Sighting

Government House in Ganeshkhind is also where Anna Liberata de Souza, the subject of this chapter, lived and worked for eighteen months from 1865 to 1867 as an ayah to Mary Eliza Isabella Frere, Bartle Frere's daughter. In the winter of 1865, when Mary accompanied her father, the governor, on an official journey through the Deccan, she recorded the stories of *Old Deccan Days* from Anna.

As I stood in the library, captivated by the book, I quickly turned the pages and saw a pencil sketch of Anna. On the next page was Anna's autobiographical narrative, titled "The Narrator's Narrative." A first reading tells us this story: Two generations before her, Anna's family had been Lingayats, members of a Hindu sect that worships the deity Shiva. Her grandfather had moved from Calicut to Goa, at that time a Portuguese territory, where he had converted to Christianity, and consequently become ostracized by his family. Like many Goan Christians, Anna's grandfather and father had served in the British army; her grandfather had been a *havildar* (sergeant) and her father a tent lascar,[3] and both had won medals in the battle of Khadki in 1817. At some point the family had settled in Poona. After a childhood that lacked nothing, Anna's destiny changed when she was married at twelve and widowed at twenty. With two children to raise, she became an ayah to British families. Already fluent in Marathi, Malayalam, Portuguese, and Konkani, Anna quickly learned to speak, read, and write in English. A year before Anna narrated the stories, her only son drowned in a river accident in Poona. Anna's narration ends on a philosophical note about the turns in her life.

As I browsed through the stories in the book, I remember being struck by the (curiously transliterated) phrase "mera baap re" (my dear father) and the name "Guzra Bai" (garland lady). I imagined how Anna might have told the stories at least partly in Marathi, the language of my childhood; the book inspired my MA thesis. The storied landscapes of nineteenth-century India continued to fascinate me.[4] Ten years after I had first seen the book, the spell of *Old Deccan Days* returned. It took me to the British Library in London, where in the Oriental and India Office Collection (OIOC) I found the hand-written manuscript of *Old Deccan Days* and some correspondence between Mary Frere, various other individuals, and John Murray, the publisher.[5] At the John Murray Archive (then held in London but now at the National Library of Scotland in Edinburgh), I found a trove of decades-long correspondence between the Frere family and Murray. Thus began my efforts to unfold the map of the making of *Old Deccan Days*.

Old Deccan Days: The Shaping of the Book and Its Voices

In early March 1867, after thirty-three years in India, Bartle Frere returned to England for good with his wife and their two older daughters, Mary and Catherine. He had become quite a favorite of Britain's royalty and Parliament. Mary brought with her a nearly completed manuscript built on Anna Liberata de Souza's stories. And Anna's oral stories, which she had heard from her mother and her grandmother, traveled across the Arabian Sea, curved around the Cape of Good Hope, sailed up the Atlantic, and came to be fitted to a new life as a book commercially published on London's Albemarle Street.

About seven months after they had arrived in London, Bartle Frere seems to have written to the publisher John Murray with a query about publishing his daughter's manuscript. In a letter dated October 15, 1867, Murray accepted, adding a word of caution about tempering expectations, as the market was flooded with books for children. Three days later Bartle Frere indicated that his daughter would accept, with pleasure, Murray's "very handsome offer to publish the Indian fairy tales at [Murray's] cost and risque [*sic*], on condition of giving her half [the] profits in the event of its succeeding."[6] The letter puts on display right away the entrepreneurial spirit and creative talent of the Freres: "As regards illustrations, I think my daughter would prefer its coming out at first without profusion of them—which might make it more a picture than a story book. But if it ever reached a 2nd edition, she and her sister Katie would be able to furnish many illustrations of scenery and figures such as you describe." And so a partnership of the prominent was sealed. Frere's political stock was high, and he carried a reputation as a formidable statesman of the British colonial government. The John Murray publishing house had been in the business for a century. It had published authors of the stature of Charles Darwin, Jane Austen, Henry James Coleridge, David Livingstone, and Lord Byron and produced the trademark John Murray handbooks and travel guides, much used by travelers to Britain's colonies.

This collection of Anna's stories debuted in 1868 in London. Subsequent editions came out in 1870, 1881, and 1889, and the fourth edition was reprinted in 1898.[7] The third edition (1881) settled on a structure that gave the book its permanent identity. This edition begins with a "Preface" that Mary Frere wrote when she was thirty-six years old. She recounts the circumstances in which Anna narrated the stories and describes the manner in which she had recorded them. The next is Bartle Frere's "Introduction," where he tries to elaborate authoritatively on Hindu beliefs and practices supposedly underlying Anna's stories for an English audience. The elaboration relies on his personal experiences in the Maratha country and his knowledge of European ethnology. Then comes "The Collector's Apology" by Mary Frere, containing her guarded defense of the stories against perceptions of Indian character. In addition, she provides a brief statement on transcription and orthography.

But the tour de force is "The Narrator's Narrative." It is Anna de Souza's life story, which Mary assures the reader "is related as much as possible in [Anna's] own words of expressive but broken English."[8] Mary compiled and edited this story from conversations with Anna over the eighteen months that Anna worked for the Freres. Anna's twenty-four stories follow immediately after. The literary English of the stories, ironically, has nothing in common with the curated "broken English" of "The Narrator's Narrative" that has just preceded them. The irony may be explained by the manner in which the stories were transcribed: as Mary heard each story, she took notes, then she wrote up the story and read it back to Anna to check that she had "correctly given every detail."[9] So we may with some certainty, then, say that the diction of the twenty-four stories is Mary's/European and the characters and the plots are mostly Anna's. "The Narrator's Narrative" presumably provides just that touch of colloquial flavor, while the stories, with Anna's presence dissolved, satiate the narrative tastes of Victorian audiences.[10] In all this, it is critical we remember that Anna's "broken English" is in fact an accomplished act of translation. If Anna has narrated these stories in English, it means that she has translated a cultural world into an alien language system and renegotiated her cultural fluency for Mary's benefit.

The book concludes with "Notes" and a "Glossary" (from the second edi-tion onward). In two longish notes in the section under "Notes on the Nar-rator's Narrative," Bartle Frere raves about the heroism of British troops in the battle of Khadki ("Kirkee") and defends the economic policy of his government, respectively. Mary's single note provides a translated text of two of Anna's songs. Finally, the "Notes on the Fairy Legends" are glosses—sanctimonious micro-sociologies—by Bartle Frere on six of the stories and by Mary Frere on one story. Twenty Indian words form the glossary that closes the book. Five full-page hand-drawn illustrations, one of which is a portrait of Anna Liberata de Souza, are interspersed. This was the polished book I had chanced upon in the library.[11]

Reinterpreting Anna through Sense Reading

Earlier writing on *Old Deccan Days*, mine included, came to the conclusion that it was a pioneering effort in ethnography: it presented a play of multiple voices in a fascinating heteroglossia; Mary Frere displayed a rare empathy for the depictions in the stories; and above all, the collection contextualized Anna the narrator with an autobiographical narration.[12] There were also some ironies in the book. Fellow anthropologist Kirin Narayan and I both noted that while Anna had "space" in the collection, it was not clear that the financial success of *Old Deccan Days* had improved her life. While she had a "voice" in the collection, it was severely mediated by both Freres, father and daughter. Despite these ironies, I admired the collection for its rarity as a new genre, and lamented that its methodology had not been emulated by even one of the dozens of collections of oral narrative that succeeded it in colonial India.

But the story I tell in this chapter takes a different turn. In 2016 I stumbled across a passage in a nineteenth-century memoir that changed my percep-tion of both Mary Frere and *Old Deccan Days*. The memoir by Marianne North, a British woman traveler and botanical painter, described her expe-riences in India and Sri Lanka. North tells us that in 1878, ten years after *Old Deccan Days* was published, she ran into Anna in one of the bungalows of Government House, Bombay. Anna was then working for the family of Richard Temple, the governor of Bombay. Here is how she describes Anna:

> The old ayah Miss Bartle Frere has made famous as the story-teller in her *Tales of Old Deccan Days* [sic] sat on the doorstep. People there said, the old lady was quite guiltless of any of the stories imputed to her; that the only thing she was famed for was idleness and a habit of

getting drunk on Sundays, when she said: "I Christian woman; I go to church." But Sir Richard Temple promised the Freres to keep her, and he did. I liked the old lady, as she never worried me by putting things tidy, but sat picturesquely on the door-step and told me of the wonderful things she had seen. She tried to persuade me to take her on my next travels with me: a female John! bottle and all![13]

At this time, *Old Deccan Days* was in its second edition and continued to be a runaway success in England, but its financial success had clearly not reached Anna. North's denigrating remarks about Anna jolted me. Had I, in my earlier engagement with *Old Deccan Days*, been overly impressed by the apparent authorial generosity of the book? The autobiographical "Narrator's Narrative" had seemed singularly refreshing against the dehumanizing representations of Indians rife in colonial documentation. Had I unwittingly seen Anna Liberata de Souza through the eyes of a reading practice that is unaccustomed to admitting people like her as anything other than subaltern? Even if such a reading practice were to recognize Anna as a *speaking* subaltern subject, it would still allow us to see her only as an especially articulate servant whose life story provides nothing more than a rich social context for the audiences who read the stories she told.

Two questions surfaced. First, did Anna mean anything more to Mary than an old storytelling ayah, a source of unmined Indian lore? It is unquestionable that Mary was enthralled by Anna's stories—even writing to her from England for clarifications on names and seeking details on the Calicut song—and felt that the stories pushed back against prevailing negative images of India in England.[14] She writes:

> It is remarkable that in the romances of a country where women are generally supposed by us to be regarded as mere slaves or intriguers, their influence (albeit most frequently put to proof behind the scenes) should be made to appear so great, and, as a rule, exerted wholly for good; and that in a land where despotism has held such a firm hold on the hearts of the people, the liberties of the subject should be so boldly asserted as by the Milkwoman to the Rajah in little Surya Bai . . . or to meet with such stories as the Valiant Chattee-Maker, and "The Blind Man, the Deaf Man, and the Donkey," among a nation which it has been constantly asserted, possesses no humour, no sense of the ridiculous, and cannot understand a joke.[15]

At the same time that Mary admired the stories, there is a tint of condescension in her tone. Mary says that she (or Bartle Frere) has provided expla-

nations for things in the stories that could be rationally explained, but for
things that are beyond rational explanation, Anna is "the sole authority." But
when Anna translates "Seventee Bai" as "Daisy Lady" (to help Mary understand
shevanti, chrysanthemum, in the language Mary knows best), Mary comments
that no botanist "would acknowledge the plant under that name," and when
Anna describes a place called "Agra Brum" as the "City of Akbar," Mary opines,
"No such province appears in any ordinary Gazetteer."[16] (Anna must have meant
Agra Bhum, the land [*bhumi*] of Agra, where Akbar's tomb lies.) But neither in
the archives nor in the book do we see signs of a sustained relationship that
could rescue an instrumentality of purpose. Nor do we find Mary expressing
toward Anna the coeval ethics that makes fellow beings *fellow* beings.

The second question was provoked by Anna's disquiet. Mary, anxious that
stories such as Anna's would be lost if they were not written down, appeals,
"Will no one go to the diggings?"[17] But Anna has a different view on the problem of the disappearance of stories and storytelling. To her, writing down
oral stories is hardly the solution, for it destroys the integrity of the stories
and ruins the aesthetic experience altogether:

> It is true there are books with some stories something like these, but
> they always put them down wrong. Sometimes, when I cannot remem-
> ber a bit of a story, I ask some one about it; then they say, "There is
> a story of that name in my book. I don't know it, but I'll read." Then
> they read it to me, but it is all wrong, so that I get quite cross, and make
> them shut up the book.[18]

Anna's discomfort is not limited to the "wrongness" of textualization, even
as she finds herself entangled in it. It is the project of colonial modernity
itself—its economics, its education, and its promise of progress—that causes
Anna greater disquiet.

I retraced my steps in the archive, confronting the well-known limitations
of colonial records: photographs, travelogues, fiction, minutes, reports, and
surveys materialize Anglo-Indian person and policy in diverse ways, while
the experiences of Indians are subject to recovery and recoverability, a process frequently needing the midwifery of special disciplines. The manuscript
of *Old Deccan Days* presents its own complications as a colonial record. It is
very close to the published version of the book, though it does not contain
Bartle Frere's introduction (which, one of Mary's letters to John Murray tells
us, was "delayed" and would reach him separately). While the stories in the
manuscript are lightly edited—recall that Anna's voice recedes in them—
"The Narrator's Narrative" is heavily edited. It explicitly displays Mary's
stitching together of discontinuous snippets that were gathered across eigh-

teen months into a linear narrative. Numerous numbered hash marks designate blocks of text that are assembled into the chronologically ordered narrative of Anna's life that appears in the book. Perhaps all chronologies intrinsically, inescapably have a fictive quality to them. Yet when the past is remembered disjointedly over time in the form of musings or as responses to contexts and questions, the sense of the person that emerges is different from the sense that comes from the tighter logic of a chronologically ordered story. Mary's seamless composition renders Anna as someone who once had a happy childhood of "plenty" but had become a hapless ayah, dependent on the goodwill of English Christians.

I began to revisit the same colonial record—the same archives, the same book—with a different instinct, more attuned to an ethics of recognition and acknowledgment. Rereading the elided material in Mary's handwritten manuscript helped me punctuate the record differently. With the chronology now disrupted with new pauses, the narrative acquired alternative meanings and affect that come from intuition, what the French phenomenologist Henri Bergson calls the "receding and vanishing image which haunts [the mind] unperceived . . . in order to furnish 'explanation.'"[19] Against the Kantian insistence that the intellect is the fountain of *all* knowing, Bergson says that while "intellection" gives us insight into physical operations, intuition takes us to the "inwardness of life." This intuition is that "instinct that has become disinterested, self-conscious, capable of reflecting upon its object and of enlarging it indefinitely."[20] The intuition is sympathetic in that it helps me see, for instance, the many shades of orange between red and yellow and thereby *sense* the spectrum of possibilities of color. The result of interpreting through intuition is a *sense reading*, a term I adapt from Michael Polanyi. In the theory of meaning that Polanyi calls tacit knowledge, "inarticulate meaning of experience [Bergson's intuition]" is the "foundation of all explicit meaning." Tacit knowing proceeds on sense giving and sense reading. Sense giving is the search for the words that will express the meaning I want to convey. Sense reading (akin to figuring out what that strange shape in the garden at night could be) is the striving to understand a text from "an inkling of a meaning" in it.[21]

My sense reading reveals an Anna who is robustly independent and audacious. She shows that life, with all its comeuppances and happenstances, could still be lived fully and happily, without either the largesse of colonialism or its opportunities for labor. Colonial modernity turns out to be a ruse. Christianity too, Anna shows, could still be salvific for her, but without its exerting a dominant control over the everyday arts of religious imagination. A sense reading reveals an Anna to whom dignity and belonging mattered more than increased colonial wages. This Anna is ultimately sovereign because her speaking ability is indestructible and empowers her to critique and defy, and to create and dream. Even when Marianne North ran into her a decade after the book had found lucrative shores, the much older Anna was just as keen as before to narrate her stories and travel to new places.

Anna Liberata de Souza: Identifications

Old Deccan Days cast Anna in the mold of the "old ayah," disregarding the way she saw herself. The image of an old ayah figures prominently in Anglo-India's nomenclature for Indian domestics. The belabored logic of this nomenclature is anonymity, typification, and repetition.[22] Memoirs and letters, novels and manuals in the hundreds talk about "the ayah" or "old ayah" (a ladies' maid or children's nanny) without mentioning her name and speaking of her as belonging to a class of individuals with a fickle moral makeup. Nonetheless, an ayah's boundless capacity for care and love was seen as indispensable—indeed, restorative—for English children growing up in India. For instance, the imperial writer Rudyard Kipling, whose imagination is celebrated for its exquisite detail and nuance, felt destitute in England without his ayah, who had been his first muse. "In the afternoon heats," Kipling recalls, "before we took our sleep, [the ayah] or Meeta [meaning "bearer"] would tell us stories and Indian nursery songs *all unforgotten.*" And yet, Kipling fails to tell us her name even after he had the opportunity to meet her again in his late twenties. He does not seem to know. She was just Ayah.[23]

Actually, by 1818, when Mrs. Sherwood published her narrative on Indian servants *The Ayah and Lady: An Indian Story*, the ayah had already become a paradoxical necessity in the Anglo-Indian household, the so-called domestic empire. She was much needed but strategically distrusted. After the Indian Uprising of 1857–58, the domestic empire became more authoritarian in keeping with the aggressive tenor of British rule in India. By the time Anna worked for the Frere family, ayah protocols were well in place.[24] Soon, adding to journalistic, anecdotal, and fictional accounts,[25] prescriptive manuals on the Anglo-Indian domestic economy systematized duties and wages for an ayah, all based on the understanding that she was a lesser human. Memsahibs like Catherine or Mary Frere headed the domestic empire in mansions such as government houses and officers' bungalows. British homes in India, and in other colonies, ran on the energy and resourcefulness of sizable contingents of overworked and ill-treated natives who were often compared to wild animals and wily semi-humans by their British employers. Frequently, like the nameless "Ayah," they were simply referred to as Meeta/ bearer, Bheeshti/water carrier, Chaprasi/sweeper, Mali/gardener, Dhobi/ washerman, or Chokra/errand boy. The definitive ayah *shastra*, or manual, was *The Complete Indian Housekeeper and Cook* (1888) by Flora Anna Steel and Grace Gardiner, which codified the ayah's role, programming her diurnal existence. A sampling:

> Her mistress's room done, the ayah will see that the bathroom is set in order, squeeze out the sponge, dry and fold the towels, etc. . . . When the order is given for luncheon, she will take hot water to her mistress's room, and at the same time ask what dress she proposes wearing in the afternoon and evening. At dusk she will go to the bearer for candle and lamp, draw the curtains, if necessary light the fire, and be ready on her mistress's return.[26]

In line with this colonial outlook on Indian domestic servants, reviews of *Old Deccan Days* were ambivalent about Anna while they widely praised Frere's accomplishment. One review, perhaps stinging from Anna's criticism of the rising prices of everything under British rule, including guavas, calls her "this uneducated Anna Liberata de Souza, living and developing her brain on guavas."[27] For other reviewers, Anna is simply "the old woman" with a "very singular and amusing piece of autobiography."[28] A reviewer who appreciates Anna says, "If this woman *still lives*, it may convey to her a true pleasure, *in the evening of a life* which has had sore troubles, to know that she has made thousands of English children happy, and that here, if not in her own land, her name will be remembered with feelings of lively gratitude."[29]

Amidst these crowds of evening silhouettes of the ayah figure, how did Mary depict Anna, the ayah whose life story she had sought out? After all, unlike Kipling and many others, Mary does not refer to Anna simply as "Ayah." She names her. But in my understanding of how names embody persons, Mary's naming remains sophisticatedly disembodied. In 1879, in a letter, Elizabeth Price, wife of the missionary Roger Price, excitedly shares with her children that she had met Mary Frere, "the writer of 'Deccan Days,'" at Governor's House in Newlands, a suburb of Cape Town in South Africa. Price says, "She told me about her old ayah—how she would squat upon the ground, and recount all these stories from memory while she wrote them down."[30] We do not know if Anna was named in this conversation, but the manuscript of *Old Deccan Days* is suggestive of what Mary actually thought. Among the sheets is a note written in 1872 that she marks "Paragraphs to be inserted in the Collector's Apology after the words 'City of Akbar.'" These paragraphs per se did not make it into any edition of the book. Instead, an intriguing modification appears in the preface to the third edition of 1881. Mary's 1872 note describes the manner in which Anna narrated the stories:

> If she was interrupted whilst telling a story by another person coming into the room or by a question being asked, the thread of memory would be broken, and she would be unable to go on unless all that she had just been saying was repeated to her or she herself repeated it without interruption from the commencement. It was as if by a strong effort of memory the mind was forced back into the past and if the present intervened the spell was instantaneously ~~broken~~ destroyed. Anna generally sat on the floor whilst talking, often with an entranced, far-away look on her face, as if she were actually seeing at that moment, all that she was describing. . . . As her grandmother died when Anna was 11 years old, it is perhaps the [*sic*] rather surprising that she remembered as much as she did of what she had heard from her than that she remembered no more.

In the 1881 edition, Mary reworks and publishes the paragraph for the first time:

> While narrating [the stories], she usually sat cross-legged on the floor, looking into space, and repeating what she said as by an effort of memory. If anyone came into the room while she was speaking, or she was otherwise interrupted during the narration, it was apparently impossible for her to gather up the thread of the narration where it had been dropped. And she had to begin afresh at the beginning of her story as at the commencement of some long-lost melody. She had not, I believe, heard any of the stories after she was eleven years old, when her grandmother had died.[31]

The earlier description, more poetic, more empathetic, has diminished into the commonplace Anglo-Indian perception of ayahs. Gone is the sense that Anna's "far-away look" means that she was entranced and "seeing" the stories come alive, and gone is the expression of admiration that Anna could remember so much. Instead, in the reworked description—the one that became public—Anna stares vacantly: her memory of the stories is feeble.

Anna, however, imagines herself very differently. In the "Narrator's Narrative," she tells us that listening to her sing, her father and brothers used to say, "That girl can do anything!" I hear the echo of that line in another confident remark of Anna's. Looking back at how she had been trapped in the life of an ayah, she says, "If I'd I been a man I might now be a Fouzdar."[32] A *faujdar* was either a commander in the Mughal army or a chief of police in British India. Anna's paternal grandmother suffuses her narrative: her grandmother is physically strong, has a capacious memory, is an inventive caretaker of her grandchildren, telling them countless colorful stories. I could relate. I was deeply attached to my maternal grandmother, whose quiet assertiveness and practical wisdom I grew up admiring. And I was told often that I was the living image of my paternal grandmother, who had died in my father's childhood, and whose death anniversary coincides with my birthday. Similarly, Anna recollects: "It was after my granny that I was named Anna Liberata. . . . [She was a] a very tall, fine, handsome woman and very strong. . . . Her eyes were quite bright, her hair black, and her teeth good to the last." Married to a *havildar* in the British army, she went with the regiment wherever it marched, going "on, on, on, on, on."[33]

There is the strong suggestion that Anna believes she resembles her grandmother—the same name, the same dark hair, the same love for storytelling, and the same resilience in the face of hardship. Anna proudly states, "a great deal hard work that old woman done."[34] Anna's mother (who knows fewer stories than the grandmother) does hard labor outside the home to earn money for the family. She is no less feisty than Anna's grandmother and minces no words in standing up for herself. When quizzed by her husband why she had spanked little Anna (who had taunted Gypsies), she retorts: "If you want to know, ask your daughter why I punished her. You will then be able to judge whether I was right or not."[35] It is this abundance of memories of the hardworking, independent, and principled women in her family, and not the Anglo-Indian construction of "poor old ayahs," that shapes Anna's self-perception.

Anna's memory of time is lucid. She tells Mary that her grandmother lived till she was 109 years old (although Mary inexplicably strikes out the 109, changing it to "about a hundred" in the manuscript) and her mother till she was ninety. Anna was seven when she got a pet dog, eleven when her grandmother died, twelve when she got married, and twenty when she was widowed. And yet it is a matter of great surprise when she does refer to her own age: Did Mary never ask, or was that detail elided? The manuscript, with its insertions and juxtapositions made in the interests of narrative flow or "relevance," disregards Anna's precise understanding of temporality in relation to her own life; it obfuscates the chronology of Anna's life so that it is impossible to be certain about Anna's age.

And yet—Lear had fumed, 'Age is unnecessary'—to settle for Anna simply as an old ayah would be to disavow her personhood. So let us discern Anna's age through her statements: "My husband was a servant at Government House—that was when Lord Clare was Governor here. When I was twenty years old, my husband died of a bad fever."[36] At face value, this would imply that Anna's husband died when he was a servant in Clare's house. Lord Clare was governor from 1831 to 1835. If Anna had been twenty sometime during these years, she would have been born between 1811 and 1815.[37] This calculation, however, is inaccurate.

The handwritten manuscript shows that the sentence "My husband was a servant at Government House—that was when Lord Clare was Governor here" has been *inserted* before "When I was twenty years old, my husband died of a bad fever." This conflation leads us to assume a synchronicity that in fact does not exist. If we move this insertion to the only other place where Anna mentions her husband, we get the following composite: "Then I was married. I was twelve years old then. My husband was a servant at Government House—that was when Lord Clare was Governor here." This rearrangement makes Anna *twelve* (and not twenty) during Clare's governorship. From this, we get a first range of dates for when Anna could have been born: 1819 to 1823. We get an additional clue from another detail she provides Mary. When Anna lost her husband at twenty, her brother-in-law (who was a personal valet to General Charles Napier in Sind) invited her to Sind (now Sindh). Since Napier was in Sind from 1843 to 1847, Anna would have been twenty years old sometime in this period. This now gives us a second range of dates for her birth: 1823 to 1827. The overlap of these two ranges (1819–1823 and 1823–1827) allow us to pinpoint her year of birth as 1823. She would have been forty-two when she started to work in the Frere household in 1865.

Anna's portrait in the book drawn by Mary's sister Catherine shows her with youthful features and jet-black hair (of which Anna is rather proud). In a letter to John Murray while the first edition was being readied, Mary mentions a photograph they have of Anna but says that the hand-drawn "likeness of 'Annie' (the narrator) is *much* more like her than the photograph."[38] The youthful "likeness" further persuades me that Anna was in her forties at the time of the portrait. In 1878, when Marianne North was belittling her as

FIGURE 3.   Anna Liberata de Souza. Reproduced from Mary Frere, *Old Deccan Days* (London: John Murray, 1868), xii.

"the old lady," fifty-five-year-old Anna was still expressing her love for travel and stories, just as she had declared once to Mary Frere. Calcutta, Madras, England, and Jerusalem were still on her dream itinerary. She told North about "the wonderful things she had seen. She tried to persuade [North] to take her on [North's] next travels."[39] If she saw herself as I sense her, then when she died in 1887, she died young.

The Deccan Sojourn

"I have often been asked under what circumstances these stories were collected?"[40] writes thirty-six-year-old Mary in the two-page preface to the third
edition of 1881. As she describes the official tour during which the collection of Anna's stories was inaugurated, we come face-to-face with a strange
absence. Anna is present through the description of her mannerisms of narration, but as fellow sojourner she is absent. To get a sense of Anna's experiences of the intense journey, we must turn to the very account that has
created the absence.

It had been a little over a year since eighteen-year-old Mary, the oldest of
the five Frere children, had arrived in India with her mother, Catherine, to
join Bartle Frere. Shortly afterwards, Catherine returned to England to be
with the younger children, leaving Mary in charge of the domestic management of Government House in Bombay—or, during the monsoon, in Poona.
This was a task she executed "with a tact and power singular in so young a
girl," her sister Georgina proudly recounts, "owing to a very human interest
in her fellow creatures, which took no narrow view of life and of its possibilities under all sorts of conditions, and she enjoyed the opportunities of meeting Native ladies in their Zenanas and Missionary workers at their Stations,
as much as 'Society' in its more usually accepted sense."[41]

The journey through the Deccan turned out to be stunningly instructive
for Mary, far exceeding her private education at Wimbledon. The governor
and his daughter, and a few British officers, were supported by a retinue
of six hundred retainers—cooks, camel divers, elephant mahouts, horse
grooms, tent pitchers, and so on—and a multitude of assorted animals.[42]
From Poona, they went south in the direction of Satara and then to Kolhapur, continuing on to Belgaum and Dharwad. At Bijapur they turned north.
From here, Bartle Frere hoped to make it to Sholapur "in three marches."[43]
From Sholapur, they took the Grand Indian Peninsula Railway and returned
home to Government House in Poona.

"I chanced to be the only lady of the party," Mary writes. "Anna Liberata
de Souza, my native ayah, went with me. . . . As there was no other lady in
the Camp, and I sometimes had no lady visitors for some days together, I was
necessarily much alone."[44] (Georgina shares that Mary was also afflicted with
ophthalmia during the three-month sojourn.)[45] One day, "tired of reading,
writing and sketching," Mary asked Anna, her "constant attendant," to tell
her a story. "This [Anna] declared to be impossible," but Mary persisted.
"You have children and grandchildren, surely you tell them stories to amuse
them sometimes?"[46] And Anna told her the first of the twenty-four stories

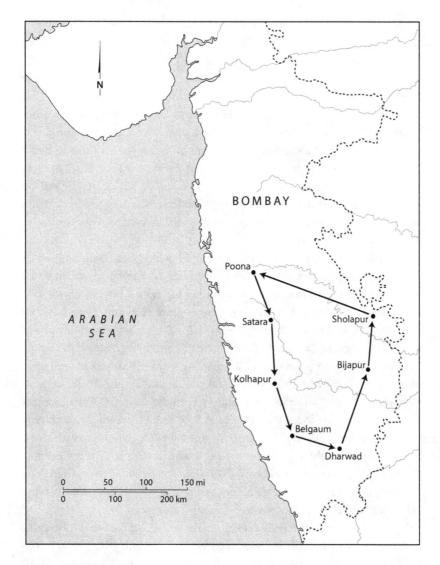

MAP 2. Anna and Mary's Deccan sojourn, 1865
Source: Map by Bill Nelson. Based on information from J. G. Bartholomew, *The Imperial Gazetteer of India: Bombay Presidency*, Volume 1. (Oxford: Clarendon Press, 1909).

that bustle with human heroes and supernatural beings entangled in tricky predicaments. Mary's preface recounts the thrills of the expedition: In Kolhapur, she met the Rani in the palace. In Satara, she saw Shivaji's famous sword ("Bowanee," she calls it) which the goddess Bhavani had given him; in Karad ("Kurar"), the Buddhist caves; in Belgaum, the ruins of Jain temples; and in Dharwad, the nawab's cheetahs hunting antelope on the plains.

Bijapur ("Beejapore") seems to have almost overwhelmed her. Here she saw the Pearl Mosque and the "Soap-stone" Mosque; the "vast dome" of the "grand Mosque," which was "thirteen feet larger in diameter" than the dome of Saint Paul's in London; the eleven-ton sixteenth-century gun so big "a grown-up person can sit upright"; the shrine with its three hairs of the Prophet Muhammad's beard; and the massive library whose contents her father had "rescued" and relocated to the India Office Library in London.[47] We see her taking it all in breathlessly, caught between, on the one hand, rehearsing the arch-trope of orientalism that reproduces "the East" as a site of seductive paradoxes—barbarism and civilization, for example—and on the other, quite naturally experiencing wonder at the staggering diversity and richness of story and landscape. Anna's stories would have fit into this larger experience of foreignness and wonder.

There is little doubt that at the same time Mary was continuing to be imperceptibly groomed in the everyday praxis of empire in which Anna could be only an attendant, a necessary utility, but not a companion—despite the predicament of their being the only two women in a camp of six hundred men. Empire, as Partha Chatterjee reminds us, "was not just about power politics, the logic of capital, or the civilizing mission, but instead was something that had to be practiced, as a normal everyday business as well as at moments of extraordinary crisis, by real people in real time."[48] Tellingly, in the manuscript of *Old Deccan Days*, Mary revises the sentence "Anna Liberata De Souza, my native ayah, *accompanied me*" to "Anna Liberata De Souza, my native ayah, *went with me*."[49] Vast privileges and protocols were available to the governor's daughter—"the only lady," as she has learned to see herself—in an imperial government in post-1857 India. The Indian Uprising had been ruthlessly contained eight years before this journey (with her father playing a significant role in its suppression), and the avaricious British Crown had replaced the mercenary East India Company, whose sun had set in the east.

While Mary's journalistic reminiscence is graphic and attentive to minutiae, it betrays the habitual obliviousness Anglo-Indian writings show toward domestic servants. An anonymous article in *Temple Bar*, a leading literary magazine, confides, "We take little notice often of our servants in India, discussing things before them as we should not do before English servants; forgetting sometimes that they are not dummies, but living men and women, and perhaps taking an intelligent interest in all that is being talked about."[50] Mary shows no curiosity about Anna's experiences during the journey (which would not have afforded to Anna any of the comforts available to her) and certainly keeps no record of them. But if we draw on Anna's narrative to punctuate the "Preface" and imagine some of *her* experiences during the journey, we understand the "circumstances under which these stories were collected" in a markedly different sense. Anna becomes present, and not merely as the attendant who relieved the tedium of the journey for a young English lady.

For instance, Mary tells us that when they reached the Krishna and Bhima Rivers, the sahibs and the memsahib crossed safely in wicker-basket boats, while the native men and animals either swam across or used open rafts. How did Anna, the only other woman in the retinue, ford river waters? Did the sight of the river remind her of her handsome son who had drowned in the Mula River near Poona just "last year"? Sometime during the making of "The Narrator's Narrative" she tells Mary, "That was my great sad."[51]

As they passed through Bijapur and Dharwad—places that are historically important to the Lingayat community to which Anna's family once belonged (a point that Mary herself notes)—did the sites somehow resonate for Anna? Kolhapur, where Mary recorded Anna's first story and later sent it on to her younger sister in England, would surely have viscerally reminded Anna of the terror of the 1857 uprising, when she and her previous British employer had escaped in the middle of the night. She had fled with her two small children. Mary does not reproduce Anna's story about the Kolhapur escape in "The Narrator's Narrative." The allusion appears through Anna's remark, "but I've told you before about all that."[52]

This image of a widowed young mother, running with her children, scared for their lives, is the image that stays with me as I read "Punchkin," the first story that Anna narrates (which Mary initially titles "An Indian Story"). It is about a smart princess named Balna, who through a series of misfortunes is abducted from her room in the palace by an evil magician called Punch-kin, who has turned her husband and his six brothers to stone. Punchkin separates Balna from her beloved baby son and imprisons her for twelve years in a tower because she refuses to marry him. When the son turns fourteen and learns of his history, he sets out in search of his parents and uncles. Donning a disguise with the help of a gardener's wife, he finds his mother in the tower and comes up with an elaborate rescue plan. "Do not fear, dear mother," he assures her.[53] Eventually he rescues her and the rest of his petrified family by turning the magician's magic against him and killing him. It is a story of a mother who is at last reunited with her son. I am transported to "The Narrator's Narrative," where Anna describes her son to Mary: "He was such a beauty boy—tall, straight, handsome—and so clever . . . and he said to me, 'Mammy, you've worked for us all your life. Now I'm grown up. I'll get a clerk's place and work for you. You shall work no more but live in my house.' "[54]

Mary tells her publisher John Murray that this story was the hardest to transcribe and write up because of the "many repetitions" it contained.[55] Was it hard for Anna to narrate too? Or was it one she immediately recalled for its echoes in her own life? I wonder, also, about Anna's halting style, mentioned earlier. Narration was an "effort of memory," Mary concludes, but she also says in the unpublished paragraph in the handwritten manuscript that Anna seemed as if "entranced." Does Anna's manner of narration connect to her own views on how we remember and how we forget? "I'm afraid," she tells Mary, "my sister would not be able to remember any of [the stories]. She has had much trouble; that puts those sort of things out of people's heads." After her son's death, she tells us, "I can't remember things as I used to do, all is muddled in my head, six and seven."[56] Anna, wearied by the memory of self-altering loss but also enlivened by the magic of the stories she is telling, reminds us that narration is in essence a fuzzy art, mingling real-life experiences with conjured enchantments. Anna is deeply present during the Deccan journey, which in the final account would need to acknowledge that it was a journey that was experienced by two women, although in vastly different ways.

A Frere Family Venture: Anna Disappears

Back in palatial Government House in Poona (and, after the monsoon, in their Bombay home), Mary rewrote Anna's stories, seeking clarifications, she informs readers, from Anna. Anna continued to tell her stories—we may assume—in one of the inner familial spaces, which she was allowed to enter as an ayah, the only servant who had access to all rooms.

And then in England, in the Frere home at Wressil Lodge, Wimbledon, Surrey, the publishing of *Old Deccan Days* quickly became a robust family venture for the Freres. The archivist of the Murray archive in London told me, "In fact it seems the whole Frere family was writing to Murray and they appeared to be great friends."[57] As I went through thirty years of this correspondence, which spanned four editions of the book, a universe of negotiations and discussions about topics from pictures to profits emerged. Among all these letters, there are precisely two references to Anna. The first asks whether it would be better to use a photograph of Anna or a sketch of her made by Katie, Mary's sister. The second reference notes in passing Anna's death in Ganeshkhind. In a larger discussion about what additional information should go into the fourth edition, Mary Frere writes to Murray, "I could add a word or two if wished about my dear old ayah's death—but that would not be necessary but could come into a later edition."[58] That is it.

The first edition was carefully curated to present the right look and feel, in line with the family's understanding of Anna's stories—and, indeed, of India. As the book moved through editions, and especially after Bartle Frere's death in 1884, Mary's tone becomes more directive about everything from the timing of a new edition to marketing strategies. In an annotation on one of her letters, John Murray writes a brusque note: "Impossible. Wd [Would] be a regular take in. Book must be very materially changed to justify being called a NE [new edition]."[59]

Mary was perhaps not easy to work with. In the Littleton papers at the University of Witwatersrand, I found a curious letter from W. F. Littleton, who was private secretary to Bartle Frere in South Africa. Littleton, writing from Cape Town to his mother in England in 1879, complained that Lady Frere and Miss Frere "are fussy, meddlesome, inconsiderate to a degree; inconsequent and stupid."[60]

The illustrations to the book were done by Katie, who had arrived in India soon after Mary and Anna's Deccan journey. Katie had perhaps joined Mary when Anna told the stories in Government House. Her thumbnail sketches bookended the stories. "Two narrow gold lines" on the cover would make the book "look unusual," she suggested to Murray (through Mary). Mary elaborated:

> My sister has been trying a *great many* different designs for a title page— but has not succeeded in getting anything to her satisfaction. She tried introducing palm trees on the sides—and alligators, and snakes—but without gaining the effect she wished. She then tried sticks for the framework tied together with snakes. But this looked so common a design. She thinks it would have a good effect to have all the people and principal objects in the different stories collected together in a chain interwoven with a sort of light tracery of branches and leaves. . . . She begs we send you the enclosed little attempts at snake twists. No. II we thought the most satisfactory. The corners are made of a lotus and three leaves, and the little snake fills up the gap."

The many cobras, the lions and tigers, the twisted snakes, the sinuous vines, the owls and fortune-tellers, and the dusky maiden bathing by a pool provide the oriental aura of the book. As Mary presents the final image for the book, a note of embarrassment creeps into her tone: "This little cobra twisted into an M, my sister is particularly anxious should, if serviceable, be put into one of the nooks or corners which have been left unprovided for in the little design sent by Mr. Whymper![61] It might she thought either go at the end of the list of contents, or at the top of the 'Collector's Apology.' "[62]

The M stands for Mary, and it appears on the outside cover of each of the five editions; the book has now become fully hers. Or so we think. Yet if we "sense read," we know that the collection is animated by Anna's spirit, and we also see an audacious irony at play in "The Narrator's Narrative." Anna, a supposedly lowly ayah lost in the pages of the book and the verandas of Government House—a grand symbol of the British Crown—turns out to be an outspoken critic of the economic progress claimed by imperialist policy, subtly challenging one of the most powerful governors of colonial India.

Government House and the Phantom of Economic Progress

Government House was the pet project of Bartle Frere. Lavish in concept and style, Government houses were an architectural feature of the global British Empire. In India, the oldest of these were built in Madras by Robert Clive (governor 1798–1803) and in Calcutta by Richard Wellesley (governor-general 1798–1805). During the tenure of the East India Company, when it was intent on squeezing out every bit of profit, and when the British were still half-kneeling to the ruling Mughals, the Company's directors disapproved expensive building programs. After the British Crown took over the company, however, government houses came to be seen as representing imperial authority and were hence architecturally designed as imposing structures that commanded panoramic views and contained native labor.[63]

Tipped to be the governor-general of India, which he ultimately never became, Bartle Frere began his long tryst with India when he landed in Bombay in 1834 after an adventurous land passage through Egypt. Both his grandfathers had been MPs for Norwich and Arundel, and he had been sent to the East India College at Haileybury (the recruitment academy for the East India Company), from which he graduated with distinction.[64] In India, he rose rapidly through colonial ranks—private secretary to the governor of Bombay, political resident of Satara, chief commissioner of Sind, and finally governor of Bombay. In 1844 he married Catherine Arthur, daughter of the then governor of Bombay, to whom he was private secretary. Bartle Frere's heavy footprint is also seen in those things that colonialism likes to credit itself for: development projects such as canals for irrigation, trade fairs, the Sind Railway, and the Oriental Inland Steam Company, and even the first adhesive postage stamp in India, in 1852, called the Scinde District Dawk. But—from an imperial perspective at least—it was Frere's role in suppressing the Indian Uprising of 1857–58 (he speedily sent troops to Punjab, taking a calculated risk on Sindh's security) that secured him a knighthood and a prized appointment to the viceroy's executive council for three years.[65]

The construction of Government House began in 1865 with projected costs of £175,000 and a timeline of a few years. But soon, cotton prices crashed following the end of the American Civil War, and the British colonial government ran out of funds. The project was halted for several years. The building was finally completed in 1871 at nearly six times its projected cost. When it was finished, Government House—with its hundred-foot tower—sat in the center of 512 acres of land in Ganeshkhind in the midst of a colonial development. Trees lined the roads, and ornamental terraced gardens surrounded British-style bungalows for officers.

The four-hundred-foot-long Government House itself stretched north-south and had two double-storied wings connected by a central portion. In the south wing and the central parts were some of the large public spaces—a durbar area, a formal dining room with an arched ceiling, a ballroom, and an arcade opening to a large conservatory. Banquets and receptions and "Ladies at Home" socials were held here.[66] Guest bedrooms were on the upper floor of this wing. The larger northern wing housed the governor's office and his private residence. The north wing was connected to the east wing via a 250-foot underground tunnel, at the end of which was the kitchen, the store, and the servants' quarters.[67]

FIGURE 4. Visible part of the tunnel in the Government House that connected the north wing to the east wing. Photograph by Akshayini Leela-Prasad, February 2020.

In addition, four bungalows for the governor's staff, a guardroom with an ornate clock tower, European-style barracks for the governor's band, stables and coach houses were placed around the main building. One traveler notes that the building was a "Palace—if not quite a thing of beauty and joy for ever, at least a very imposing structure, with noble tower and fair frontage—state apartments of the grandest—conservatories, gardens fresh and blooming—placed on a commanding site, with a view over the undulating plains and strange tumultuous scenery of the Deccan."[68]

There was evidently no problem housing servants in these vast bungalows. Edmund Hull's vade mecum for Anglo-Indian domestic life notes that the great advantage with Indian servants is that "no provision has to be made with regard to their board or lodging." Hull instructs that only one servant should sleep in the house at night—on a mat in the veranda. The cook could sleep on a shelf in the kitchen. The horse keepers should sleep with the horses in the stables, "always."[69] Anna would either have lived in one of the servant outbuildings or slept in the verandas of the north wing of Government House in Ganeshkhind, where Mary could have called her at will.

Bartle Frere had his critics to contend with, though. The British secretary of state for India censured the enormous expenditure on Government House in Ganeshkhind.[70] When the Prince of Wales visited India in 1875 (a tour that Frere had principally organized), Bartle Frere faced a few taunts standing in the very Government House that he had commissioned and supervised.[71] His defense was that "he had built a very fine dwelling for future Governors, that he had acted within his legal powers, that he was not insubordinate, and that he had not spent all the money at his disposal."[72] Naturally, Frere did not need to allude to the fact that Government House had been built amidst the debris of Bombay's great financial crash of 1865. When the cotton mills in Manchester were suffering during the American Civil War (1861–1865), Frere encouraged the cotton trade in India. Markets boomed and prices all around rose. Inflation crippled the common person in India. The *Gazetteer of the Bombay Presidency* recalled the change in prices of common grains in those years: "Since 1842, *jvari* [millet] and wheat had risen more than 150 per cent, linseed about 50 per cent, and *kardai* or safflower and other chief oil seeds more than 200 per cent."[73] But worse was in store. Following the end of the Civil War, cotton prices dropped dramatically, the financial markets crashed, and the Bank of Bombay collapsed. People laid off by companies in Bombay returned to their villages, and Bombay's population dropped by 21 percent.[74]

The lower cadres of Anglo-Indians like railway engineers complained about the economic policies of the English. But right there, on the veranda of Government House, there was a vocal critic telling the governor's daughter herself how colonial economic policy had in fact depleted the quality of everyday life. Anna Liberata de Souza furnishes a quotidian then-and-now arithmetic of this depletion. Prior to the rule of the British,

> we were poor people, but living was cheap, and we had "plenty comfort." In those days house rent did not cost more than half a rupee a month, and you could build a very comfortable house for a hundred rupees. Not such good houses as people now live in, but well enough for people like us. Then a whole family could live as comfortably on six or seven rupees a month as they can now on thirty. Grain, now a rupee a pound, was then two annas a pound. Common sugar, then one anna a pound, is now worth four annas a pound. Oil which then sold for six pice a bottle now costs four annas. Four annas' worth of salt, chillies, tamarinds, onions, and garlic, would then last a family a whole month, now the same money would not buy a week's supply. Such dungeree as you now pay half rupee a yard for, you could then buy from twenty to forty yards of for the rupee. You could not get such good calico then as now, but the dungeree did very well. Beef then was a pice a pound, and the vegetables cost a pie a day. For half a rupee you could fill the house with wood. Water also was much cheaper. You could then get a man to bring you two large skins full, morning and evening, for a pie, now he would not do it under half a rupee or more. If the children came crying for fruit, a pie would get them as many guavas as they liked in the bazaar. Now you'd have to pay that for each guava. This shows how much more money people need now than they did then.[75]

There is another point that Anna makes: "The English fixed the rupee to the value of sixteen annas; in those days there were some big annas and some little ones, and you could sometimes get twenty-two annas for a rupee."[76] A rupee was a silver coin and an anna a copper coin. The value of a silver coin depended on the market rate of silver on any given day. Similarly for copper coins. Depending on the fluctuations in the rates of silver and copper, when one exchanged a silver rupee for copper annas, a rupee could sometimes fetch more than sixteen annas—and sometimes less. In two ways, Anna's remarks strike at a fundamental self-justification of colonial rule, which was that the empire would improve the natives' quality of life, a self-justification whose duplicity was stoked most vigorously by Lord Dalhousie (1812–1860), under whom maximum territorial acquisition had occurred in British India.[77] First, Anna exposes how the quality of life has actually deteriorated with colonial policy. Second, she criticizes the standardization of the rupee to sixteen annas, a move that curtailed the monetary elasticity of the rupee and robbed Indians of their agency in exchanging the rupee for annas when *they* determined it was best, that is, when the exchange rate from rupees to annas was optimal. Bartle Frere bristles at Anna's trenchant assessment of the economy. He attempts an explanation in a note that largely falls back on dismissing her remarks, which he says are "very characteristic" and a "specimen of a very widespread Indian popular delusion."[78] We may nevertheless say that Frere's invocation of "popular delusion" is itself "very characteristic" of his approach to Indian sensibilities and culture. The trope of dismissal serves England's self-image as civilized and civilizing, terms whose "usage necessarily also presupposed and demanded the existence of the institutions of the modern European state, and its goals, values, and practices, ranging from the pursuit of material progress to Civilized manners and clothing."[79] But the trope serves England's treasury, too, for it is well known that, as Gauri Viswanathan says, in the bigger picture, "however much parliamentary discussions of the British presence in India may have been couched in moral terms, there was no obscuring the real issue, which remained political, not moral."[80] Anna effectively showed Bartle Frere, the governor of Bombay Presidency, that English rule was an economic disaster for Indians like her.

Figments of English Literacy

A starlit sky on a clear wintry night, a wayside shrine to a Hindu deity, stories describing extraordinary lands and creatures, visits to the bazaar with her mother, hours in the sun taming pets: these are some of the everyday contexts of Anna's childhood, and through them we can begin to understand the distinction she makes between getting an education and acquiring reading and writing skills. Anna's distinction holds up the myth of English-language literacy, a key signifier of colonial modernity. Education, for Anna and her siblings, was in and through the everyday. There were no schools she could go to when she was growing up. A formative presence was instead Anna's grandmother, whose stories were her teaching tools. Anna says: "About *all things* she would tell us pretty stories—about men, and animals, and trees, and flowers, and stars. There was nothing she did not know some tale about." For example, she taught them to identify the constellations using their story names: Three Thieves, Hen and Chickens, or the Key, for example. How would Anna and her siblings ever forget the Pleiades cluster when it is remembered as the "Three Thieves climbing up to rob the Ranee's silver bedstead, with their mother (that twinkling star far away) watching for her sons' return. Pit-a-pat, pit-a-pat, you can see how her heart beats, for she is always frightened, thinking, 'Perhaps they will be caught and hanged!'"?[81]

Anna's grandmother turned to the same starlit sky to teach them about their Christian faith—the cross, the ascension, and so on. A falling star meant the death of a great person, and good persons were the steadiest and brightest stars in the sky.

Learning also unfolded through an abundance of curiosity and through osmosis. Perhaps there was something powerful for Anna in watching her grandmother, a devout Catholic, stop to pray at wayside shrines to Hindu deities, saying, "May be there's something in it."[82] It taught Anna that to be able to say "maybe" was a matter of self-confidence and openness, not fear and ignorance. The interflow between Roman Catholic and Hindu worship practices should not surprise us. Kristin Bloomer's ethnography shows that three women in Tamil Nadu who experienced Marian possessions were all "familiar with the widespread practice of deity and spirit possession in popular Hinduism."[83] The metaphor of siblings is part of local vocabulary to describe relations between Syrian Christian saints and Hindu temple deities, Corinne Dempsey finds in Kerala. A bishop tells Dempsey that the parishioners of his home church consider its patron, Saint George, to be the "brother of Visnnu from a nearby temple."[84]

But the compatibility between Catholic and Hindu approaches to the sacred through images and iconographic presence did surprise Bartle Frere as he psychoanalyzed the "practical belief of the lower orders" of Hindus.[85] The compatibility was also missed by Mary Stokes, who notes in *Indian Fairy Tales* (1880) that the Hindu and Muslim narrators who told stories to her and her daughter rarely mentioned the names of Hindu deities. Stokes concludes skeptically, and erroneously, that Anna, in contrast, "almost always gives her gods and goddesses their Hindu names—probably because, from being a Christian, she had no religious scruples to deter her from so doing."[86]

Anna does not share these concerns. Years after her grandmother is no more, and Anna looks back, she is able to agree with her that *maybe* the extraordinary people of the stories did exist in the world at some time, even if not anymore. But Anna's immediate surroundings of course included others with whom she had to learn to coexist: Gypsies, for instance. Prancing alongside her mother in the bazaar, she calls them "dirty," "nasty" people who "live in ugly little houses." The comment draws a sharp reprimand from her mother: "Because God has given you a comfortable home and good parents, is that any reason for you to laugh at others who are poorer and less happy?" Anna's mother educates her by constructing an ethical relationship *in the present* between Anna and the "other" Gypsies.

Anna's childhood vignettes do something rather bold. They disrupt James Mill's assertion that Indians confused historic pasts and fabulous stories and consequently lived in a decadent present. Mill said, "The offspring of a wild and ungoverned imagination, they bear the strongest marks of a rude and credulous people whom the marvellous delights, who cannot estimate the use of a record of past events, and whom the real occurrences of life are too tame to interest."[87] It is to Mary's credit that she presents to English readers the opportunity to engage Anna's reflections on her upbringing, reflections that offer a sophisticated interpretation of history, and of life itself, as in-between-ness: between the real and the fantastic, between the possible and the plausible, between memory and imagination, and between oneself and another.

Although Anna did not go to school when she was growing up, Poona and Bombay were beginning to see a burgeoning of schools, and by 1865–66, the Bombay Presidency had nearly one hundred schools.[88] Anna herself had spent "a great deal" to send her son to school, and perhaps Rosie, her married daughter, was now talking about sending her children to school.[89] The "school" would probably have been some version of the Anglo-vernacular school—where a largely European curriculum was taught in both English and Indian languages to Indians.[90] Emboldened by the 1813 Charter Act, Bartle Frere's predecessor and hero Mountstuart Elphinstone had rallied to set up "native schools" that broke away from the missionary-led Bombay Education Society (BES). Elphinstone had proclaimed, "There exists in the Hindu languages many tales and fables that would be generally read and that would circulate sound morals," and these could be used in textbooks with the proviso that the government "silently omit all precepts of questionable morality."[91] Elphinstone's sententious endorsement notwithstanding, in Anna's view it was precisely the redaction of Indian stories that ruined them. Such compilations, rather than being educative, "leave out the prettiest part and they jumble up the beginning of one story with the end of another—so that it is altogether wrong."[92]

But beyond the annoying misrepresentation of Indian oral narrative, Anna challenges the (much-debated) grandiose imperial notion that by learning English, Indians would embark on a path of "progress."[93] She would not have been aware of Thomas Babington Macaulay's call for the formation of a class of brown bodies with English tongues (brown sahibs) to serve the interests of English administration in India, but she knew from hard experience what English-language learning could do for *her* economic class: "I know your language. What use? To blow the fire? I only a miserable woman, fit to go to cook-room and cook the dinner." Her words throw me back to the stifling dungeon-like kitchen and pantry of the bungalow I grew up in. Thus, knowing English gave Anna at most the opportunity to become an ayah, moving from one Anglo-Indian house to another no fewer than eight times.

The first woman who employed her had taught her English—adding to all the languages Anna already knew—but even when Anna learned it well, her brother-in-law, who we recall invited her to come all the way up to Sind to work in the home of General Charles Napier, could only promise her the job of an ayah (an offer Anna declined).

Did Anna's realism about the retooling of Indian stories, and about schools and schooling, expose the hollowness of the modernity promised by colonialism? "Now I'm grown up I'll get a clerk's place," Anna's son assured her after completing his English-language education. How far could "English" schooling take a young man of Anna's economic class in the decades when she was raising her children? At least in 1832, the French botanist and traveler Victor Jacquemont, reporting on schools in Poona, describes a curriculum that focused on English, mathematics, carpentry, "Making Plans," and surveying. One can see how the brazenly utilitarian curriculum was doing nothing more than oiling the human wheels of the colonial machinery. Jacquemont observed that the government was the only employer. The *Gazetteer of the Bombay Presidency* notes, "It was cruel to give poor children a high training, pay them to learn [both teachers and students were paid] and then to leave them without work."[94] Tellingly, when Jacquemont visited, a Portuguese student who was one of the best in the school asked to be hired as his servant. English schooling was designed to teach the language of servitude.

Yet colonialism had closed for Anna's son the routes taken by Anna's father and grandfather. "My grandfather couldn't write, and my father couldn't write, and they did very well," she tells Mary. They had, without knowing how to read and write, done honorably in their professions, provided "plenty comfort" for their families, and ensured happy childhoods for their children.

I return to a letter that Mary Frere hurriedly wrote to Murray on October 20, 1870, on receiving the proofs for the second edition, which she saw bore the new title *Fairy Legends of the Deccan*. Dismayed, she argued:

> I would be very grieved for the title to be altered. 1st because it is the same book, and should therefore I shd. think have the same title. & I would no more willingly call the same book by a different name than I would call myself by a name that was not my own because it sounded prettier—besides (to my fancy) "Old Deccan Days" having been presented at Court, and made her debut in Society will have had all that trouble for nothing. I have to begin making friends on her own account again, if she changes her name. Then, to our Bombay ears, Calicut—whence the legends came, is not the *Deccan* but the *Concon*—

though the book may rightly be called "Old Deccan Days"—as being these legends told to Anna de Souza in old days in the Deccan (by her grandmother & by her to me). And "Old Deccan Days" seems to me a name that keeps in the memory easily. Not too long to say at a breath & to a certain extent distinguishes those ever-be upheld Tory principles of which you and my Father are such staunch supporters, and as one protest against the Ever shifting radicalism now so much in vogue I hope it may not be deemed advisable to change the Title of Old Deccan Days.[95]

As I concluded in my earlier work, "the alliterative assonance of the title *Old Deccan Days* was about more than just the aesthetic of sound. The deep identification Mary Frere felt with the book coalesces into the practical anxiety that the 'new' book would cease to be associated with her name unless she made strong efforts to keep the association explicit."[96] Ultimately, we realize how ironic Marianne North's conclusion was that Anna was the "old ayah Miss Bartle Frere has made famous."

A greater irony is that the record that smothers Anna in one part is the very record that allows us to discern her presence. If we follow that presence, Anna Liberata de Souza is the "girl who could do anything." She is outspoken, expressive, and un-enamored with the glitter of colonial modernity. It is not a small matter that when she was made an offer that would have paid her almost twenty-five years' worth of her ayah's pay in India,[97] she firmly refused, honoring her better sense of belonging and dignity:

> One lady with whom I stayed wished to take me to England with her when she went home (at that time the children neither little or big), and she offered to give me Rs. 5000 and warm clothes if I would go with her; but I wouldn't go. I a silly girl then, and afraid of going from the children and on the sea; I think—"May be I shall make plenty money, but what good if all the little fishes eat my bones? I shall not rest with my old Father and Mother if I go"—so I told her I could not do it.[98]

Pune, without the Ouija Board

In January 2018, I was in a hotel room in Guanajuato, Mexico on academic work when I got a call on WhatsApp. It was Trevor Martin from Pune. Although I had not been in touch with him for more than thirty years, I had turned to Trevor, a native Punekar and a former Jesuit priest, who had been my father's MA student in the English department in Pune during the 1970s. Trevor had a lead. Was this the piece of information for which I had looked for years? Over the course of my writing this book a curiosity had turned into an obsession: *Where had Anna been buried?* If I trusted the line in *Old Deccan Days* below the image of Government House that had arrested me decades ago, Anna had died in Government House, Ganeshkhind, on August 14, 1887. I told him Anna's story. He was excited. "I'd love to help," he said. As with archival records, burial records and graves of Europeans had been very easy to find. Holkar Bridge, Khadki War Cemetery, more choices. New Poona Cemetery in the 1880s did not allow Indian Christians to be interred there, as per new burial laws, we learned. A newsletter of the Diocese of Western India reported in 1881, "Next year we shall be obliged to provide a Cemetery for ourselves, as the Government have issued an order that in the Poona New Cemetery no native Christians can be buried."[99] Promisingly, somebody had donated a plot of land for natives to be buried in Ganeshkhind in 1882.[100] But nobody in Pune seemed to know about it, though everybody I asked voluntarily visited sites and pored over records.

After much legwork, Trevor had learned that Catholics of Portuguese origin in colonial India had mostly been buried at the Church of the Immaculate Conception, commonly known as City Church. He was now calling to say he had found out that the church had scrupulously maintained burial records. He and a friend who had become interested were going to look at them. There was a chance that although she was not Portuguese, Anna as a Roman Catholic would have been buried there. Trevor sent me images of burial entries from around 1887. The entries were in exquisite calligraphic Portuguese on large yellowed ledger pages. I do not know Portuguese, so each time I saw the name "Anna" or "de Souza," my heart raced. (These are common names in Portuguese). At Duke, I studied these entries with Larissa Carneiro, a Brazilian colleague. Sadly, there was no entry for Anna. My husband, Prasad, was in Pune at one time, and he too visited various graveyards. At Holkar Bridge cemetery the keeper said: "You're here to look for the record of the Goan lady, right? We didn't find anything. We looked and looked. But I'll keep searching." By "we" he meant that Trevor had already visited the cemetery. My brother, co-accomplice at Ouija board sessions in our childhood, put me in touch with Vincent Pinto, his friend from their Indian Air Force days. Vincent, a former intelligence officer who now lives in Pune, said, "I'd love to be involved in such a historic search."

Historic. My search, though still open, concludes for the moment with the realization that the sense of Anna I have pursued is the very sense that has motivated others to help "find" her. Like me, these persons, unconnected with my project, feel justice is served when we are able to grasp a sense of a person—belonging, perspectives, creativity, struggle—that is beyond what can be captured by a label or a category, and in so doing reimagine the past with more equity and dignity. Without my childhood beliefs, but with the intuitions, I am coming to believe that it is time to invite Anna Liberata de Souza's spirit to the Ouija board that, at the end of the day, history itself is.

CHAPTER 2

The History of the English Empire as a Fall

P. V. Ramaswami Raju

It was July and the southwest monsoon had arrived in Hyderabad. As the car idled in standstill traffic on a waterlogged road with bubbling potholes, I mindlessly scrolled through my phone. Suddenly the whooshing of the wipers and the rumble of the rain were interrupted by the electronic beep of an email message. "Dear Dr. Leela Prasad," it said:

> I came to know about your work on ethnography in colonial India, in an article under *Madras Miscellany*, "When the Postman Knocked" by S. Muthaiah. I am glad to inform you that the great-grandson of P. V. Ramaswami Raju, P. V. Sundaresan, resides in Chennai. I have informed him about this and very soon you will be hearing from him with more information on P. V. Ramaswami Raju, who had written *Pratapachandra Vilasam* and *Sreemad Ramanatha Rajangala Mahodyanam*. By now you must be wondering who I am? I am the grandson of P. V. Ramaswami Raju's son's first cousin, P. V. Bhaskara Raju.[1]

The message was signed by Dr. T. D. Babu and included a phone number.

I almost jumped out of the car to dance in the rain. The email was a response to an article published *ten* years earlier. In 2003 I wrote to Mr. Muthaiah, a historian of colonial Madras (now Chennai), who authored a regular column called "Madras Miscellany" in the regional edition of *The Hindu*, a leading national daily. I was hoping he could help me find biographical information on P. V. Ramaswami Raju (1852–1897), who had written plays, essays, poems, fables, social drama, and comedies in English, Tamil, and Telugu, and even translated Shakespeare into Tamil. Years ago, Muthaiah had published a similar query that had helped me find information about Pandit S. M. Natesa Sastri; this time there had been no response. I pursued every biographical trace in Ramaswami Raju's writings: records of the Department of Sea Customs in the Tamil Nadu Archives, the barrister rosters of London's Inner Temple, and the employment records of University College London, for instance. I learned a great deal about where he had worked and what he had written. But I still did not have a sense of him that perhaps his descendants could provide. And now, ten years later, like a little paper boat that startles you in a street stream, a channel I had considered closed had been opened by Dr. Babu's discovery of a newspaper clipping that he had misplaced.

I called Dr. Babu immediately. A marine biologist and founder of civic organizations in Chennai, Babu connected me to his uncles, Ramaswami Raju's great-grandsons, Mr. P. V. Sundaresan, a retired senior executive in a private company in Chennai, and Dr. P. V. Ramamurti, a retired professor of psychology and dean at Sri Venkateshwara University, Tirupati. A few conversations and some days later, taking up their invitation, I showed up in Chennai with copies of all the books by Ramaswami Raju that I had collected over the years. I met Babu at an intersection just off the Royapettah High Road. He had agreed to take me to Sundaresan's house, which was only a short distance away but would have been tricky for me to locate. "I've managed to get hold of this," Babu said, showing me a copy of Ramaswami Raju's Tamil musical play—the first play in Tamil—*Pratapachandra Vilasam*.[2] Sundaresan was waiting on the front steps of an airy modern structure tucked behind a canopy of old trees and a fitness center. Within minutes we were chatting in Telugu over a special celebratory homemade lunch with Sundaresan's children and grandchildren, in honor of our shared connection to their erudite ancestor. Ramaswami Raju, I learned, belonged to a Telugu-speaking family that had its roots in colonial Madras, with an ancestral connection to the village of Vallam in Panruti *taluk* of the Cuddalore district of modern Tamil Nadu. (The *taluk* and the village names supplied the initials P. and V. in Ramaswami Raju's name.) Traditionally Rajus are a peasant landowning community, sometimes affiliated with the Kshatriya (warrior) caste order.

Ramaswami Raju wrote in what we may call a "double register," a style he perfected. The double register is a creative strategy that simultaneously speaks in two voices, two languages, sometimes across two cultures, creating meanings and suggestions that ripple in many, even counter-flowing directions. The result is more than satire; it is a theater of being, by which I mean two things. First, Ramaswami Raju's writings reveal the persona of a raconteur who is, at different times (and sometimes all at once), a political critic, an ironic humorist, a spiritual seeker, and an enchanted enchanter. There is thus in his writings the constant presence of an allusion to *something else*—a something else that creates a near invisible adjacency of meaning beyond the worlds indexed by the words. Second, there is the theater of English rule in India with its dramatis personae and its presumptions. Imperialism as a category of rule troubled Ramaswami Raju throughout his life. Its imperatives and impulses were founded on a colossal arrogance that presumed the right to possess and dispossess persons and property. If English empire fortified itself at least in part through a belief in its higher moral ground, its civilizational superiority, and its unvitiated past—all infused into the Macaulayan idea of "English history"—Ramaswami Raju sought to destabilize these foundational constructs through a sophisticated double register that seemingly praised and simultaneously critiqued empire's practices. In his last piece of writing, an essay on "the religious life of Hindus," he says: "The causes of the greatness of England have been summed up by some in three words—Christianity, Commerce and Conquest. St. Paul's Cathedral, The Bank of England and the British Parliament may be said to be the emblems of the three great causes. The British people are really proud of these."[3] As I will show, the double register often also opens up life worlds in which Europe is not the center, and sometimes is even subjugated to an Asian center. I argue that through moral rescaling and geopolitical reorientation, Ramaswami Raju was already engaged in the task of "provincializing Europe."[4]

As I immersed myself in Ramaswami Raju's writings and interacted with his family in Chennai over the years, two distinctive biographies of Ramaswami Raju began to converge. I began to understand the lightning-like political audacity that characterized his voice and the lotus-like sovereignty of his self.

A Lightning-Like Audacious Voice

I caught my first glimpse of Ramaswami Raju through the introduction that Henry Morley, professor of English literature at University College London wrote for Ramaswami Raju's *Tales of the Sixty Mandarins* (1886). Morley says:

> He is a graduate of the Madras University; he is a Member of the Asiatic Society; and he had just been called to the bar at the Inner Temple when he left England for India, and left the manuscript of these tales in

my hands. We had come into friendly relations at University College, London, where he was Lecturer on Tamil and Telugu in the Indian School for the training of Selected Candidates for the Indian Civil Service.[5]

Ramaswami Raju had gone to England in 1882 to study law at the Inner Temple (one of four professional associations in England for lawyers). The entry in the student register of the Inner Temple describes him as "P. V. Ramaswami (aged 30) of Madras, India, BA, formerly Inspector, Sea Customs, Madras, the eldest son of P V Ramaswami of Madras, Government Superintendent of Salt." The entry notes that he was "admitted [to the Inner Temple] on 4 November 1882, and called to the bar on 29 April 1885."[6] I learned from Sundaresan that after Ramaswami Raju had returned, he became a successful advocate in the High Court of Madras.

In the little over two years of his studentship, from late 1882 to early 1885, Ramaswami Raju, perhaps to support himself, applied for the position of lecturer in Telugu and Tamil at University College London. His application tells us that he had been "headmaster, Pachhiappah's High School, Conjevaram [Kanchipuram], Madras; till recently Examiner to the University of Madras—Tamil and the Uncovenanted Civil Service—Telugu."[7] Pachhiappah's High School was a private school founded in 1846, prestigious as the first non-missionary Western-style educational institution funded by a Hindu trust, and reputed to be a feeder school for the University of Madras.[8] Colonel R. M. MacDonald, the director of public instruction for the Madras Presidency, wrote in his testimonial, "A copy of the 1879 Report of the school at Conjevaram shows that that the attendance had risen from 140 to 203, the matriculation class from 4 to 10, and the quality of work and discipline reflected great credit on the headmaster, Mr. P. V. Ramaswami Raju." Other testimonials effusively praise Ramaswami Raju's expertise in Tamil, Telugu, and Sanskrit.[9] The search committee's report concludes with a quotation from one of the testimonials: "I can scarcely conceive a rival candidate in the essential points."[10] Ramaswami Raju also offered to teach Tamil and Telugu to British officers who were preparing for their postings to India. In the archives of University College London I found an 1883 letter by Ramaswami Raju. It triggered a strange sense of déjà vu regarding my own experiences of living in Edinburgh as a child and in London as an adult. Perhaps it was the nameless awareness of being brown in England, even though a hundred years separated our experiences. The letter is addressed to an unnamed "Sir." Ramaswami Raju says: "Telugu is my 'mother tongue' and Tamil is the Indian language in which I graduated at Madras. I need hardly observe that

I should be able to afford you special facilities to converse fluently in these languages and make your progress in the literature of such as satisfactory as possible before you leave for India."[11]

Ramaswami Raju's political views had already begun to show in a tongue-in-cheek manner when he was just twenty-four. *Lord Likely* (1876), a play he had written six years before he landed in London to study for his law degree, is ostensibly a lost-and-found story of a young marquis who, as a baby, is presumed to have drowned in a shipwreck. The play, set in London, is a sly critique of British policy and conduct in India. The central characters are Sir Strictly Sternface (a retired governor of India), Lady Homely (a former memsahib), Sir Dreadful Dash (a failed colonel returned from Algeria), Sir Stingy Lucre (a Kentish baronet), and Quicklash (a former key official of British India). A couple of the minor characters are General Sir Hasty Crack Caput and Major Mincemeat. These caricatured archetypes of colonial figures become quasi-real as Ramaswami Raju stages British rule and its ruination of India, pointedly in two "aside" scenes. In one, two clownish characters, Gog and Wire, bring the baronet Sir Stingy Lucre to the ex-governor Strictly Sternface's mansion.[12] In their banter, Gog and Wire describe Strictly Sternface as someone with a calm countenance. He is the sort of ruler who, "how'er low his position at first," would convert a country—as he did "the country of the mogul in the Indies"—into such a paradise that the devil himself would want to tempt another Eve in it.[13] This motif of the fall from paradise is one that Ramaswami Raju found tremendous political use for—as we will see in his long narrative poem *Sreemat Ramanatha Rajangala Mahodyanam* (The Auspicious Story of the Great Park of the English Raj).[14] In fact, in a preceding "aside" scene, a teacher named Simon Twaddle conducts a class in a "subterranean vault in the City." Twaddle describes in graphic shorthand the fall of Adam and Eve in paradise: Eve "ate up the forbidden fruit" and Adam "got a wigging." He then lists other biblical events—Cain "cut down" his brother Abel and the Lord cursed his blood"—and rhetorically asks the pupils Cockrifle, William Hiccup, and Quickshear, "Now, tell me if Evil then is not a right bequest to the race?" Twaddle's lecture for the day focuses on how theft, housebreaking, and robbery are "necessary institutions" for the existence of society, where "polished crimes are all the fashion of the day." The lesson concludes with a review of the main categories of theft—"theft simple and theft compound"—that are "sanctioned by Acts of Parliament" and common law. Twaddle's *summum bonum* teaching, though, is that liberty is the Briton's birthright. So innate is the Briton's love for liberty that every English cat can mew lectures on it to "many a tyrant abroad."[15]

To return to Gog and Wire, after they show a general confusion about the location of India, speculating that it is possibly somewhere "between the Spice islands and the continent discovered by Captain Cook," Wire declares that India is that "country that's covered all over with temples, Brahmins, and wealth." The group is joined by Quicklash, a former official in India, who begins to show the baronet around the mansion. It is "a little museum in itself," he declares. Actually, it is full of the loot that the governor has brought back from India. The walls are decked with hunting trophies, which include the head of a great horned buffalo, the skin of a leopard, and the tusks of an elephant. The ivory-handled dagger "*had* from a great Rajah" (my emphasis) also festoons the wall, along with a "collection rare of birds and shells and pictures, and baubles and trinkets and other toys gathered in the east." It is hardly an innocent reference. Ramaswami Raju was surely aware of the Museum of India in the headquarters of the East India Company in London. Until it was dismantled in 1861 and its exhibits dispersed across various locations in London, the museum displayed Indian booty from "intricate ivory carvings, jewel-inlaid daggers and spears, gorgeous fabrics, rugs and carpets" to "a replica of the tomb of the founder of the Sikh Empire Runjeet Singh," "an effigy of the Muslim ruler Nawab Schurff smoking a hookah," and "thousands of models of ordinary Indian people 'clad, or half-clad, or unclad' cooking, conjuring, digging, exercising, juggling, snake-charming and weaving."[16]

Quicklash—his name suggestive of his method—quickly chronicles his political successes. He boasts: "Pray, who was it that wrote the Minute that gave the Sirdar Thulwar Singh his due? Who was it who suggested to Sir Strictly that the only mode of giving peace to the province was deposing the prince Zulum Shah, and putting on the musnud [*masnad*: throne], in his stead, the Prince Puppet Jah Bahadur?" The thin fictionalizing of names barely provides cover from the rain of allusions; instead it creates a spate of adjacent meaning. All too real are the English *shikars*, the great hunts that depleted India of its wildlife;[17] the broad plunder of things and species such as Tipu Sultan's ivory-handled dagger, a spoil of the Fourth Anglo-Mysore War of 1799.[18] This war, in fact, generated several trophies for the British monarchy (which one can see today for a steep fee at the Tower of London's Jewel House or the Victoria and Albert Museum). Quicklash's boast brings to mind a composite of allusions to the insidious politics of Company rule. First, in 1848–49, Lord Dalhousie, the governor-general of India from 1812 to 1860 (who uncannily resembles Sir Strictly Sternface),[19] aggressively suppressed the Sikh rebellion in Punjab. He then had his foreign secretary, Henry M. Elliot, draw up a vengeful treaty that stripped the nine-year-old

Raja Dalip Singh of Punjab and all his jewels including the Koh-i-noor diamond and wrenched him from his mother, Rani Jind Kaur, a feisty regent
who was quickly exiled.[20] Does Ramaswami Raju's character Quicklash contain a trace of Elliot, who was also a bricolage chronicler of Mughal history?
The second allusion could be to an earlier event of 1838, when the British
deposed the Mughal emperor Akbar Shah II ("Prince Zulum Shah" in the
play) and replaced him with his son Bahadur Shah Zafar ("Prince Puppet Jah
Bahadur")—who became the "last Mughal."[21] Incidentally, Elliot was assistant to the political resident and commissioner at Delhi in 1830.[22]

On a first reading, Lord Likely appears to be similar to Ramaswami Raju's
other early plays Urjoon Sing (1875) and Maid of the Mere (1879), as it imitates
nineteenth-century English drama, teeming with themes from English literary history and social custom that would have been alien to its author's lived
experience. Indeed, an English reviewer, identified by the initials H. T. W.,
concluded contemptuously that Lord Likely was an instance of failed mimicry
of high British social life by an overimaginative Indian litterateur.[23] Yet mimicry in power-stratified contexts is not the imitative aspiration that H.T.W. so
naïvely thinks it is. Mimicry is a political act. It is, as Homi Bhabha has said,
"the sign of a double articulation; a complex strategy of reform, regulation,
and discipline, which 'appropriates' the Other as it visualizes power. . . . The
menace of mimicry is its double vision, which in disclosing the ambivalence
of colonial discourse also disrupts its authority."[24] The historical exposé demonstrates how Ramaswami Raju's play is more than mimicry; it employs a
double register. Lord Likely unfolds between allegory and satire and performs
"English speech" to deconstruct English conceits about empire. Through
Twaddle's pedagogic method and the underground training center, Ramaswami Raju deploys the theme of Christian transgressions to enumerate the
closet routines of British imperialism. And via Quicklash's walk through the
museum-like rooms of the ex-governor's house in London, the very seat
of colonial exercises, Ramaswami Raju orchestrates a recollection—a recollection that not only names, describes, and makes visible the moral and
economic inebriety of colonialism but also makes the colonizers themselves
inadvertently confess it.

If the idea of England occupies Lord Likely, which Ramaswami Raju wrote
while in India, it is Asia that rules the imaginary of his Tales of the Sixty
Mandarins, which he completed during his two years in London. Just as Old
Deccan Days had announced itself with the image of an imperial Ganesha,
Sixty Mandarins arrived in 1886 with its own "Eastern" aura: a green and gold
cover with colorful Chinese figures carrying golden satchels, a title in letters
that look like bamboo sticks, and a Chinese lantern on the spine. The illustra-

tions in the book were done by one of Britain's best-known illustrators of the time, Gordon F. Browne, who illustrated books such as Daniel Defoe's *Robinson Crusoe* (1885), Jonathan Swift's *Gulliver's Travels* (1886), and Washington Irving's *Rip Van Winkle* (1887). (Browne's famous father, Hablot Knight Browne, known as "Phiz," had illustrated Charles Dickens's work.)[25] The book is reminiscent of the frame-narrative format of well-known Eastern story collections such as the Sanskrit *Kathāsaritsāgara* (Ocean of Story) and the Arabic *Alf laylah wa-laylah* (A Thousand and One Nights). In *Sixty Mandarins*, a Chinese prince has sixty learned mandarins (wise men) for friends, each of whom tells him a story. At the end of each narrative, the prince pithily sums up the story and what he gleans to be its moral. The summing-up inspires another mandarin to tell a different story, sometimes expanding on the prince's interpretation of the previous one. And so it goes until all sixty mandarins have told him a tale.

When I discovered *Tales of the Sixty Mandarins* amidst other collections of tales that were published around the same time, I expected Ramaswami Raju to rehearse the obsessions of colonial-era anthropologists and comparative mythologists: *In which province were these tales found? How do they relate to (so-called) classical motifs? What do they reveal about the physical attributes and the social and religious mentalité of a people? Where on the ladder of civilization are they positioned?* Instead, his colleague Henry Morley's introduction to the book tells us: "This is a real book of new Fairy Tales. Gatherings of the legends of the people, partly Indian, partly Chinese, have been touched by the genius of the writer, himself from the East, who brings his own wit and fancy to the telling of his tales, and is *as ready to invent as to hand down tradition.*" In his preface Ramaswami Raju writes:

> In a country like India, or China, where people from all parts of Asia, if not the world, meet for commercial purposes, there is free interchange, not only of commodities, but also of ideas. In the course of such friendly communion, not seldom the speakers cite proverbs, tales, and traditions, by way of argument or illustration, in the way best suited to the special subject of discourse. Listening to such talk, not to speak of higher paths of research, is one of the chief sources from which stories like these might be drawn. . . . It may be added that the difficulty of tracing the origin, or recognising the position [of these tales] or their parallels, in "the lore of the learned of the land" will . . . be found to be very great.[26]

Furthermore, so difficult is this task that scholars too would be baffled about the origins of the stories and perhaps not even recognize them. Yet,

says Ramaswami Raju, stories and proverbs are told and heard in Asian mar-
ketplaces and along the bustling trade routes that connect the many regions
of Asia—and with that we are left to presume that Ramaswami Raju places
himself in those circuits where ideas are exchanged and cross-cultural observations occur. At such a crossroads, the question of scientific origins and
genealogies and types of humankind becomes secondary—in fact worth-
less—to the absorption and creative transmission of narrative. To make his
argument more potent, he tells us how nonplussed the Arabic scholars whom
he consulted about "The Story of the Caliph Haroun Alraschid and His Fool"
had been. As much as it seemed to *resemble* the stories in which Caliph Harun
al-Rashid and Zubeida appear in the "Arabian Nights Entertainments," they
said, it was not to be found in it or elsewhere. He then defers to the authority
of a mysterious "Wazeer Abdul Ali" of an equally mysterious "Three Maha
Mondon Pur" who says that "so far as such popular tales go, it matters not
whether they are anchored firmly like great ships in the havens of the writings of the learned, or floating like stray waifs on the seas of the traditions
of the people, provided they fulfil the triple conditions of being wholesome,
entertaining, and instructive."[27] In short, stories are not for debating origins
and types; they are for pleasure and learning.

In setting the stories in an Asia that ranges from China, Japan, and Korea
to Morocco and Algeria, from Uzbekistan and Azerbaijan to the islands of
Indonesia, Ramaswami Raju suggests a political vision that gives us, in Wang
Hui's words, "the possibility to create new narratives of 'world history.'"[28]
Imams, sheiks, and sultans, Arabian princesses, rabbis, Buddhist monks,
ordinary humans, animals, and other creatures populate the panoramic Asiatic geography of the tales. The prince's mandarin friends narrate out of a
cosmopolitan memory that crosses customs of regions with recorded (and
contested) histories of places such as Samarkand, Algiers, Kashgar, Alexandria, and Bihar. In the process, they draw attention to Asia as a parallel zone
of entry into world systems of economy, politics, and cultural and religious
flows. As Prasenjit Duara notes, such flows were "nothing short of world
transforming."[29] We might alongside note a visceral irony: it is in the colonial metropolis of London, probably consulting its prodigious libraries, that
Ramaswami Raju conceptualizes such a turn away from a Eurocentric view
of history.[30] The story "The Famous Book on Alchymy," for instance—and a
classic instance—is about the now lost city of Balkh (in modern-day northern
Afghanistan), a city that was among the world's greatest cultural centers in
late antiquity (its pre-Islamic name was Bactra, in Greek), and the birthplace
of the renowned thirteenth-century poet Jalāl al-din Rūmī. As Arezou Azad
notes, Balkh was "the missing link between the western and eastern Iranian

worlds, at the crossroads between the 'Iranian' and 'Turkic' peoples of the north, at the western fringe of Buddhism, the mythical death place of Zoroaster (or Zarathustra, the prophet of the ancient Iranian Zoroastrians), and the cradle of Sufism."[31]

Ramaswami Raju's story takes for its background the historically established Arab invasion of Balkh in the early eighth century. The plot, though, possibly fictionalized, is about how a prominent library of Balkh was destroyed. The story tells us that this library held a book on alchemy composed thousands of years ago by a magician-philosopher who was born in Ethiopia, trained in Egypt, and settled down in Balkh practicing "the religion of Zartusht."[32] Then, artfully using popular legends about the destruction of Alexandria's library, the story describes how the invading Arab general commands that all books in the Balkh library be burned; those books that repeat what the Qur'an says are redundant, and those that do not are heretical. The general, however, comes to an agreement with the Jewish people of Balkh (known to have historically lived there) about preserving the book on alchemy. The book is sacred to Balkh's Jews, but since they cannot raise the money to keep the bargain, the famous book of alchemy is burned after all. (The view that the second caliph Umar ibn al-Khattab [r. 634–644] had ordered the destruction of the Alexandrian library and said words to that effect had been debunked as a polemical myth,[33] but it seems to have given Ramaswami Raju fabular material.) What is striking about the story is not how it makes up its fiction but how it constructs Balkh itself—as a learned city between the pre-Islamic and the Islamic and as a space in which Buddhists, Jews, Muslims, and Zoroastrians robustly coexisted—at least before the Mongol conquests of the thirteenth century. The reference to alchemy immediately calls up Balkh's prominent place in ancient Egyptian traditions of alchemy. The formidable Arabic scholar and alchemist of the eleventh century Abu Ali Ibn Sīnā (Latinized, Avicenna) tells us his father was from Balkh.[34] In this manner, as the stories in *Sixty Mandarins* unfold maps of Asia's pasts, we are taken to a world of abundant interactive history in which Europe is included as a player with a role but not as a director, center stage.

If we look for a center-staging of Europe in *Sixty Mandarins*, we will find it in an especially satirical story called "The Virgin from Velayet," in which the sultan of Damascus, in the hope of transforming his country into the free and enlightened place that he has heard Velayet, in England, to be, seeks to marry a virgin from there—and thus brings home his English sultana. "The political relations between the East and the West have given rise to some amusing tales," explains Ramaswami Raju in the preface, blandly continuing, "The nucleus of this story was found among a section of the Indian peasantry, and must have arisen from that good-humoured representation of Western ideas and institutions, which very often recommends itself to their rustic and unsophisticated hearts." The sultana, who, Victoria-like, takes "great interest in the welfare of her subjects," guides the sultan in the process of a seismic transformation, undoing many indigenous institutions so that "all arts of civilized life" could begin to flourish in Damascus. While this is going on, the sultan asks his English sultana if they should not also replicate the British Parliament in Damascus. He observes:

> Of course, in your country, the members of this body, as you said, appear to spend a great part of their time in factious declamations and hair-splitting harangues. Again, there appear to be two parties in the body, one saying "no" to every "yes" of the other, out of sheer party spirit and jealousy. When one party gets into power, the other goes about the country inflaming the hearts of the people against their successful rivals till they pull them down and step into their place.[35]

The sultan proposes a solution to prevent the parliamentary problem: summarily execute any member of Parliament who talks for more than five minutes, including himself, the head of state. (I am reminded of the Red Queen in Lewis Carroll's *Through the Looking-Glass*, which was published in 1871 and became immensely popular at the time. The Red Queen's "solution," like the sultan's, is to cut people's heads off constantly.) With this observation, Ramaswami Raju maneuvers the story in the direction of lampoon. The story ends with the resigned sultana declaring that a "naturally" despotic regime could never become a democratic one. But it is hardly lost on us that the story is also describing the autocratic measures of imperial polity and the power-grubbing and self-serving habits of British parliamentarians. Such a model of Parliament deserves to be muted, the sultan seems to say, if not made extinct.

A Lotus-Like Sovereignty of Self

It is unclear when exactly after 1885 Ramaswami Raju returned to India. But what can be said with certainty is that after he returned, the political cosmopolitanism that had marked his work began to converge with his interest in Hindu sacred narrative and philosophy. The conversation introduced a dramatic new voice in his writing. The lightning-like strikes in his work were now also complemented by a complexity best encapsulated in the image of the lotus, which is one of the most celebrated symbols in Hindu, Buddhist, and Jain art, mythology, and spiritual practice. As the art historian Stella

Kramrisch describes it: "With its root in the mud, its stalk traversing the entire depth of the waters on which it rests its leaves, its flower open to the light of heaven, the lotus belongs to this world and those below and above, to light, earth and water. Its open flower emits a fragrance of the subtlest vibrations."[36] These qualities of the lotus have given it a commanding presence as a symbol of sovereignty in Sanskrit poetry. David Smith writes: "The lotus is a support, a provider of coherence, moving through the content of the poem with a binding and strengthening force. Through its pervasive invasion of the subject matter of *kāvya*, it creates a poetic universe that obeys its own laws—or should we speak rather of a universe that simply succumbs to the dominance of the lotus and does not question its obtrusive presence."[37]

As I spoke to Sundaresan[38] and Ramamurti,[39] the two great-grandsons of Ramaswami Raju, perhaps the last generation to know the family's stories about him, I became conscious that the hundred years that had passed since Ramaswami Raju's death had distilled the family's memories. Oral ancestral memory rarely exists as a singular, disembodied diachronic narrative. Rather, it is a collection of vital synchronic impressions composed by different tellers who find resonances between their own lives and those of their ancestors. Sundaresan had heard stories about Ramaswami Raju from his father, and Ramamurti from his father, his maternal grandfather, and Sundaresan's father. Their recollections did not contradict but expanded on and added to each other's, touching their own lives in different moments in different ways. I present here a pastiche of impressions.

"Ramaswami Raju's setting sail to London was itself a great achievement. . . . [H]e came from a middle-class family with meager resources, and it was with financial assistance from known sources that he finally set sail," says Sundaresan in a biographical note he wrote up for me after we met in Chennai in July 2013. But before he left for England, Ramaswami Raju promised his mother he would be a vegetarian (possibly to avoid beef and pork, I suspected, as traditionally the Rajus are not vegetarian). It was a practice he continued even after he returned. The going in London was not easy either. "It was believed that for survival in London, Ramaswami Raju wrote and sold poems and stories," Sundaresan's note said. When we met next in April 2014, I shared with him my finding that Ramaswami Raju had taught Telugu and Tamil as a part-time instructor at University College London and at Oxford. We wondered whether the numerous Indian stories by Ramaswami Raju that appeared in *The Leisure Hour*, the popular Victorian-era magazine, were related to his monetary struggles.[40] His financial fortunes, however, seem to have improved after he returned to Madras. In a detailed email account, Ramamurti wrote in July 2018: "My father told me Ramaswami

Raju was given a large estate in Royappettah that included the area of the present Royappettah government hospital, neighbouring wooded areas that extended nearly to the present area where Sundaresan lives. Ultimately, [the family] gave a good bit of the land away to the government retaining only some houses and area in and around where Sundaresan now lives." This was the house I had visited. Both great-grandsons say that the government gifted this land in recognition of Ramaswami Raju's achievements, but I wondered whether the gift was also in appreciation of the Telugu and Tamil training he provided to prospective officers of British India. Ramaswami Raju had also flourished as a barrister, becoming a civic-minded citizen of colonial Madras who, I was told, donated away much of his wealth and property to charitable trusts and public welfare institutions.

Ramaswami Raju's command of Sanskrit came through an early transformative spiritual experience. According to Sundaresan, his great-grandfather's spiritual experiences "began long before he left for England." It was curious that Ramaswami Raju seems to have chosen not to allude to these experiences directly in any of his writings. As Sundaresan had heard it told, this is the story of the mystical experience:

> One night Ramaswami Raju had a strange dream. He dreamt that the next morning, a *bhikshu* [spiritual mendicant] would knock on his door asking for alms. The *bhikshu* would be no ordinary *bhikshu* but a very learned Brahman. As the dream had predicted, a *bhikshu* came calling. Ramaswami Raju told the *bhikshu* that he knew he was a learned man and asked if he could please recite the Ramayana. The *bhikshu* told him that he had had a similar dream and that he would be glad to recite the Ramayana. It would take a month. When should he start? Ramaswami Raju said, *"Shubhasya shigram"*—good deeds should begin at the earliest. After the thirty-day recital, Ramaswami Raju wrote a shorter Ramayana in Sanskrit verse.[41]

Babu, who was listening to the conversation, added, "I've heard that the *bhikshu* wrote *bijaksharas* [sacred mantric syllables] on his tongue." I was reminded of the popular story about the great poet Kalidasa that my mother told me—a story that cannot be found in critical commentaries on Kalidasa. The goddess Kali, the story goes, was so moved by his hapless circumstances that she wrote on his tongue, and Kalidasa, who knew no Sanskrit, was transformed into the legendary poet who came to shape the literary history of Sanskrit poetry. Ramaswami Raju himself does not mention any formal training in Sanskrit, though his testimonials observe that he was not only competent in Sanskrit but also wrote Sanskrit plays, which were performed by the Sanskrit Dramatic Society in Madras. The great-grandsons had no doubt. Ramamurti said, "My maternal grandfather told me that PVRR was a Sanskrit scholar; he used to host scholars from Benares and discuss spiritual matters with them."

The story about the *bhikshu* is also about Ramaswami Raju as a spiritual inquirer. Ramamurti recalled:

> Sundaresan's father used to tell me that when he was young, he had accompanied Ramaswami Raju [his grandfather] on a pilgrimage. First to Badrinath, and then onwards to Kedarnath, Kailash, and Manasarovar [pilgrimage sites in the Himalayas]. They used to travel during the day on ponies and rest for the night in *dharamshalas* [pilgrim guesthouses]. It was a description I enjoyed listening to. . . . My grandfather also told me that Ramaswami Raju was spiritually oriented and used to communicate with trees on his long morning walks.

Ramaswami Raju had called his estate Temple Garden, a name that brought to my mind Ramaswami Raju's stay at London's Inner Temple. In fact, Sundaresan had told me on one of my earlier visits that in the evenings, Ramaswami Raju used to go up to the roof of the building, which he later donated to the government (and is now the Government Royapettah Hospital). He would isolate himself there and meditate. "Some divine force guided Ramaswami Raju," mused Sundaresan. "The memories are all now fading. But his blessings are definitely there on this family. We feel it."[42]

The Great Park: A Sacred Ethos for a Profane Empire

England, "that little island which is but a particle of earth in the great sea, the hideous home of eternal unhappiness," is where native Englishmen live "without any form of enlightenment like wild animals."[43] How did this audacious statement escape censure? In fact, the statement is one among many that abound in Ramaswami Raju's remarkable long narrative poem titled *Srīmat Rājāṅgala Mahodyānam, or, The Great Park of Rajangala* (the English Raj), which he began publishing in 1894 when he was an advocate in the Madras High Court.[44] *The Great Park* was Ramaswami Raju's magisterial ambition. In his words, it was meant to be "an account of the origin and rise of the Angala [British] Empire on Earth in Samskrita verse (25,000 thousand stanzas) with Angala [English] translation."[45] The "account" was never completed. Ramaswami Raju died in 1897, three years after he published the first segment—1,500 Sanskrit verses with a parallel English translation of text that had been conceptualized to be of a length comparable to that of

Valmiki's Ramayana. Nonetheless, these 1,500 verses express a grand idea—the originating moment of the English race—and in the process, a view of "history" both from below and from above. This unfinished narrative, a swan song for all we know, can also be read as the final account of an individual whose literary immersion and fluency in a Western episteme had never, at the end of the day, co-opted the flourishing of his religious personhood and eclectic literary self. *The Great Park* carries the resonance of Ramaswami Raju's transformative experience with the *bhikshu* who had initiated him, using mantras, into the Ramayana.

Synoptically, the 1,500 verses of the unfinished narrative are a flashback. The central narrator is the elephant-headed god Ganesha, the proverbial scribe of the epic the Mahabharata, who tells a story to Ramodwitiya (Rama II), the emperor of a prosperous country called Samnaya Bharata in some future time. Ramodwitiya hears the story and commands that it be written down and disseminated across the universe as a sacred text whose reading bestows well-being and prosperity upon all listeners. In this flashback narration, the English empire is long over, and many rulers have come and gone, the fall of each brought on by a corrupt and self-serving leadership. In Ganesha's narration, the originating moment of the English race happens through a dramatic fall from heaven: In the grand heavenly court of Indra, the king of gods, a spectacular performance has been arranged in honor of two special guests, the mighty god Shiva and his equally powerful wife, Parvati. As the performance reaches its climax, a celestial musician (*gandharva*), who is the lead harpist, strikes a wrong chord in a drunken stupor. Darkness immediately shrouds the court. For this cataclysmic mistake, Indra expels the *gandharva*, cursing him to live "without a name" on earth, on a miserable "little island," which we discover is England. The fallen *gandharva* is the progenitor of the English people. With abundant digressions into magical lands and other histories, and with only 1,500 verses of the hoped-for 25,000 verses completed, we do not get to hear the story of how the British established an empire in India or a narrative of India's Mughal past.

With "the English race" being the subject of *The Great Park*, the narrative curates two ways of speaking within and across the Sanskrit and English texts, intermingling praise and critique, and the sacred and the secular. It is in this text that I see most vividly Ramaswami Raju's political voice—which I described earlier as lightning-like—illuminate the sovereignty of his self, which I find is lotus-like. In *Lord Likely*, we saw how English characters in an English play themselves inadvertently lampoon English imperialism, and in *Sixty Mandarins*, we saw how a "collection" of Asian tales defies imperial disciplines of anthropology and comparative mythology while dislodging

Europe as the center of the world and world history. Here in *The Great Park*, the double register is enabled by what I call "absent translation," a strategy of translation in which certain details or features are deliberately left untranslated without altering the plot. Only a reader literate in both Sanskrit and English will see the innovations involving syllables and semantics that are available in literary Sanskrit and liturgical Sanskrit but are absent in the English translation that Ramaswami Raju provides alongside. Giridhara Shastry, a friend and former professor of English and Sanskrit at Sri JCBM College in Sringeri, Karnataka, translated for me selected verses of Ramaswami Raju's Sanskrit text to compare against Ramaswami Raju's own translation.[46] Ramaswami Raju's translation is literally accurate, but it is marked by an "absent translation" that is missing not because of self-erasure or incompetence. Rather, "absent translation" is a strategic narrative choice that allows an author who is also the translator of the same work to position the texts in two worlds, each conveying a different resonance.[47] The juxtaposed Sanskrit and English texts create an "unprecedented [third] poetic space" and allows a reader who knows both languages and cultural worlds to see and hear different things across the two texts, in the contrast between them. The bilingual reader, in short, is able to perceive how Ramaswami Raju has represented a risky subject between and across two texts. We could say of Ramaswami Raju's poem what Velcheru Narayana Rao and David Shulman say about the translational accomplishment of the fourteenth- to fifteenth-century Telugu poet Śrīnātha: "The interactive presence of these two languages creates a third."[48]

In addition to absent translation, a second strategy that facilitates *The Great Park*'s double register is Ramaswami Raju's choice to use an aesthetic form that allows colonial power to be critiqued within a structure of piety and praise. The *purāṇa* is arguably that form. The dominant mood and narrative quality of the Sanskrit text of *The Great Park* reflect a *purāṇa*, a genre of Hindu sacred narrative whose recitation is associated with spiritual merit and well-being. Technically, the definition provided by Amarasimha, a fifth-century lexicographer, has become the notional definition of a *purāṇa*. According to this definition, to be a *purāṇa*—primarily an oral genre—a text should display five signature features (*lakṣaṇa*), called the *pañcalakṣaṇa*. First, it should narrate stories about the creation of the universe; second, it should describe how this universe is destroyed and re-created; third, it should tell stories about the genealogies of gods, mortals, and *rākṣasas* (demons); fourth, it should herald the arrival of a progenitor of a new age; and fifth, it should document the dynastic history of a ruler. These five distinguishing marks do not form a rigid structure that circumscribes a *purāṇa*; instead, as Narayana Rao points out, the five features must be thought of as forming a flexible framework that allows diverse materials to be molded to "create a world and a worldview."[49] Unfolding through dialogues between seekers and seers, a *purāṇa* enacts its ideological commitment to a worldview that could be sectarian or place-centric, taking and transforming topical events and offering new ways of looking at the present, the past, and the future.

It is easy to locate *The Great Park* in this narrative scheme. It regales readers with the story of the origin of the English and their empire in India; it takes us through lavish descriptions of both prosperous and fallen lands, charts battles and magical maps through which we are ushered by a progenitor called Mahamangala, the first Englishman; it links earthly history to cosmic events; and it presents lineages of key figures. This intermeshing of cosmological occurrences and this-worldly events is so pervasive in Indic and Indo-Persian narrative traditions—whether *itihāsa*, or *kathā*, or *caritra*, or *qiṣṣa*, to mention only a few genres—that it is important to take it seriously. Rao, Shulman, and Sanjay Subrahmanyam remind us that when, for instance, the catastrophic moment in the conflict between the eighteenth-century raja of Bobbili (present-day Andhra Pradesh, a story I return to in the next chapter) and the French coalition is recounted by the Telugu narrator through the metaphor of a "fateful cockfight," we need to think "in terms of history that includes independent insets, syncopation and whorls."[50] In other words, colonial rule is rendered differently "present" through *itihāsa-purāṇa* techniques of past-narration.

Our first step into *The Great Park* is through the gates of a mandala, which is a sacred diagram.[51] This is the first page of the book, the only page that encases its text in a special visual arrangement, and the only page that is exclusively in Sanskrit. (The other pages feature both the Sanskrit text and its English translation side by side; see figure 5.) A rectangle with decorative borders contains two sections, the first called *ādeśa* (proclamation), and below it the second, called *upadeśa* (instruction). These two sections together spell out the lofty intent of the work and set its tone. The proclamation sanctions the publication of *The Great Park*. The Sanskrit text provides the reader with a vivid description of the court in which this proclamation is made. The court is in an enchanted city called Maha Mondon, which is part of deeply interconnected cosmic and human landscapes.[52] Maha Mondon, nestling on the banks of the Ganga, is the city of the goddess Vindhyachaleshwari. It is a part of the Himalaya-adorned (*himavatālaṅkrita*) country of Samnaya Bharata, a land with a rich heritage. Samnaya Bharata is on the continent of Dharma (Dharmadvīpa), which itself belongs to the world of matter (*bhautikolōka*)

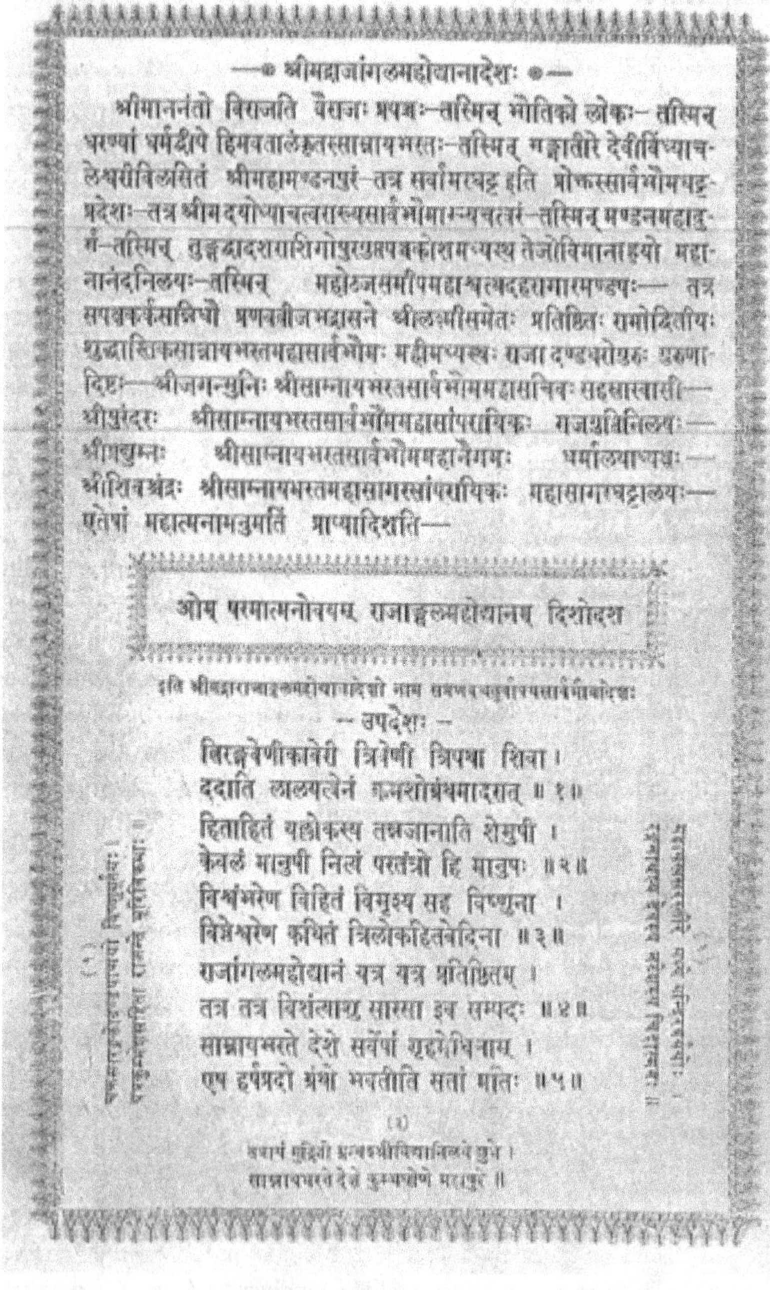

—❋ श्रीमद्राजांगलमहोदयानादेशः ❋—

श्रीमानन्ततो विराजति वैराजः श्रपञ्जः—तस्मिन् भौतिको लोकः— तस्मिन्
धरण्यां धर्मदीपे हिमवतालंकृतसाम्राज्यभरतः—तस्मिन् गङ्गातीरे देवीविद्याच-
लेश्रवीविलसितं श्रीमहामण्डनपुरं—तत्र सर्वोमरपट्ट इति प्रोक्तसार्वभौमपट्ट-
प्रदेशः—तत्र श्रीमदयोष्णाचलतस्यसार्वभौमाम्पञ्चतवं—तस्मिन् मण्डनमहाद्वा-
र्गे—तस्मिन् तुङ्गद्वादशराशिगोपुरप्रपञ्चकोशमप्यस्य तेजोविमानाद्ययो महा-
नानंदनिलयः—तस्मिन् महोज्वलसमीपमहाश्वदहरागारमण्डपः— तत्र
सप्तक्वर्क्वसन्निधौ प्रणवबीजभद्रासने श्रीलश्रीसमेतः प्रतिष्ठितः रामोदितीयः
शुद्धासिकसाम्राज्यभरतमहासार्वभौमः महिमप्यस्थः राजा दण्डभरोष्ठकः उरणा
दिष्टः—श्रीजगन्मुनिः श्रीसाम्नायभरतसार्वभौममहासचिवः सहसास्वासी—
श्रीपुंदरः श्रीसाम्नायभरतसार्वभौममहासांपरायिकः राजश्रविनिलयः
श्रीगद्युम्नः श्रीसाम्नायभरतसार्वभौममहानैगमः धर्मालयाच्यः—
श्रीशिवश्रद्रः श्रीसाम्नायभरतमहासागसांपरायिकः महासागरपट्ट्रालयः—
एतेषां महात्मनामुमर्तिं प्राप्यादिशति—

ॐ परमात्मनोवयम् राजाङ्गलमहोदयानम् दिशोदश

इति श्रीमद्राजाङ्गलमहोदयानादेशो नाम समस्तपञ्चतापरसार्वभौमादेशः—
—उपदेशः—

विरज्जवेणीकावेरी त्रिवेणी त्रिपथा शिवा ।
ददाति लाल्यत्वेन जनशोऋषमादरात् ॥ १॥

हिताहितं यल्लोकस्य तज्जानाति शेमुषी ।
केवलं मानुषी निलं पश्वंप्रो हि मानुषः ॥ २॥

विश्वंभरेण विहितं विमृश्य सह विष्णुना ।
विश्वेश्वरेण कथिते त्रिलोकहितवेदिना ॥ ३॥

राजांगलमहोदयाने यत्र यत्र प्रतिष्ठितम् ।
तत्र तत्र विशंलाद्य सास्सा इव सम्पदः ॥ ४॥

साम्राज्यभरते देशे सर्वेषां गृहधेधिनाम् ।
एष हर्षप्रदो ग्रंथो भवतीति सतां मतिः ॥ ५॥

(१)

स्वयर्थं मुद्रितो प्रन्यश्रीविद्यानिलयेव युक्ते ।
साम्राज्यभरते देशे कुम्भघोणे मदातुरे ॥

FIGURE 5. Mandala. Reproduced from P. V. Ramaswami Raju, *Srimat Rajangala Mahodyanam, or,
The Great Park of Rajangala* (Kumbakonam: Sree Vidya Press, 1894).

in a radiant universe (*vairāja prapañca*). The city is a perfect architectural mandala with named concentric squares and circles that eventually take us to the twelve-gated palace of the sovereign and righteous emperor Ramodwitiya. (Note that the name means Rama II, an allusion to the reputedly perfect reign of Rama of Ayodhya [*rāmarājya*].) Seated on a resplendent throne with his consort Sri Lakshmi, Ramodwitiya is holding court in a grand hall. Noblemen and sages surround him. Commanded by his preceptor and with the approval of his four learned teachers—Jaganmuni (the prime minister), Purandara (the commander), Pradumnya (the chief businessman), and Sivaschandra (the naval chief)—Ramodwitiya issues the proclamation.

The proclamation is set apart in its own embellished box in the middle of the page. It says:

Oṃ *paramātmanōvayam rājāṅgala mahodhyānam diśodaśa.*
We, descended from the supreme soul, command that [this book] *The Great Park of the English Empire* be spread in the ten directions.

The traditional prefix *Om*, the primordial sound signifying consciousness, makes the proclamation function like a mantra or a sacred utterance, and since, in puranic geography, the ten directions encompass the universe, the reach and potency imagined for the book become clear. A succeeding sentence clarifies that *The Great Park*'s realm is the limitless cosmic empire (*sārvabhoumadeśa*), which is held up by four great statements (the *mahavākyas*) and the syllable *Om*. Given Ramaswami Raju's interest in Vedic literature, the "four great statements" would very likely refer to the four Upanishadic "essential" statements believed to describe the unity of consciousness.[53] The book's ambitious geographic imaginary is ratified by a succeeding section called the *upadēśa*, teaching imparted by a guru to a disciple—a common feature of a puranic text. The metaphor of sacred expanse continues through this teaching: *The Great Park*, we are told, was planned by the creator Brahma after consulting the god Vishnu. A few other declaratives follow: Human intellect cannot know what is good and bad for the world, but the god Ganesha, the remover of obstacles, knows, and being the archetypal scribe, he narrates *The Great Park*. The holy rivers, Kaveri in the south and Ganga in the north, cherish and distribute this work. Wherever *The Great Park* is respected and recited, prosperity will enter as waterfowl enter a lake. And finally, it is the opinion of good people that *The Great Park* will become an object of joy to all householders in the land of Samnaya Bharata.

This teaching is then enclosed between two-line verses just as a mandala's innermost point is secured by protective boundaries. These verses extol the sacrality of the place where *The Great Park* has been printed—"Sri Vidya

Press, in the city of Kumbakonam, Madras." Kumbakonam is no ordinary city in Hindu sacred geography. It is the home of a large holy lake and temples to many forms of Vishnu. In effect, cosmic contextualization, mystical pronouncements, and visual cues irrefutably establish the identity—and authority—of the Sanskrit text of *The Great Park* as a puranic text. It recasts a mundane place into a sacred space by recovering memories of the landscape and extolling its virtues.

The last page of the book, which provides the English translation of the first page, is a complete contrast to the first. Unlike the first page, in which a purely Sanskrit text is contained in concentric rectangular mandalas, the last page is exclusively in English. The puranic tenor of the first page is now absent. The mandala-like boundaries have been (mostly) dispensed with. Instead, information such as Ramaswami Raju's credentials, his degrees, and the titles of his books, and details of his installment-pricing scheme, are provided. Indeed, this page seems to be more like an advertising brochure, which Ramaswami Raju probably intended it to be—"the language of the gods in the world of men," rather literally speaking.[54] The translation of the proclamation itself is literal and almost unintelligible: "Pranava—From the Supreme Soul (are) we—Rajangala Mahodyanam—Ten corners." This incoherent English translation withholds the semantic import of the mantra for an English (that is, a foreign) audience, making the mantric aura of the Sanskrit proclamation available exclusively to Sanskrit readers. In fact, the only three pieces of text enclosed in mandala-like borders on the last page are the sacred proclamation, the names of the gurus, and the name of the sacred city in which the narration occurs. These reflect visually what the author regards as the poem's sacred core. I return later to this point about how Ramaswami Raju controls sacrality by inserting mantras into the Sanskrit text (but not into the translation) and by determining where in the narrative the mantras should end. At this point, the text becomes non-sacred. This exercise of control over the textual aura is a sovereign act.

The real departure from the first page's tightly contained puranic ethos is the command that the emperor Ramodwitiya and the four learned teachers issue to the author of *The Great Park*, a command that is absent on the first page. These authoritative figures—of the king and the gurus—who are "ardent admirers of British rule have ordained that the work should assume a purely Indian character, that no word other than Samskrita should be found in it and that it must take the form of a narrative of the acts of Angala history by Ganesa to a spiritual Indian sovereign in a great city named Maha Mondon." Admiration for the British notwithstanding, the gurus commission a work that is nationalist in language and spirit. This account of "the origin and rise of the Angala (British) empire on earth," we are further informed, is structured as a Great Park (*mahōdyānam*) with five groves (*brindam*). The groves are named Narmabrindam, Mangalabrindam, Shishthabrindam, Varunabrindam, and Yashobrindam. Ramaswami Raju draws our attention to the fact that the initial syllables of the groves' names—na-ma-śi-vā-ya—constitute the five-syllabled (*pañcākṣari*) mantra invoking Shiva.[55] Chapters are referred to as "trees," *drumas*. Ramaswami Raju was able to complete 1,500 verses of only "the first grove," the Narmabrindam.

The metaphor of a park for an account of the English empire is a masterly literary choice. From the fifteenth century, English royalty deliberately cultivated large parks as private hunting grounds, which continue to be the property of the royal family. It was only in 1851 that London's eight royal parks were opened up to the public, providing access as an act of royal grace but with no rights of use.[56] Ramaswami Raju, living in London and familiar with English society, surely could not have missed the emblematic connection between parks and British monarchy. Even though Indian literature of earlier periods, especially Sanskrit and Persian, is full of garden landscapes that contribute to the mood and motif of the aesthetic work, Ramaswami Raju conjures something novel by organizing the story of English rule in India around the metaphor of a great park. The five parks of *The Great Park*, taking their names from Hindu sacred syllables, are now part of an *Indian* ethico-religious landscape—in which British history unfolds as one phase of a puranic history.

The main text begins with endorsements by acclaimed contemporaneous Sanskrit scholars, indicating the intellectual community to which *Rajangala Mahodyanam* belongs. Its author, we learn from these testimonials, is not an ordinary author; he is specially endowed to bring a park to life by enchanting it with cosmic time, events, and auras. The glowing letters that accompanied his application for the position of Telugu lecturer at University College London pale into bread-and-butter testimonials as we read Pandit Sri Teagarajadhvari's praise:

[Ramaswami Raju is an] eminent poet. . . . [He] is (also) well-versed in English and [he] has a sound knowledge of the principles of that great law which guides the rulers of the earth. He who knows English well rarely knows Samskrta equally well. This Ramaswami is indeed conspicuous as one deeply learned in both the languages. Proficiency in English, surpassing skill in Samskrita composition, a sound knowledge of ethics, elegant taste, charming poetical power—all these are apparent in this work.

Pandit Raghavarya, who is the author of "a commentary on the great work *Lakshmi sahasram*" and resides "on Pattarachary Street in Kumbakonam," is of the opinion that "the learned who scrutinize this work will see that it is not inferior in style to the Ramayana."[57] The family's stories of Ramaswami Raju's devotional life come to mind.

I turn now to five moments that illustrate the working of the double register in the narrative, drawing on Ramaswami Raju's prose translation of the Sanskrit verse text. At times I draw on an independent translation to highlight "absences" in Ramaswami Raju's English translation.

The First Moment: Mantra as a Textual Boundary

The narrative begins in the realm of the gods. Ganesha has just finished invoking the gods and is meditating, when the four sons of Brahma, the god of creation, approach him. They have a question for him: Could he, the wise storyteller with a long memory, explain how it had transpired that the Angalas who were but

> inhabitants of a little island had overtaken the entire earth. There is no sea where there is not some ship of theirs; there is no mart where they do not derive great profit from trading; there is no kingdom of which the head does not seek their friendship; and there is no measure of world-wide utility which is carried out without their aid. Many, who were counted brave and honorable on earth, have been conquered by them just as inferior birds are subdued by falcons. Even Bharata, the great country that has been protected by divine power, was subdued by these manly and energetic people. Wherever the invincible Angalas go endowed with dominion, the earth soon seems to smile with prosperity.

The awe, which is significantly limited to colonial success in commerce and conquest, turns to incredulity as the sages continue: "By those, who know the ancient history of the world, [the English] are said to have been originally living in the forests without any form of enlightenment like wild animals. How is it that such fame has been acquired in this world by people so described?"[58] The provocatively phrased question sits waiting for an answer while Ganesha digresses to narrate the puranic story of the churning of the ocean of milk from which Lakshmi, the goddess of prosperity, rose to the surface. He tells us that as she emerged, "the lotus with a hundred thousand petals, effulgent like the sun, where the goddess took birth, shone forth with the sea," and the gods announced that Lakshmi is the "architect of the well-being of the entire universe."[59]

Interestingly, the Sanskrit reader's entry into the poem is through the opening word *namashivaya*, the Vedic invocation to Shiva as the "supremely auspicious one" who inhabits the elements and is consciousness itself. (The mantra, we recall, provides the logic behind the names of the five books of *The Great Park*.)[60] In Ramaswami Raju's English translation the mantra—which Ganesha recites—is nominally translated as "Salutations to Siva," but a reader who knows both Sanskrit and English immediately recognizes that the potency of *namashivaya* as the five-syllabled mantra (*panchakshari*) is lost in translation. This dynamic of fullness and absence between the Sanskrit text and its English translation continues. I discovered further that the story of the birth of Lakshmi titled "Lakshmisambhava" in Sanskrit also encodes the twenty-four-letter Rig Vedic verse commonly known as the "Gayatri mantra": *tat savitur vareṇyam bhargo devasya dhīmahi dhīyo yo naḥ pracodayāt* (I meditate on that most desirable divine illumination; may the radiance of that light awaken my intelligence).[61] The Gayatri mantra is considered by

> Indian sages, saints, and practitioners to be *the* most powerful mantra of purification and transformation known to the *yogic* traditions. . . . It is an invocation for enlightenment that can have the effect of drawing other individuals into the same state. The repetition of the *Gayatri* mantra creates a unique series of vibrations that integrates a person's mental awareness with deeper levels of the unified energy system that is believed to be at the core of being.[62]

If one reads the first syllables (which appear in bold) of the twenty-four verses of this chapter vertically, one would be reciting the Gayatri (see figure 6). To illustrate, *ta sa vi*, the first syllables of the Gayatri, help form the first words of the first three verses (*tapas, samudre,* and *viṣṇus*). In fact, the Gayatri mantra resonates *throughout* the work. From the second chapter onwards, each chapter's first syllable is once again from the Gayatri, and in this manner the "sound" of the Gayatri permeates the text. Since the mantra is absent in the English translation, the potential for a transformative meditational experience of the text is precluded for the English-only reader. Sanskrit readers who may choose not to avail themselves of the mantric experience can still participate in the literary play within the Sanskrit text. Without com-

तपस्वाध्यायनिरतास्तास्सर्वे देवाः प्रहर्षिताः ।
अखण्ड सागरे विष्णुं समद्रमथने परा ॥२६॥
समुद्रे भाति देवेश रत्नजालं महाद्युषम् ।
तस्मिन् वरेण्यमस्मन्यं कृपया दाह्यमर्हसि ॥२७॥
विष्णुर्देव्या सुमहतीं नित्यमात्मगदिरिशताम् ।
उवाच त्वं महाभागे भवरतमउत्तमम् ॥२८॥
तुश्या सा करुणा प्राह किं रूपं खलसब्ये ।
तवेप्सितं तदेवेश वक्तुमर्हसि सांप्रतम् ॥२९॥
वं प्राह ततो विष्णुः क्षीरसममितप्रभम् ।
श्रुत्वा तं सर्वलोकानां मङ्गलं महदाचर ॥३०॥
रेखा चान्द्रमसी दीक्षा यथा भाति शरद्धने ।
तथा दचार करुणासागरे रूपमद्भुतम् ॥३१॥
निखिले जगदम्येष निनिमिषमवेक्षत ।
तां तव सर्वभावेन परयानन्दरूपिणीम् ॥३२॥
यं ह्रास्य फलमिलाड्डुर्यायचक्रनिरीक्षयताप ।
तपसः फलमिलाहुर्मुनियोब्रह्मवादिनः ॥३३॥
भद्रं सर्वस्य लोकस्य समुतपन्नं ममोद्यमात् ।
इत्याह संसारत् वेधाः परमां शक्तिमात्मनः ॥३४॥
गोबा बिंदशर्सेचानामेवं प्राहशतक्रुः ।
भागधेयस्य मे वरं फलमुत्पन्नमीदृशम् ॥३५॥
देवस्तां समितः प्राह विष्णुः कस्य तपःफलम् ।
भद्रे खमसि सेजाता प्रसन्ना क्षीरसागरे ॥३६॥
वचः प्राह पुनर्देवी निलं तव ह्रदिस्थिता ।
तवाद्यब्रह्मासाद्य जाताहं क्षीरसागरे ॥३७॥
स्यन्दनं वृषभे दिव्यमारुह्यप्राह्यवान् शिवः ।
देव्या यदर्क तच्च्ययमित्याह पुरुषोत्तमम् ॥३८॥
धीमन् सद्गुणतनया भार्या ते परमाङ्गना ।
सञ्जाता सर्वलोकस्य कर्तुमत्यन्तमङ्गलम् ॥३९॥

मङ्गलेब महादेवी सर्व सम्पत्प्रदायिनी ।
इति पर्वतराजस्य छता प्राह शुभं वचः ॥४०॥
हितार्थं सर्वलोकस्य जातेयमिति सादरम् ।
जयस्सर्वैब संह्रद्य दिवि चास्सस्साङ्गाः ॥४१॥
धिया वरेण्या पृथिवी प्राह वान्र्यं सगद्वदत् ।
अहं वसुमती चनमननेव ममेश्वराः ॥४२॥
यो गदेव्याधाबीर्य विश्वलोकस्य तत्वतः ।
इत्याहुर्हस्तमुन्नम्य देवा रत्निप्रोगमाः ॥४३॥
यो ग्वतामी दर्शी तस्याश्शुला संकीर्तिता खरेः ।
पाणिना परिजग्राह तां विष्णुस्सर्वरोभनाम् ॥४४॥
नलिनं शतसाहस्रदलमादित्यसन्निभम् ।
स्थानं यत् जन्मनो देव्या निराज ससागरम् ॥४५॥
प्रहर्षमतुल लेभे पद्मकिञ्जल्करेणुयिं ।
लिर्गं देवी समासाद्य लीलया विष्णुरात्मवान् ॥४६॥
चोदितास्तस्यवाक्येन सर्वेलोकासमद्रुहः ।
त्वं लक्ष्मीरिति तां देवीं प्रणेषुः परया मुदा ॥४७॥
देयाविष्णोर्महाभाग श्रुलेव देवतापर ।
सन्निधौ सर्वलोकानां प्रतिजह्रे यशस्विनी ॥४८॥
या वाच्या देहिनां लोके सर्वां शकिमतां मयि ।
तामई सर्वभावेन कऱोमि सफलां सदा ॥४९॥

FIGURE 6. The bold letters shown vertically form the Gayatri mantra. Reproduced from P. V. Ramaswami Raju, *Srimat Rajangala Mahodyanam, or, The Great Park of Rajangala* (Kumbakonam: Sree Vidya Press, 1894).

promising a semantic translation, mantras nonetheless create experiential and aesthetic boundaries between the texts and their readerships, and when uttered aloud, they create resonances.[63]

The Second Moment: English Character, Virtue, or Vice?

The story of the birth of Lakshmi becomes an occasion for an exposition on the rule of righteousness. Ganesha declares, "It is righteousness that protects valour, strength, riches, glory and fortitude. Kingly power and greatness shine forth exceedingly only when maintained by righteousness." As long as the kings of Samnaya Bharata were ethical, prosperity "resided" in Samnaya Bharata. But then the rulers "swerved from the path of righteousness," and the country became vulnerable to foreign invasion by "energetic people outside the pale."[64] We could speculate that the "foreign conquerors" are eleventh-century Ghaznavi invaders; such speculation raises the question of whether Ramaswami Raju was presenting a Hindu nationalist view that painted Indian history in terms of "pre-Islamic glory and the unceasing trouble that came to reign ever since the Muslims came to the subcontinent."[65] I am not persuaded, however, that Ramaswami Raju held such a view. That would require us to disregard the cultural cosmopolitanism of *Sixty Mandarins*, whose lively stories draw on global Islamic cultures; it would also require us to disregard Ramaswami Raju's precocious foregrounding of the British betrayal and looting of Sikh and Mughal rulers in *Lord Likely*. And it would mean that we disregard the Hindu-Muslim alliances depicted in Ramaswami Raju's play *Urjoon Sing, or, the Princess Regained* (1876), which pivots on Rajput princes marrying the Mughal emperor Jahangir's daughters in the presence of Thomas Roe, the East Indian Company official who represented the British monarchy in Jahangir's court. (In fact, in this play, Jahangir challenges a Catholic missionary about the Christian denunciation of Islam and especially the Qur'an.) In short, *The Great Park* asks that it be read through the literary inspiration not of a Hindu nationalist but of a *pauranika*, a narrator of myths, who used story and sacred utterance to categorically maintain that all arbiters of justice had to be morally incorruptible to deliver justice.

To return to our story, with the corruption of the rulers of Samnaya Bharata and their consequent decline, the stage is set for the entry of English rule. As a teaser, Ganesha sums up the accomplishments of English rule in broad strokes. He says: "It has filled with people many lands that had no people in them before. It has become the protection of many weak kingdoms. It has relieved the oppressed from bondage. It has given liberty and happiness to all people without distinction." Just as we begin to think that this description of an enlightened despot reflects the text's internalization (and indigenization) of a Millsian ideology, it distances itself from that possibility by declaring that nothing human can explain the might of the English; the English empire was made possible by Hindu gods who ordained it. Ganesha argues that the English themselves assert that "if [they] should lose Bharata, they should lose their greatness in this world" and that "Bharata is the brightest jewel in the imperial diadem." In short, we have a new reading of the jewel in the crown: the crown exists because of the jewel. Ganesha, the ever credible narrator, tells the sages that before they are misled by rumors about the moral depravity of the English, he would ask them to note "four great qualities" of the Angalas: "straight-forwardness, truthfulness, a natural love of justice, and fruitful gratitude." These noble qualities, he says, in fact counter the gossip of "ignorant people" who believe that Vishnu would take up an *avatāra* to destroy "English hordes." After all, Ganesha reminds us, "what man is there who is without a fault and who has been born sinless?"[66] We find ourselves engaging a crafty secondary text that uses rumor to place English rule on a slippery axis between virtue and vice. The sages are now even more eager to hear the rest of the story. But Ganesha tells them that the full story could be told only in a fitting venue and that venue is the court of Emperor Ramodwitiya, who rules in the resplendent earthly city of Maha Mondon, located somewhere between Varanasi in the east and Allahabad in the west.

The Third Moment: The Myth of History

And so, disguised as ascetics, the four sages and Ganesha proceed to Maha Mondon. As they journey through the country of Samnaya Bharata toward its capital, Maha Mondon, and the palace, the holy troupe is wonderstruck seeing the gilded domes, the palaces, and the parks; they marvel at the spectacular thriving of art and pleasure and science and law. Everybody is happy doing their duty, peace prevails, and the king and queen are humble but authoritative and just. In contrast to the disputable goodness of English rule, Ramodwitiya's rule is marked by a moral perfection: "This great ruler had attained the position of the arbiter of the earth for the good of the whole world by the consent of all races." We learn further that "in this court, the great emperor presides as a protector of the law surrounded by wise men and himself hears the petitions of his subjects and administers justice. Master and servant, the rich and the poor, the high born and the low born, all see the law equally dealt out at this court."[67] This ideal court presents a stark contrast to the messy Anglo-Indian judicial system with its contrived texts, judicial hierarchies, and culturally incompetent and racist dispensations of law.[68] As a lawyer in the Madras High Court, Ramaswami Raju would have known the Anglo-Indian legal system very well.

But, we might ask, why does the story have to be narrated "in the presence of the emperor?"[69] Why should Ramodwitiya's court in Samnaya Bharata be the venue that befits the narration of English history, and why not Indra's court in heaven or Shiva's abode in the impenetrable Himalayas, surely more appropriate locations for the holy crew? The answer to these questions has broader implications for how Ramaswami Raju constructs *the political* in a dual register. The temporal ruler Ramodwitiya and his officers—ministers, the commanders, tributary representatives, and other judicial and political functionaries—are the most fitting audience as well as agents to hear and enact a particular political theology. This theology's central assertion is twofold. The first premise—which we have already encountered—is that temporal sovereign power is divinely given. (Thus English empire could not have been possible without the intervention of Hindu gods.) The second is that consequently, such power obligates the sovereign to govern righteously and justly. Conceptualized this way, political power is a sacrosanct power, its abuse sacrilegious. Ramodwitiya himself states: "The sovereign that falls from the path of justice undoubtedly falls from everything. Is not justice said to be the centre of the wheel of this world? The wise have said that the sovereign is the centre of the wheel of state; his efficient ministers are said to be the firm spokes of the wheel; his subjects content with his rule are the circumference. Thus by mutual support turns the wheel of state."[70]

Further, the earthly location for the narration of the story about the English empire allows Ramaswami Raju to conflate several kinds of mythic narrative and make a counterstatement about history itself, dominantly imagined as linear and Eurocentric. Implicit in the conflation is Ramaswami Raju's argument that there are many ways of constituting the past and arriving at its many meanings, and many ways of linking temporalities—for instance, the distant future (represented by Ramodwitiya's reign), the forgotten past (represented by a primitive Angala race), and the authorial present (evoked through Ramaswami Raju's awareness of world events). Myth, as scholars of mythology note, is not, as it is in common parlance, a euphemism for an untruth or a delusion.[71] Instead, Wendy Doniger argues that a myth is a special kind of narrative that "combines distant and near views . . . is greater than the sum of its parts . . . expresses cross-cultural human experience . . . and expresses both an idea and its opposite, reveals—or sometimes conceals— certain basic cultural attitudes to important (usually insoluble) questions, and is transparent to a variety of constructions of meaning."[72]

As Ganesha recalls the mythology of Samnaya Bharata, dwelling on its political order and its ethico-economic prosperity, he also constructs a mythology of English antecedents. Through these welded mythologies, Ramaswami Raju reconstructs the idea of English history. The early English, Ganesha tells the listeners in Ramodwitiya's court, were once a people "devoid of all wealth" who dressed in barks, skins and leaves and lived in "caves, bushes and hollows of trees." Their country itself was made up of "dense forests infested with carnivorous animals." They earned their daily bread and did not possess the ability to discern good from evil as other civilized races did. At last—in line with narrative's political theology—divine grace willed prosperity and fame on the English. They began to build invincible ships that "with hulls and wood and iron, capacious holds, manned by warriors skilled in the ways of the sea vomit terrible fire that burns adverse hosts, like giantesses that are sprung out of the sea for the protection of the [English]." England's naval capability matches the disposition of its people:

> Its invincible warriors have, by various means, conquered many prosperous countries and established by their might a boundless empire over which the sun never sets—which is unprecedented and productive of infinite happiness to mankind. . . . The learned men of this island, who know many sciences, who are ever impelled by the desire to discover the subtle truths of nature, proceed higher and higher in their career of research . . . in a manner peculiarly their own. . . . [Its] able and enterprising merchants possessed of a potent love of wealth, have gathered the treasures lying scattered over the world in many forms and amassed them in an exceedingly magnificent style in their own country. The men and women inhabiting this island are mostly truth-speaking.[73]

Yet, ultimately, this is a description that equivocates. Lurking in the admiration is a shadow that falls on English claims to enlightenment and rationality, to urbanity and advancement. Phrases such as "potent love of wealth," "mostly truth-speaking," and "proceed higher and higher in their career of research . . . in a manner peculiarly their own" punctuate the narrative of the glory and accomplishments of the English. English conquest "by various means" is subtly juxtaposed with Ramodwitiya's rule "by the consent of all races." The contrasting utopian description of Maha Mondon backhandedly suggests that the flourishing of India was plentifully possible and secure without colonization. The wonder that is Samnaya Bharata exposes the fiction of progress on which the English empire was founded. Implicit in Ramodwitiya's not knowing that the English had once ruled his country—

clearly *that* history does not seem to have been chronicled in traditional royal genealogies—is the fall of the English empire in India. In this double register where the English empire, long gone, is remembered in the court of a king in the future of time, it is myth that makes history visible. The myth of Ganesha's visit to an earthly realm, the myth of English civilization, and the myth of a Hindu utopia enable not one but many constructions of history, showing the hollowness of the supposition that historical consciousness and its emancipatory possibilities were exclusive to Europe. The Sanskrit text, with its puranic tenor, the mantras with their potential to enlighten, and the mandala-like sacred arrangement of text draw on a sensibility that is outside European thinking; European thought and experience at best provide the raw material for the narrative.

The Fourth Moment: New World, Old Serpent

Ramaswami Raju recognizes that a story of "the British Empire" is incomplete without reference to Europe's colonization of the Americas.[74] Ramaswami Raju anticipates modern scholarship that recognizes that this colonization is a story of "immigration, slavery, and disease" that left "90 to 99 percent of the [indigenous] population dead in two generations."[75] As Ganesha describes the continents (using Sanskrit names for each), one of the sages asks whether he could narrate the story of how Mahodyama ("Man of Gigantic Enterprise—Columbus) discovered America. In Ganesha's telling, Columbus, a native of Hitastalas (Italy), resolves to prove that the earth is spherical for the "good of the world" and proposes to the Spanish king Ferdinand (Dharma Vardhana) and queen Isabella (Dharma Vardhini) that he would sail "westward" till he finds land.[76] After he overcomes ecclesiastical opposition to his plan, Isabella agrees to sponsor his expedition.

A long and eventful journey that includes the near mutiny of his crew brings Columbus to lands occupied by indigenous peoples. He quickly plants "with his own hand the banner of the Supunias [Spain]." When the natives offer hospitality and friendship, Columbus "exclaim[s] with astonishment— 'How can these be said to be uncivilized who possess such an excellent character by nature?'" Wandering around, he "saw here a beautiful waterfall, there a winding stream, at one place a lake resonant with the music of aquatic birds, at another place woodlands with verdant turf and trees, creepers and bushes . . . and exclaimed with delight, 'The world is but the picture of one artist!'" One might almost like Columbus for his fledgling ethnological sensitivity. But Ramaswami Raju's characteristic double register returns: Praise for a problematic subject is quickly felled by a word or a line or a twist in the plot. Columbus, preparing to return to Tejodwipa ("Continent of Light": Europe), assiduously begins to collect "all that is peculiar to the land," a sample of every botanical and animal species, in an unmistakable colonial act of illegitimate acquisition.[77] Ramaswami Raju's description of Columbus's collecting zeal indexes the beginnings of the story of a networked European capitalism that fueled the colonial enterprise—Mahodyama, Columbus, after all, is a "Man of Gigantic Enterprise." As Daniela Bleichmar notes:

> Botanists and ministers alike hoped that a better-known and efficiently administered empire would furnish rich revenues by allowing Spain to compete with trade monopolies maintained by other nations. The Dutch, for instance, controlled the pepper, cinnamon, and nutmeg trades, while the French did the same with coffee and the British with tea. This climate of international economic and political competition created opportunities for naturalists to sell their services to interested patrons. Botanical expertise became a highly valuable form of knowledge: in the eighteenth century, botany was big business and big science. . . . Over the course of the eighteenth century, natural history became a global project, and European naturalists hungered for observations and specimens from distant parts of the world.[78]

When his shipmen propose that, in addition to plant and animal samples, they also help themselves to a few natives who would present a "strange and novel sight," Columbus gives a lofty moralistic speech about how all men belong to their own homes and families and hence should not be abducted. But Ramaswami Raju is not quite done with the narrative about the colonization of the Americas. The natives, Ganesha tells us, are themselves so overcome by Columbus's radiant nobility that they swim out to the departing ship in the same way that "iron is attracted by magnet." They implore Columbus to take them along with him, and to this entreaty Columbus says, "So be it." Everybody on the ship is enveloped in adoration for Columbus, and the journey back to Spain with samples is smooth.[79]

Ganesha immediately seeks forgiveness for using the simile of iron and magnet: "This simile is not proper. The wise should forgive its use. The qualities of the good and the great certainly exercise a nobler and lovelier method of attraction in respect to men's minds than that of magnet towards iron." The narrative apology is timed well because it is offered too late: Ramaswami Raju has succeeded in alerting us to the clank of shackles. And it is the kind of apology that does not restrain more unflattering metaphors such as the proverb "The serpent enters the hole made by the white ants," which Ramaswami Raju uses to describe the English advent in North America.[80]

The Fifth Moment: The Fall

The climax of this unfinished poem centers on how the English got their progenitor. The scene is the celestial court of Indra, where Shiva and Parvati are expected to visit. A grand reception has been organized for distinguished delegates, and Indra's staff has rehearsed an elaborate protocol of entry and hospitality. There is much tension in the air, as they cannot afford to have anything go wrong, given the exalted status of the guests. At this event, the *gandharvas*, heavenly musicians, are expected to perform. The minister of the *gandharvas*, who is also the son-in-law of the king of the *gandharvas*, is called Mahamangala. Unfortunately on this momentous day, he gets drunk and forgets all about the event. Reminded by his wife, Sreevardhini, he scrambles and just in time manages to join the performing troupe with his harp. As the concert unfolds, "the movable and immovable in nature stood intent on listening . . . mountains danced . . . the trees in the woodlands embraced one another, oceans overstepped their limits and went back after congratulating the earth; the rivers came back reversing the course of their limpid waters, carnivorous animals . . . adopted holy lives." In the midst of this serene music, a terrible thing happens. Sudden darkness descends on the court. All three worlds are shaken with alarm. Horrified, Indra cries, "What is this?" The sage Narada, famous diagnostician, says, "Out of the lips of Mahamangala a wrong note has proceeded; from that this great disaster has happened to the three worlds."[81] Upon Indra's command, the Wind quickly removes Mahamangala from the hall. This dismissal returns the performance to harmony.

After the event, Indra summons Mahamangala and curses him:

On earth there is a cold and desolate island in the western ocean, which is an expanse of perpetual snow. Dense forests resounding with the yelling of carnivorous animals and mountains and marshes make it impassable. It is surrounded by a sea ever rough with waves lashed by tempests. There water does not flow; fire does not burn vigorously; the sun does not shine which is ever shrowded [*sic*] by masses of clouds. There the midday which is generally as bright as twilight (in other places) suddenly becomes night enveloped in dismal fogs. Long days in summer, protracted nights in winter, in a moment wind, in a moment rain, in a moment thunder, make that little island, which is (but) a particle of the earth in the great sea, the hideous home of eternal unhappiness. There, fallen from heaven, reside for interminable years in the form of a man ever addicted to liquor and flesh-eating. . . .

As through your folly you forgot my timely word, you shall totally forget your former history. . . . [Y]our all-exterminating act has destroyed
your name also; therefore without a name bear the burden of your
miserable existence.[82]

Upon hearing the curse, Mahamangala lets his harp fall, but it is caught
by Sreevardhini. Mahamangala becomes speechless. Sound has great significance in *The Great Park*, which begins with *Om* (the *praṇava*), the original,
generative sacred sound. Indra admonishes Mahamangala:

> Where a singer does not exercise self-control and act with retentive
> memory, earnestness and purity, there, sounds prove highly hurtful to
> him. Just as the world of matter is made of fine particles of matter,
> the world of sound is made of fine particles of sound. Natural acts
> like coughing, laughing, talking and weeping arise in all animals by the
> union of particles of sound. A sound mispronounced by a guardian
> of sound is known as a wrong sound which is capable of destroying
> everything.[83]

By this logic of cosmic sound, if Samnaya Bharata is born of a perfect primordial note, then the birth cry of the Angalas is a discordant one, an *apas-
vara*. It is a commonplace sound like talking or sneezing.

Sreevardhini feistily protests and Indra, relenting, reduces the earthly
exile to a few centuries. He gives her three magical gifts—a suit of armor,
a helmet, and a lance—gifts that remind us of medieval English romance
heroes. She is still not satisfied. She laments to Indra, "How can I, who have
thus received a holy name and many benedictions from you, follow a nameless husband?"[84] A minor drama ensues involving politics between celestial
teachers and students and husbands and wives. Indra answers Sreevardhini's prayer and showers six names on the now nameless Mahamangala:
Speethari, Pingaloddama, Mitaharsha, Mitotsuka, Yogi, and Janmabala. But
the teacher of the gods, Brihaspati, thinks that Indra has made a mistake in
pronouncing the names and has therefore given the name Mitotsuka inadvertently. He corrects it by conferring a seventh name, Hitotsuka, on the
still speechless Mahamangala. At this, Brihaspati's wife, Tara, points out
that in correcting Indira, Brihaspati himself had gone wrong. After a heated
argument between Tara and Brihaspati (in which Tara questions his knowledge), she tells Mahamangala that among his friends, he will be known as
Amitasharsha and Amitotsuka, and among his enemies he will be Ahitotsuka.[85] This is an interesting strategy by Ramaswami Raju, since these three

names can be read both positively and negatively, serving to offset the other insulting epithets.

Ramaswami Raju provides these names in the English text as proper nouns, transliterated, not translated. The reason for the absence of translation becomes clear: not one of the ten names is flattering. Giridhara Shastry helped me unpack the uncomplimentary semantics.[86]

1. *Spheetari*: *Spheeta* means bloated, increased, or numerous. *Ari* is enemy. Literally, *spheetari* would be "one whose enemies are increasing or numerous."
2. *Pingaloddama*: *Pingala* means tawny, monkey-like, ruddy. *Uddama* means unrestrained, intoxicated, bold, dreadful, or vain. So *Pingaloddama* would mean an "unrestrained monkey." (In many regions of pre-independent India the English were popularly called red monkeys; for example, *kempu koti* in Kannada or *lal bandar* in Hindi).
3. *Mitaharsha*: *Mita* means limited; *harsha* happiness. Thus, "having limited happiness."
4. *Mitotsuka*: one who feels little emotion.
5. *Yogi*: trickster, conjurer.
6. *Janmabala*: one with natural (brute) strength.
7. *Hitotsuka*: self-interested.
8. *Amitaharsha*: one whose happiness is unbounded (alternatively, one who is unboundedly concerned with one's own happiness).
9. *Amitotsuka*: one whose curiosity is unlimited (alternatively, one who is meddlesome).
10. *Ahitotsuka*: eager to harm others.

Understandably, the names do not pacify Sreevardhini. Let us look at the final verses of *The Great Park*:

Thereafter Sreevardhini respectfully addressed Indra, "O Lord, the names bestowed graciously by you, the preceptor and his consort are all of special distinction. They are like branches. How can a tree, cut at the roots, bear branches? (verse 463–64)

The name given in the childhood ritually in the presence of his father is indeed the real name and all other names are ornamental. (verse 465)

That name is the root of the tree of renown; that is dear to all beings. Is not the love for one's own name, home and land natural? (verse 466)

O wise one, are you not aware of the real nature of the course of action of the one who cuts the roots of a tree and adorns its branches?" (verse 467)

And thus abruptly ends the unfinished project of *The Great Park* or *Rajangala Mahodyanam*. Without a name that links them to ancestors, the English are without history—nameless in the Great Park, and rootless heads of an empire destined to wither. The origin of the English in the fall from heaven reads like a strategic subversion of Milton's "Man's first disobedience" in that Great Park, and of Shakespeare's "special providence in the fall of a sparrow"—lines from bards who epitomize the very identity of England. As far as British imperialism is concerned, *The Great Park* erases the independent identity of the British as an exceptional power; it creates a moral caesura in the narrative of British glory. Empire is not the consequence of English agency; rather, *The Great Park* insists that the rightful provenance of all power and justice is divine providence. By incorporating into a Hindu mythos the origin of the English race from a fallen progenitor, it renders the very idea of "English" history impossible. Ramaswami Raju did not merely refute the refrain of English historians that ancient India did not possess a historical sense. He reversed it.

The Tamil Nadu Archives in Chennai is a red colonial-era building that dates back to 1909,[87] a building that went up eight years after Ramaswami Raju died. It sits diagonally opposite Chennai Central Station on Gandhi Irwin Road in the Egmore area. Mr. Rajendran, the helpful chief archivist, met me outside the building, understanding, as only an archivist does, why I was so keen on reading Ramaswami Raju's obscure plays. To read Ramaswami Raju's writings during those humid afternoons in this colonial building, with its high ceilings and its long-stemmed fans tirelessly making a clicking noise, was quite different from reading the Mary Frere papers in the British Library in London. A passage I had circled with pencil in my photocopy of *Urjoon Sing* stands out: Jahangir asks Thomas Roe (of the famous inaugural tax grant "and all our woe"): "Sahib Roe, what kind of people are you? Do you brave danger? Love your homes and friends? Hate a lie? Like a war?" These lines summed up what had most disenchanted Ramaswami Raju about colonialism: its moral repugnance. Another set of lines is from a scene where Roe waxes rhapsodic about Shakespeare, and Urjoon Sing responds, "Perhaps, a Kalidoss?" (Kalidasa).[88] The accomplishment—or the hope—of the unfinished *Great Park* is in inventively deploying gods to make possible meta-historical tellings of history that are both equitable and rooted in everyday life.

CHAPTER 3

The Subjective Scientific Method

M. N. Venkataswami

About 420 kilometers southeast of the south Indian city of Hyderabad, in the eastern part of the state of Andhra Pradesh, is the city of Kadapa. Near Kadapa, in the small town of Gandi, where the hills border the river Papagni, is a temple to Hanuman. According to legend, in the time of the Ramayana, Hanuman strung a garland of golden flowers between two hilltops to mark a resting spot for his beloved Rama and Sita. Today the garland is not visible to ordinary people. Another legend surrounds Gandi dating to modern times. In 1827 Thomas Munro, the governor of Madras, who was traveling in this region, which then belonged to the Madras Presidency, saw the garland. Intrigued, he asked his assistants why there was a golden rope hanging up there in the hills. There was silence. Then an old man dared to tell him that those who could see the golden garland were blessed, but they would also die shortly. As it turned out, Munro died from cholera while still encamped in the region. Today in the main hall of the temple, Munro's picture hangs along with images of gods and goddesses.[1]

For a long time, this was the only story about Munro's death that I knew. Then I read another Munro story in a collection called *Tulsemmah and Nagaya: Folk-Stories from India* (1918). This story was less reverential:

Mundrole Saheb or Dora as Sir Thomas Munro, the Governor of Madras, was termed—was sent by the English on a political mission to the Nizam of Hyderabad. He negotiated much too favourably to the Nizam and Englishmen came to know of this. Munro too, while returning to Madras, became aware of the fact and being greatly afraid of the anger of his countrymen and the ignominy he shall be put to, took out his emerald ring off the finger and rubbing it on a stone with a little water and mixing the paste in water he drank it off and thus put an end to his life on the way. The English, with a view to perpetuate his unworthy conduct to posterity, set up his statue in Madras open to the skies, the crows and other birds of the air making dirt throughout the year with impunity.[2]

The avian transgression is unpunishable, and after all, the British precipitated it. I was to learn that rambunctious, not reverential, was the word that rightly described the author of the collection in which this story about Munro appears. I discovered him in 2003 in a secondhand book store in the Charing Cross area of London after a day looking at the Frere manuscripts in the British Library. A book intriguingly titled *Life of M. Nagloo: The Father of the Hotel Enterprise in the Central Provinces, and Head Goomastha to the "Mahanadu"* (1908; second edition 1929) caught my eye.[3] Its author was Nagloo's son "M. N. Venkataswami, M.R.A.S., M.F.L.S." (Member of the Royal Asiatic Society and Member of the Folk-Lore Society). The hand-signed copy, which I now possess, includes a date, January 29, 1931, and a note that marks it as a gift to a Reverend Marsh, who I later learned was an American Baptist missionary in Markapur (in what was then the Madras Presidency). "COPIES OF THE BOOK," we are told in uppercase letters, "CAN BE HAD FROM THE AUTHOR." It would take me seven years to track the enigmatic addresses mentioned in the book ("The Retreat, Hyderabad" and "The Hermitage, Secunderabad") and to discover Venkataswami's living descendants. I tell the story of this search at the end of this chapter.

M. N. Venkataswami (1865–1931) was a solitary figure in scholarly circles of his time and is practically unknown today. That night in London, I read Venkataswami's fascinating story of his father, Nagaya. I had read nothing like this before. Nagaya belonged to the caste of bamboo weavers, the Medaras, who were considered Untouchable by "upper castes" in those days. Venkataswami recounts how Nagaya became an enterprising hotelier amidst the turbulent events of post-1857 India, a time when India, for all practical purposes, was irrevocably altered. After reading the biography, I became obsessed with tracing Venkataswami's other writings and discovered that there were only a few extant copies of his books. Because of the treacheries of printing presses and the Musi floods of 1908 in Hyderabad, only a

FIGURE 7. M. N. Venkataswami. Reproduced from M. N. Venkataswami, *Heeramma and Venkataswami* (Madras: S.P.C.K, 1923).

handful of copies remained. In fact, the eminent historian Jadunath Sarkar remarked in a review, "A strange fatality has dogged [Venkataswami's] literary productions: nearly all the printed copies [of his books] have been successively destroyed by fire, flood or other mischance. But Mr. Venkataswami's persistence is unconquerable."[4] These lone copies are now scattered across the world—in the state library in Hyderabad, the British Library in London, the library of the Asiatic Society in Kolkata, the libraries at the universities of Cambridge, Oxford, and Chicago, and the Cleveland Public Library, among others.

Venkataswami was the first literate member of his extended family. He was born in Nagpur (which was part of the then Central Provinces, and is now in the western Indian state of Maharashtra) and grew up speaking Marathi, the local language, and Telugu, his mother tongue. He attended high school at the Free Church Institution and graduated from Hislop College in Nagpur; both institutions were founded and sponsored by the United Free Church of Scotland.[5] Migrating from Nagpur to Hyderabad shortly after the deaths of both his father and his wife in 1893, he became a sub-librarian in the nizam's State Library (Kutubkhana Asifia) in Hyderabad, the capital of a Muslim-ruled princely dominion. Between 1900 and 1930, in addition to the biography of his father, Venkataswami had rendered a work from the Telugu oral epic tradition into English and published three collections of oral narrative and a book of short essays.[6] Although he wrote only in English, his writings are suffused with Telugu, Hindi, Hindustani, and Marathi. In a departure from his usual writing on everyday life and cultural forms, he wrote the introduction to Ralph Griffith's translation of the Valmiki Ramayana, published in the prestigious Chaukhamba Sanskrit series.

Venkataswami's story challenges our understandings of anthropology in colonial India in significant ways. Unlike the majority of Indian scholars who came from so-called upper castes, he came from a so-called lower caste; unlike most colonial-era anthropologists whose books were published by well-known publishing houses in London, he self-published a limited number of copies of his books, relying on Christian presses and printers in south India (SPCK, Methodist, Diocesan, and Solden). Although neither Venkataswami nor his family converted to Christianity, Christian missionary activity was intense among the Medara and Mala communities in south India, a fact that would have made him familiar with the press as a powerful missionary tool for disseminating Christianity. Missionary presses voluminously published Christian prayer books, catechisms, and translations of the Bible in various Indian languages, attempted to enter the lucrative market of school textbooks, and also undertook non-Christian printing work for the government and private individuals. It is hard to know whether Venkataswami paid these presses to publish his books, but we do know that during World War I, Christian presses were strapped for funds and staffing, and non-Christian publications became a revenue stream.[7] To return to Venkataswami's unusual position in colonial anthropology, unlike many Indians who "collaborated" as pandits and *munshis* with British officials, Venkataswami never played the part of assistant or native informant for British anthropologists. This chapter explores Venkataswami's authorial persona across three of the genres he wrote in: the biography, oral epic, and folktale collections. It shows how he allows the subjective to suffuse the hallowed ideal of scientific objectivity through a narrative craft that exposes the hollowness of objectivity.

The Subjective Lens, the Looking Glass of Science

By the early twentieth century, the notion of objectivity had become the totem of colonial anthropology and folklore and the sanctum of the discipline of history, where a fetish developed about "original sources."[8] In this vision, if knowledge about "other" people was to be authentic, reliable, and universally decipherable—that is, objective—it had to be abstracted from living contexts, fitted into various taxonomies standardized by European institutions. Charlotte Burne, the president of the Folk-Lore Society, insisted, "The scientific study of folklore consists in bringing modern scientific methods of accurate observation and inductive reasoning to bear upon these varies forms of Tradition, just as they have been brought to bear upon other phenomena."[9] To be considered a scientific endeavor, a collection of folklore had to gather cultural specimens (such as stories) through specified methods and provide notes and annotations. A narrative collection's scientific stock went up if it engaged debates on origins and primitive mentality and if it included a vetted typology of motifs. An index that listed beliefs, practices, and other exotica for easy reference added to its scientific utility, and its scientific aura was enhanced if the author noted that the work was the fruit of labor conducted beyond the call of duty—an image that went well with the nineteenth-century idea of the scientist, who, as the historians of science Lorraine Daston and Peter Galison put it, was the "insightful self, the diligent worker."[10]

But could a *native* anthropologist claim a scientific self? European scientists could realize the cherished ideal of objectivity through various filters on the self.[11] Native anthropologists, by contrast, could be objective only if they performed a rather fundamental negation: erase their belonging to, and participation in, their everyday worlds. In nineteenth-century anthropology, the word "native" was a retrenched category, without the complexity the term carries today.[12] Natives were invisible or voiced-over informants. After *Old Deccan Days*, there was never again a "narrator's narrative" in the hundreds of collections that followed; instead, we are more likely to see variations of "narrator's name not given" or "boy who sold eggs."[13] Further, as we will see in more detail in the next chapter, native *scholarly* expertise, necessary to advance scientific anthropology, had to be constructed on this foundation of self-denial. Thus disaggregated, dissected, disembodied, and disenchanted, "culture" in scientific anthropology could not have been more removed from those who lived and breathed it.

The "writing culture" turn of the 1980s began to systematically spell out the racist logic of scientific premises in early anthropology.[14] The logic applies equally to the politics of temporality in the discipline of history. Dipesh Chakrabarty sums up the central contradiction of the so-called scientific ("reason-based") method:

> If historical or anthropological consciousness is seen as the work of a rational outlook, it can only "objectify"—and thus deny—the *lived* relations the observing subject already has with that which he or she identifies as belonging to a historical or ethnographic time and space separate from the ones he or she occupies as the analyst. In other words, the method does not allow the investigating subject to recognize himself or herself as also the figure he or she is investigating.[15]

On the surface, Venkataswami observed many of the norms of scientific anthropology. He was a member of the Royal Asiatic Society of Great Britain and Ireland and also the Folk-Lore Society of London,[16] and like the colonial collectors, he too invoked the discourse of typology, indices, the image of the hardworking social scientist, and so on. Consider this passage from his preface to *Folk-Stories of the Land of Ind* (1927):

> For the use of the student a classification to the best of my ability has been drawn up on the lines followed for his Indian Nights Entertainments by the Rev. Charles Swynnerton; a glossary of Indian terms and copious notes to elucidate the text are also given, and to enhance the utility of the work I have given an Index on broad lines as recommended by the eminent Indian folklorist, Sir Richard Carnac Temple, [this is] a study of the Indian folklore . . . in a scientific spirit. . . . [T]he author will consider himself amply compensated for the labour bestowed on the work for a year and a half, while performing his duties of an uncongenial nature and at high pressure.[17]

But what I find interesting is the way in which he deploys the scientific. For instance, he dispassionately presents the British under a *new* tale type called "Foreign Character Series." Here we find the story about bird droppings on a statue of the well-known British official Thomas Munro.[18] In the notes he places supposedly exotic Indian practices side by side with European customs.

Thus, he blandly describes "washed his hands" as "a habit which is essential to those who eat with the fingers, not with knife and fork."[19] English, the language of scientific discourse, itself must stretch to include Indian scripts and transliterated, untranslated colloquialisms and breathe through the onomatopoeia of Indian languages. *Gulloo gulloo*, he explains factually, is the "noise caused by anklets worn by ladies," and as for *kich kich*, "rats make such noise."[20]

Through a set of writing practices and viewing techniques that can be described collectively as a "subjective lens," Venkataswami performs the scientific but obstinately refuses its racist premises. Such a lens inverts the object in a way that our gaze is directed to a human subject who is not an insulated biometric object but a living, reflecting person connected to places and things and people and phenomena. This subjective lens reveals a world of vernacular abundance, a world that overflows with acknowledgments of his parents, sisters, aunts, uncles, nephews, and cousins. It is a world energized by descriptions of everyday life with its micro-politics, local landscapes, and caste-specific practices. Kinship and affective ties connect stories to particular life moments in narrators' lives, and oral stories demand an equal hearing with the written record of things. The subjective lens also describes Venkataswami's unexpected use of the photograph. In contrast to the gospel belief of nineteenth-century anthropology that the photograph could objectively illustrate "primitive culture" beyond expository assertions from the field or the armchair, for Venkataswami, photography became a technology that gave stories form and life, their *élan vital* (vital impetus).[21]

Finally, the subjective lens also reveals Venkataswami's relationship to the English language. "I am not responsible for the language in which [the stories] are couched or clothed by reason of my being a foreigner," he clarifies in *Folk-Stories of the Land of Ind*, and elsewhere he offers variants of that sentiment: "The writer is writing in English, a tongue foreign to him," and "Absolute perfection [in English] only comes to him who stays in England be it for a season and I have never been [to England], much less stayed [there] for the sheer fact of my being one of nature's unwealthy sons."[22]

Why did Venkataswami write only in English?

I have been asked this important question many times when I have presented Venkataswami's work. I have not been satisfied to say that English was simply the language of power and he therefore aspired to write in it. To assert this would be to go against a view he held passionately: "The regeneration of my country (or any country) lies in the cultivation of the vernaculars to the highest pitch, and not in writing English although Lord Macaulay's Educational Despatch of 1833 was instrumental in giving such a liberal education or education in such a finished and fine form to some of India's sons."[23] I imagine, therefore, that as colonial anthropology began to annex a deeply familiar terrain by wrenching stories from their lived moorings, Venkataswami felt that it violated his cultural experiences. Notwithstanding that he lacked privileges of class and caste, he reclaimed that terrain, and reclaimed it in the languages of science and English—the languages of nineteenth-century Europe that depleted, if it did not destroy, the sap of everyday Indian life. These were also the very languages that sought to fashion brown sahibs whose re-formed cultural inheritance would include a hand-me-down Anglo-Saxon past and English ways. The Kenyan writer Ngũgĩ wa Thiong'o describes the parallel predicament in Africa: "The ambitious colonial scheme of reconstructing an African whose historical, physical, and metaphysical geography begins with European memory was almost realized with the production of such a native class dismembered from its social memory."[24] But only *almost*. Because raconteurs like Venkataswami, far from letting the English language sever them from their societies, expanded the language and made *it* recognize and overcome its forgetfulness of human person and memory. To write in English, therefore, was an ethical choice, a political choice, as much as it was an aesthetic choice.

In the rest of the chapter I consider how Venkataswami re-narrates the present and the past on his own terms, intertwining two dominant genres in which India was being inscribed: history and folklore.

The Subject of Biography

Life of M. Nagloo, Venkataswami's biography of his father, Nagaya, was begun during Nagaya's lifetime and published in 1908, fifteen years after Nagaya's death.[25] It was written over twelve months. Venkataswami's financial circumstances allowed him to print only a hundred copies of this edition, which he privately published after much delay. Unfortunately, the 1908 Hyderabad floods immediately swallowed up all copies of this inaugural edition. Twenty-one years later, Venkataswami published, again privately, a second edition, with significant additions and substantial copyediting. (This is the edition I had stumbled on in the used book store in London.)

In a remarkably dialogic process that is prescient about life story research today, Venkataswami interviewed scores of his relatives in Ongole, Vijayawada (Bezawada then), Nagpur, and Hyderabad. The family had migrated from the Madras Presidency to the Central Provinces and then to the territory known as the Nizam's Dominions. The narrative is shaped by his many conversations with his father and his correspondence with people who had known his father. Reflecting on how practices of history produce variant truths, the biography is decades ahead of contemporary historiography and anthropology. For example, Venkataswami regrets that he had neglected to get some details from his father, and that he had lost a precious book of Nagaya's testimonials. A set of notes made by a colonel through direct conversations with Nagaya was stolen. Hence, Venkataswami says, "we must fall back upon our memory" and trust sensory recall. He remembers Nagaya recalling that while returning home from his work as an errand boy in Kamptee (a cantonment station in the Central Provinces), he saw a large number of scorpions on a rock during a drizzle. This earthy, vivid memory "confirms" for Venkataswami that Nagaya had been an errand boy in a British officer's house. The earthy memory becomes, he says, a "way of filling up the gap" in the biography.[26]

The second edition of the biography is an extraordinary collation of voices. It includes a variety of responses to Venkataswami's solicitation for reminiscences. Some letter writers are indifferent toward the "Subject" (as Venkataswami refers to his father in the book), a few are condescending, and some others express admiration. Venkataswami also included two published reviews of the first edition, one by the historian Jadunath Sarkar, and the other by S. Zahur Ali, an educator and social reformer in the Nizam's Dominions. Fourteen appendices add to the vivacity of the biography: there is a poem by Venkataswami's brother to a deceased sister; an anonymous account of the "treacherous" ousting of the raja of Nagpur by the British political resident; a letter appointing Nagaya as the head gumastha (adjudicator of caste disputes); a petition from the Nayudu and Mudaliyar communities of Kampti and Nagpur to the British commissioner to strip Nagaya of his position as gumastha; a notification from the commissioner dismissing that petition; and a panegyric in Telugu on Nagaya by a schoolmaster. Flattering and unflattering anecdotes provide snappy views of British officials. The edition also contains photographs of key places and individuals. Between his footnotes and endnotes that continuously widen the scope of the narration of the "main text," I believe that Venkataswami tries to make a larger point—that life history can never be represented or contained by one telling, and that to understand that life through its various vicinities, one needs many perspectives. Fairly or unfairly, I had read Venkataswami's folktale collections through the lens of the biography and had allowed its colors to vivify his folktale collections. I retrace this journey of interpretation beginning with a detailed summary of the biography.[27]

FIGURE 8. Nagaya and Tulsemmah. Reproduced from M. N. Venkataswami, *Tulsemmah and Nagaya, or, Folk-Stories from India* (Madras: Methodist Publishing House, 1918).

Nagaya's Life Story

The family's history told in *M. Nagloo* begins three generations before Nagaya in the town of Kadapa (colonial name Cuddapah) in south-central Andhra Pradesh, the same Kadapa of the story in which Munro sighted the mysterious hilltop garland. Nagaya's great-grandfather Goona Nayudu belonged to the high-ranking landowning Kamma caste; the family used to be the silver mace bearers and wrestlers in the service of the local kings. During the terrible famine of 1783, as he lay starving, his wife and children already dead, some compassionate Malas (deemed to be lower in a caste hierarchy) fed him beef. Hearing this, the local king punished Goona Nayudu by banishing him to the "Untouchable" caste of Medaras, basket weavers. Medara Goona Nayudu moved to Ongole, where the local Malas accepted him. He married a Mala woman, and they had a son named Govindoo. Although orphaned at a young age, Govindoo prospered. He became a government contractor supplying bullocks to the British infantry during the last battle of Srirangapatnam (1799) and the campaign against the Maratha Holkars in 1804. When Wellesley asked Govindoo if "he wanted anything" in reward for his services, family lore records that he said: ' "I have all, Sir. I do not want anything." '[28] Govindoo made enough to eventually build a tile-roofed house and purchase a few acres of land outside Ongole. His end was sudden: he was savagely attacked in a lane on his way home after defeating higher-caste competitors in a village competition—and died, ironically, on Vijaya Dashami, the festival of the goddess Durga that celebrates the victory of good over evil. The family all across Ongole, Bezawada, Nagpur, and Hyderabad stopped celebrating the festival.

After Govindoo's sudden death, his wife and young son Polaya were cheated by many people and lost most of the family's fortune. Polaya did not enter his father's business. Instead, he learned sorcery from a sorcerer from the coast of Malabar, farther south, and also cultivated his interest in Telugu literature. Polaya became famous for his skill in healing and his public discourses. But famines stalked the family once again. The 1823 famine depleted his wealth, and the 1833 famine ruined the family. Venkataswami remarks, "Ongole, indeed the whole southern country, has not witnessed such a dire calamity before or since."[29] Desperate, Polaya participated in a raid on a government granary, was caught, and was sent to prison to serve a three-month sentence. He continued to heal fellow prisoners. But halfway through his sentence, he died. Venkataswami reports two versions in family memory about the cause of this death. The first version blames the deplorable state of British prisons, where prisoners were starved, tortured, and kept in extremely unsanitary conditions. The second version attributes Polaya's death to sorcery gone wrong. Polaya was buried on the banks of the Pennar River. It is said that on the night he died, all the "devils, ghosts, and disembodied spirits" to whom Polaya, being jailed, had not been able to keep his promises gathered at his house and created a pandemonium.[30] His mother and his wife, scared out of their wits, gathered all his sorcery books and burned them in a big fire.

It was under these circumstances of poverty and sorrow that Nagaya, Polaya's son (Venkataswami's father), was raised. Nagaya—who was born in 1828 and was barely six when his father died—was one of three to survive among the ten children born to Polaya and his two wives. The family lost everything it ever possessed in repaying the loans it owed to a Christian mission in Ongole. Nagaya's two sisters were married into native families of Ongole. The younger sister moved to Madras and the older to Jalna in the northwestern part of what was then the Nizam's Dominions. Polaya's two wives took the young Nagaya to Hyderabad in the mid-1830s, where they both soon died of cholera. Nagaya's older sister and her husband brought the orphaned Nagaya to Jalna, where they took up domestic service in the household of a British officer. Venkataswami's account pauses at Nagaya's transition from Hyderabad to Jalna. He writes, "We have seen [Nagaya], in later life of an evening and in the exhilarating moments, when he had had his usual peg of brandy and soda water, bursting out into a doggerel song, filliping his fingers before his infant offspring and recalling sad glimpses of Hyderabad." The song went, "*Sankalo pilla/Nethi meedha golla/Chadarghatoo bhata/Palmeru Saboo kittutunnadu/Kooliki potunnanoo.*" Venkataswami translates: "Child on hip/Basket on head/Way to Chudderghat/Palmer Sab is building a mansion."[31] Indeed through its everyday dialect of Telugu, the song carries the poignant image of a young mother, with her baby in a sling on her hip, setting out to work as a day laborer at a construction site. I had visited the Chadarghat area in Hyderabad many times as a college student and crossed the old bridge over the Musi to meet my mother at the school where she taught, and the song struck a chord.

The move to Jalna marks the beginning of Nagaya's self-making. After a failed marriage (and a divorce), he left on a cart for the new military cantonment of Kamptee near Nagpur in the Central Provinces. Beginning as an errand boy, he held menial jobs with various British military officers. When he was about twenty, he followed an officer to Saugor, over two hundred miles farther north of Jalna. Although in Saugor Nagaya became the *kulampedda* (head of the community), he returned to Kamptee just at the time when the Nagpur Chattisgarh railway began to run between Nagpur and Calcutta, the old seat the British Indian government. Like his forefather Govindoo, Nagaya was diligent and thrifty: "He built a tiled-roof house and two grass thatched houses in the Bandarbasti, then flourishing with Bandarawandlu [people from Bandar] or Masulipatnam men. . . [and] purchased 6 country carts that plied between the Military Station and Hyderabad in one direction and Jubbulpore on the other, on a hire of Rs. 80 to the former and 90 to 100 to the latter place."[32] In 1855 Nagaya married Tulsemmah—who came from a modest Telugu family in Nagpur—and over the years they had ten children, many of whom died young. In one especially appalling instance, the child died because of an overdose of medicine given by a negligent doctor. When confronted by Tulsemmah, the doctor laid the blame on Nagaya for having charged him for a previous carriage ride to Kamptee. (He had expected a free ride.) Venkataswami records the losses of each of his siblings poignantly.

Nagaya's Nagpur years marked a transformative period of his life. He acquired property and ran his own transportation and hotel businesses, and his life with his wife, Tulsemmah, was "singularly happy."[33] He worked for some time for a Captain Clifton of the Twelfth Lancers during the 1857–58 Uprising against British rule, during which he witnessed the ruthless practices of the British as they put down the Indians. After this tumultuous period, Nagaya worked for a judge, a forest officer, and a railways officer. The last of these jobs brought him a steady commission from the sale of timber for railway compartments and gave him a financial boost to open a small hotel on

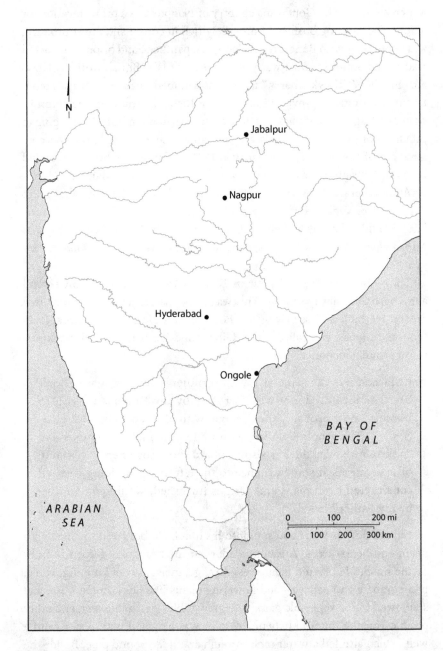

MAP 3. Nagaya's migrations
Source: Map by Bill Nelson. Based on information from J. G. Bartholomew, ed., *Constable's Hand Atlas of India: A New Series of Sixty Maps and Plans* (Westminster: Archibald Constable & Company, 1893), plate 17.

March 20, 1864. The Gondwana country of Nagpur was a prime location for a hotel and catering business. Immensely rich in cotton and forest produce, and abounding with Bengal tigers, leopards, panthers, and bison, it attracted traders and hunters. And it was well connected to the British world by How-ards Brothers' "Dawk Gharry," a horse-drawn mail carriage. Nagaya's repu-tation as hospitality provider soared when Richard Temple II, the commis-sioner of Nagpur, held the Nagpur Industrial Exhibition in 1865, bringing in hundreds of prospectors. (This was the same Richard Temple who became governor of the Bombay Presidency in 1877, and in whose house we would have our last sighting, as reported by naturalist-adventurer Marianne North, of Anna Liberata de Souza in 1878.)[34] Local folklore about the hotel grew. For instance, Venkataswami reports that one guest, a "Nayudu of Lascar-line," would get drunk and boast about his strength. *This hand has been fed at Nagloo's hotel; don't mess with me*, he would shout: *"Edi Nagloo Votailoo Chhai-yyee. Yamanukuntavoora."*[35]

The railway came to Nagpur in 1867. In 1869 Nagaya bought several acres near the railway station. This was to be his grandest entrepreneurial dream. He built a classy two-story hotel on this plot, paying almost forty thousand rupees, and called it the Railway and Residency Hotel. Venkatas-wami proudly recounts:

> Its façade was the same as the Government House at Parell Bom-bay. The idea no doubt was borrowed by my Father on a visit to Bombay, most probably the first one with his Madras bullock ghar-ries . . . The whole building with its innumerable outhouses and cookrooms and stables as also a billiard room together with a suite of apartments at some distance to the left of the building were all constructed from plans and designs furnished, would you believe, by my Father himself.[36]

Nagaya put his heart and soul into his hotel. He bordered the land with neem and henna trees. A fountain adorned the triangular garden in front of the hotel. He planted fruit trees—orange, guava, sweet lime, fig, apple, pomegranate and papaya—and flowering plants like lily, jasmine, rose, and sunflower. In the vegetable garden he grew cabbages, cauliflower, and other produce for the hotel's kitchen. The plot was irrigated with water from a well, which also fed a water tank through an underground pipe. Beside the well was a temple to Nagaya's favorite deity, Muniswaran (a form of Shiva). The hotel's lodgers were mostly Europeans who stopped at Nagpur on their way to Bombay. In fact, the railhead ensured steady Bombay-bound passen-ger traffic from Jabalpur, Mirzapur, and Allahabad.

FIGURE 9.   The Railway and Residency Hotel. Reproduced from M. N. Venkataswami, *Life of M. Nagloo (Maidara Nagaya)* (Madras: Solden & Co., 1929).

Nagaya made a fortune. His generosity was also most visible at this time. "Without putting it in footnotes and lessening the force of the narrative," Venkataswami describes his father's philanthropy. He paid for marriages and funerals in poor families, spent many hours on Sunday distributing "a good palmful of rice" or "a quarter anna copper" to alms-seekers,[37] poured sugar into ant holes, and handed out *lotas* (cups) with drinking water to thirsty travelers. He gave presents on the Muslim festival of Mohurrum to the *majeens*, *bhonds,* and fakirs, on Sankranti, the Hindu harvest festival, to troupes of women from Kamptee, and on Holi, the spring festival, to Somasi dancing girls. During the Pola festival, he gave his bullock drivers an extra day off. During the nine nights of Dassera, Nagaya rewarded his coachmen and horse keepers.[38]

Nagaya did not foresee that the fate of the Railway and Residency Hotel was tied to the capricious development of the railroad. The same trains that had brought him business took it away. In 1868 the railhead was extended to Jabalpur, and then even farther to Calcutta, establishing a direct Calcutta-Bombay line. Passengers no longer needed to come to Nagpur to transit. Nagaya's hotel suffered greatly. He became dependent on the occasional passenger and the steady income from his catering contract with the Great Indian Peninsula Railway. He opened a branch hotel in Jabalpur in 1870, and it did well until 1873. Venkataswami does not know why his father abruptly closed the branch hotel only to reopen it in 1876, when the Railway and Residency Hotel was in dire straits. Nagaya's son-in-law, who was put in charge of the reopened Jabalpur hotel, cheated him, and to complicate matters, the hotel lost its liquor license. The tottering branch hotel had to be shut down in 1878. Another hotel Nagaya opened in the nearby hill station of Panchmarhi also failed. Around this time, in 1876, the tycoon Jamshedji Tata made an offer of seventy thousand rupees to buy the Railway and Residency Hotel and its lands as a site to establish his textile factory, which later became famous as Empress Mills. But Nagaya would not sell. Then followed a ten-year cascade of lenders filing lawsuits against Nagaya to recover their debts. Ultimately, in 1879 the Railway and Residency Hotel, its contents, and its grounds were attached and auctioned. The auction fetched twelve thousand rupees. Venkataswami writes:

> This was the fall, and my father in those days lost his appetite, his gaiety had also gone, and he used to retire early to bed, touching a little food after taking little of a stimulant. There is no doubt that he brooded over the loss of the building whose construction he had watched with the glee of a child. The loss of many of his most valued articles such as the very large chandelier, the fine big billiard table, the double-horse carriages that used to run between Nagpur and Kamptee, the horses, the "sage gharries" or coaches drawn by bullock, etc., etc, might not have put him in melancholia as did the loss of his idol, the Hotel building magnificent with a fine style of architecture and commanding a partial view of the neighbouring Sookrawar Tank of old.[39]

In a final attempt to provide for himself and his family, in 1879 Nagaya established a small hotel, called the Central Provinces Empress Hotel, beside the defunct palatial Railway and Residency Hotel, which had been turned over to the railways. Venkataswami recalls that his mother's *strīdānam* (marriage jewelry) was pawned to fund his father's last venture. And he also remembers the people who came to his father's aid in these diminished circumstances: Gopal Pant Gatate, who provided the loan, and Nagaya's old friend Shaik Ismail—"one of his few true friends with a stout heart"—who was the guarantor. In 1880 Nagaya petitioned the government for a pension on the grounds that he had provided services to the state through his hotel and catering services for twenty years, at a time when the "Central Provinces [were] just arousing to commercial activity. The Hotel established was a point of civilisation as the other few points, [just as] the Telegraph Post Office, etc. are [points of civilization]." The chief commissioner of the

Central Provinces, John Morris, was a supporter of "Old Nagloo," but the proposition to provide him a life-saving pension failed because it was "bitterly attacked or opposed by Dr. Brake, the Civil Surgeon, and Colonel H. A. Hammond, the Inspector General of Police." As an "alternative measure," Morris commissioned the building of a new structure that combined the idea of a hotel and a *dak* bungalow, out of which Nagaya could run his hotel business. Nagaya relocated the Empress Hotel "on 10th August 1881."[40] In 1884, Nagaya's wife of thirty years, Tulsemmah, died, leaving him bereft of the steadiest companionship he had been gifted in his life, despite his own affairs with other women and his harsh treatment of her in his later years (about which Venkataswami is cutting).

The chronological account ends with the events of 1893. The new commissioner, Anthony MacDonnell, abruptly terminated Nagaya's lease on the hotel and *dak* building, which housed his Empress Hotel, giving Nagaya six months to leave. Venkataswami bitterly notes that the contract was issued to a German firm, Messrs. Kellner & Co., which had been operating the East Indian Railways Refreshment Rooms, an operation that displayed none of Nagaya's intimate knowledge of, and care for, clients. The notice of termination could not have come at a worse time. Nagaya had been paralyzed by a stroke. In Venkataswami's sad words, "Sir Antony MacDonnell showed himself the reverse of a man of feeling."[41] Nagaya sold his house at the same time that he was evicted from the hotel, and was moved in a *tonga* to a small rented house near the Khandoba temple, not far from his old Railway and Residency Hotel. Venkataswami—married in 1886, when he was eighteen years old—and his wife, Heeramma, cared for Nagaya during the last weeks of his life. Nagaya died on May 26, 1893—six days after young Heeramma herself had died. Venkataswami migrated to Hyderabad, and nothing in his writings indicates that he ever went back to Nagpur. And thus, through the lens of one family's experiences—its economic ups and downs, its displacements, dreams, and innovations—Venkataswami brings us face-to-face with colonial India's human paradoxes and costs, and its quotidian encounters, rarely available in imperial annals.

"Greatness" and the Biographical Subject

The oral-historical approach helped Venkataswami tell the story of the making of a self-made man, but it also helped him evince what he believed was the "greatness" of his biographical subject. In the second edition, Venkataswami published the comments of A. B. Napier, an officer in the Indian civil service to whom Venkataswami had sent a copy of the first edition. Napier wrote, "I admire your dutifulness as a son in recording the details of your father's life and from a cursory examination of the book, it would appear to contain some interesting records of persons and events connected with Nagpur, but at the same time, when I knew your father he was hardly a public character of great importance."[42] Musing on Napier's remarks, Venkataswami wonders if perhaps "he ought not to" have written his father's biography. Then he quickly asserts: "Now with reference to the estimation amongst his caste people it may be stated, that he ranked high. The qualities of the heart, which were ever predominant won them over and threw a veil over the moral breaches which at one time raised a storm of indignation of the entire community." He reminds us that from *til sankrant* to *til sankrant* (harvest festival), Nagaya's community brought him gifts of sheep and sugarcane. Somasi girls who danced each year at Holi mentioned him in their songs, which went:

Bungari Kolattamo	We sway over golden Kolattam rods.
Na Lachimi Kodaka	My Lakshmi's son [i.e., Nagaya, son of the goddess of prosperity]
Bungari Kolattamo	We sway over golden Kolattam rods.
Poowooloo boosay	The trees have blossomed
Poowooloo gawsay	The trees have flowered[43]

Napier's remarks about Nagaya's unimportance had clearly not discouraged Venkataswami. On the contrary, he called his revised second edition of the biography a "second birth" (a rite of passage generally reserved for upper-caste Hindus). That was not all. Along with photographs of the raja of Nagpur (Raghoji Rao III), the commissioner (Sir Richard Temple), and the tomb of the well-known historian of Nagpur (George Forster), he placed a photograph of the tomb of Nagaya, the pioneering hotelier. These were the makers of Nagpur. This audacious visual rejoinder to Napier does not just refuse the humiliation of erasure. It demands radical parity in the ascription of greatness.

Greatness was acknowledged by two Indian reviewers, rather backhandedly. Jadunath Sarkar and Zahur Ali, in separate reviews, admired the first edition of book for the graphic candor of its narration and its breathtaking detail. Sarkar called it a "truthful narrative," high praise in light of Sarkar's well-known commitment to "truth" in historical method.[44] Yet what arrests both Sarkar and Zahur Ali is that the biography is the story of a "pariah" by a "pariah": both reviews flash "Great Pariah" in their titles.[45] The editor of the *Modern Review,* where Sarkar's critique appeared, gratuitously comments in a headnote that Venkataswami for his "truthfulness deserves to be made Brahmin like Satyakama Javala of the days of the Upanishads."[46] Sarkar himself appreciates the complex characterization of Nagaya that balances his excesses against his generosities and concludes that despite "wealth and official favour," Nagaya remained "humble and respectful as before." But, Sarkar goes on, "This [humility] is a most admirable characteristic often noticed in low-caste Hindus who make their own fortunes." This sentiment is made more explicit when he calls on "high caste Hindus" to express "greater charity and sociality" toward "these educated Pariahs."[47] To be fair, Sarkar was reflecting a view held by one segment of the Indian elites toward what came to be called the "Pariah Problem" from the 1890s in south India. The solution to historical caste discrimination in their view lay in *social* reform, not in legislative empowerment.[48] The other reviewer, Zahur Ali, appreciates the portrait of Nagaya for different reasons: "Nagloo is indeed a very interesting personality and the interest is heightened by the fact that he appears in his 'original' Dravidian colours unsullied by *padre* purification. The ordinary fate of the *malas* [Venkataswami's ancestral community], unless they come within the missionary fold is to live and die, unseen, unknown and unlamented with not a stone to tell where they lie."[49]

Venkataswami, however, has little use for either the condescension or the patronization. Bristling at a Scottish missionary who had publicly announced that "Pariah girls" were not beautiful and so "if the caste system were to be abolished today, all the low caste Pariahs will flock in numbers to marry high caste girls," Venkataswami denounces these attitudes. He writes: "The Reader might think that we brood over our lot of being of low status, but he is mistaken. We are not brooding over our lot. We are satisfied with it, as that Being . . . has distributed equally on mankind, beauty, wealth, education, etc., without distinction of caste or creed."[50] In the teeming index of the book, Venkataswami lists the word "pariahs" with a telling cross-reference: "See Malas." And under the term "Malas" is indexed a world of anecdotes, practices, and histories.[51]

Venkataswami's observations about caste had reminded me of the famous interlocutions between Mahatma Gandhi and Dr. B. R. Ambedkar on "untouchability."[52] I wondered if Venkataswami, who had never hesitated to write to public figures, had ever corresponded with Gandhi or Ambedkar. Ambedkar's papers in the National Archives of India did not provide any leads. To my excitement, however, Sabarmati Ashram's library held letters from a single exchange between Gandhi and Venkataswami. The exchange was not about caste. What it revealed was nevertheless instructive to me and shaped my understanding of how Venkataswami viewed the biography he had written. His letter to Gandhi is dated January 1929, a few months before the new edition would have been out. Gandhi was in Ahmedabad at that time. "I beg of you to write a foreword thereto," Venkataswami requested, "after going through it from page to page—unless you have good reasons for not complying with my request [which is] not far fetched in any way." After listing names of people who had declined to write a foreword for various reasons, Venkataswami tells Gandhi:

> My book deals with many things and it is outspoken on many points, as I have to speak the truth, and people are afraid to write a foreword as by doing so they think they would be committing themselves. So I have approached you and if you are also afraid as the others [were] I would permit the book to go without a Foreword as was the case in the first edition. Lastly, I have another request to make and the request is, that you will not disclose the matter of the book much less permit it to be printed in your paper or make a reference about me in your paper or [any] other paper for reasons of my own. I hope you will comply with this request of mine unfailingly and of course with your usual kindness to all.

Unsurprisingly, Gandhi responded promptly. He congratulated Venkataswami but regretted he could not write the foreword because he was preoccupied with "matters of national importance."[53] (He was preparing for the Salt March.) Venkataswami had written to Gandhi *not* because Gandhi was, for some publics at least, a champion of less privileged castes but because his name had become associated with truth telling and the courage to commit to it.

It is clear that Venkataswami's dispute is not just with the British but also with "upper-caste" Hindus. A footnote in the biography tells us that Jadunath Sarkar had made the "minor error" of stating that Nagaya had the habit of spitting on the walls of his furnished drawing room. Venkataswami corrects this view. He writes, "It is too true that [Nagaya] retained the habit but he never spat *on the walls of his drawing room* but on the wall or a small portion of the wall to his right in the pillared verandah at the rear of the Bungalow." Equally important, however, is for him to point out that this is not a pariah peculiarity imagined by an affluent upper-caste Hindu. He writes, "It may be stated here that in these days of reason and right understanding it is a wonder to me that this very habit should be formed by an intelligent Brahmin from the Rai Bareilly district, who is an assistant of mine in a Government institution (since deceased)."[54] Venkataswami's closing words passionately state the core point of the biography: acknowledgment on the basis of greatness and not on the basis of caste.

The work is concluded, and we do not know whether the Subject of this Life by a consensus of opinion was really great enough to have a biography of his own. Opinions in the first place differ, as to what constitutes real greatness, and yet there is no doubt that the Subject of this Life had a number of qualities which were really the marks of greatness which brought him to the front rank of men. . . . When the Rev. W. E. Winks has already recorded the lives of illustrious shoemakers of his country, we thought fit to record, to the best of our ability, the Life of a Representative Mala or Pariah of our country who lived in the past century and whom we have the honour to own as our father, and if the Government of India has not thought fit to confer a title, that of a Rao Bahadur on the Subject of this Life as it did on the Stevedore Mr. P. M. Maduray Pillai, an Honorary Magistrate and Municipal Commissioner and on Mr. Aiyaswamy Pillay, D.M. & S.O., the first Indian Officer of the Madras Corporation, both being Pariahs of the Tamil country, that is no reason why we should swerve from the duty of writing the biography of our Father, the untitled Nagaya, or "Nagloo" the favourite of the Central Provinces Officers. . . . Despite the liberal dissemination of knowledge in the mother country and in the colonies and dependencies which is one of the characteristics of the Victorian age, if a Hinduised aristocratic European or a caste-ridden Hindu were to sneeringly remark, "After all it is a biography of a Mala or Pariah written by a Mala or Pariah, who is no more than one degree higher than a Madhiga or shoemaker," so what should our argument be to rebut the sneer or charge. Our argument, without offending the Reader of broad sympathies, would be an interrogation or question put in the words. "Whether a Pariah is not a man brought into existence by the Author of the Universe just as he called into being the other human creatures that go by different castes?" And if so "why talk disparagingly of the humble man and exclude him from the social organization from time immemorial?" If on the ground of uncleanliness, or rather because of being the eaters of forbidden flesh, the Burmans, the Malagasees, or the inhabitants of the Island of Madagascar, the African races, the Mohammedans (whether continental, Asiatic, or otherwise) the European nations, nay two-thirds of the human race are offenders in this respect. Yet these have their organization—call it caste organization if you please—whereby the deserving have the liberty to rise above the ranks.[55]

In choosing to tell his story as *he* chose to tell it in the light of justice, unafraid of naming people and reinterpreting events, Venkataswami takes us to David Scott's observation about George Lamming:

> For Lamming . . . the sovereignty of the imagination has neither to do with the sequestering of creativity from, nor its absorption by, the world of affairs—this would be merely bad faith. Rather an authentic sovereignty of the imagination has to do with the active will to refuse submission to the shibboleths that seek at every turn to inspire our self-contempt and our unthinking docility, and to command our understandings of, and our hopes for, what it might mean to live as a free community of valid persons.

Scott could well have been speaking about Venkataswami, who would have been an active builder of a "free community of valid persons." Such a global community (and the phrase) was the vision of the Guyanese poet Martin Carter, which Lamming explains is born out of the shared commitment to "the proximity that we have to each other, and the communality of [the] historical cargo of burden, and survival from burden, that we carry."[56]

Truth and Biographical Representation

Life of M. Nagloo takes on the central problem of "truth in history." Historians do not ordinarily turn to Venkataswami to find an answer to the question "What is history?" or "What was history?"[57] Yet Venkataswami's writings articulate what is at stake in that question and then make a choice in answering it, choosing integrity to "the subject." This integrity does not inevitably mean *bias*. Rather, in the end, integrity is the evocation of many possible truths, and not the representation of a single truth. After reading the first edition, a native of Nagpur, M. Hosanna, provided what Venkataswami calls "destructive criticisms." He advised Venkataswami to tone down details about Nagaya's love for brandy and about his affair with the "servant girl" Sayulu, to replace "Maratha Mahar women" with "Maratha women," to delete a Tamil song that has the phrase "call of nature" in it, and in general to stick to "extolling" his father, not "exposing" him. Venkataswami reproduces the feedback and challenges each of the suggestions with "why?" or "how so?" He does not modify the biography to accommodate Hosanna's suggestions. In the same way, footnotes frequently contain anecdotes with deliberate disregard for political correctness. Here is a classic example:

My father used to tell me that Sir Bepin Bose when [he] was a young man came to Nagpur to practise in the Courts he was not rich enough and as such paid reduced charges with the consent of the Hotel proprietor [Nagaya] during his stay in the Hotel for what period I do not know. But the Knight does not admit of having stayed in the Hotel for reasons he knows best and we would have struck off his name from the biography as I have done in the case of Mr. S. Ismay who said he never stayed in the Hotel, but we have no reason to disbelieve my father in the present case. So the name must stand though it does not add to the value of the biography in any way.

Venkataswami explains such choices: "In writing this biography I walked in the footsteps of Plutarch, the Prince of Truthful Biographers, giving the bright side as well as the dark side of my father's life in all candour and truth."[58]

How is this truth expressible for Venkataswami?

Sites of History

First, land and places are vulnerable to accruing inscriptions and overlapping remembrances. "Truth" in narration shows how sites are transformed by political action or social practice. For instance, Banda and Chitrakot figure in the epic Ramayana as the forest in which Rama, Sita, and Lakshmana passed their years of exile, and are sites of elaborately sculpted temples worshipped by "the pious rajas of Tiruha."[59] But they become transformed into bloodied landscapes during the 1857–58 uprising. Among the many illustrations of the layering of cultural memory is Venkataswami's description of the grand Railway and Residency Hotel building. A footnote tells us that near the site of the hotel were former gallows where prominent local criminals were hanged. He then reproduces a song in Hindustani, "sung in the bazaars," about "the Sitabaldi goldsmith Kashi's son, probably the eldest," who was evidently a criminal:

Kashi Sonar	Goldsmith Kashi
Taria baita haram	your lawless son
Kasbin ka janliya	took away the life of a prostitute[60]

In this way, Venkataswami's songs, anecdotes, images, and histories of monuments illustrate the phenomenon of change that underlies all accounts of history.

Ample History

Second, digressions in the narrative and the construction of coincidence enliven the surroundings of the biography's subject and help make an account of the past, or history, "ample." An ample history evokes a wide range of experiences, and in so doing, it allows us to perceive multiple truths that are intertwined but could remain invisible.[61] For instance, while recounting Nagaya's catering services for Sulaiman Shah (a descendant of the former Gond kings of Nagpur) and British commissioners, Venkataswami strategically digresses to describe the relationships between the Gond kings and the Marathas and then, with the Gonds fading, between the Marathas and the English. The digression enables us to visualize Nagpur as a place of rising and receding powers and Nagaya's own story as part of this ebb and flow. Venkataswami's use of coincidence juxtaposes historically disparate events, provoking new interpretations of history. For example, after describing the arrival in Ongole of the American Baptist missionary Reverend J. E. Clough, who intensified the evangelical work started by his predecessor Reverend Lyman Jewett, Venkataswami draws an unusual parallel that he himself recognizes is unrelated in geography and time. "Strange is the coincidence," he says, between the "doings here [in Ongole deep in south India] of the missionaries" and Nagaya's establishing of a hotel enterprise many years later in the Central Provinces. If Christian missionaries chose Ongole for their evangelical project because they believed that Ongole's Malas and Madigas were in darkness,[62] eight hundred kilometers away, Richard Temple, the commissioner of the Central Provinces, selected Nagpur to be developed for trade and business. (Temple, we may recall, had hosted the Industrial Exhibition in 1851 in Nagpur.) Venkataswami leaves the connection between missionary activity and business enterprise implicit. Yet this juxtaposition underlies Nagaya's argument in the twilight of his life as he sought a pension from the government: his hotel enterprise, he reasoned, should be treated as an equal participant in "civilizing" the Central Provinces, thus equating the professed civilizational goals of church and commerce. "Coincidence" is not an ahistorical construction. Instead, it helps the historian build conceptual analogies between unrelated phenomena or events and provides the irony necessary for the interpretation of history.

Narrative Justice

Third, truth in history is tied to narrative justice, a form of equity that is possible only through a many-sided narration, a narration that is prompted by the fundamental question of whose reporting yields what account of the past, and why any one account becomes the dominant version of "history." (Venkataswami, we might say, was walking several steps ahead of the "narrative turn" in history.)[63] One illustration takes for its setting the events of the Indian Uprising of 1857–58 as they unfolded in the Central Provinces. From the sidelines of this transformative event, we get Nagaya's account of the fast-paced action of the Indian summer that provoked the British chain of command into suppressing rebel soldiers in Kamptee and Nagpur. Nagaya remembers standing at night in the verandah of the brigadier general's bungalow, chatting with other servants, when the British resident, George Plowden, rushed in from Nagpur. And "getting down in great haste from his horse in the middle of the night, [he] entered the Brigadier General's room and had a close and short, evidently important talk; and [soon afterwards] all the forces were marshalled ready in an incredibly short time and marched on to Nagpore."[64] Some months later, Nagaya sees the uprising from the battlefield itself as personal servant to Captain Clifton of the Twelfth Lancers (a subdivision of the "Movable Column" led by George Whitlock). Venkataswami at first summarizes the well-known historian George Malleson's account of the events, which lauds the bravery of British generals and captains and decries the treachery of "uprising" Indians:

We have followed Malleson with incidents, details and dates of the battle of Banda and of the taking of Kirwi, and we have almost borrowed his graphic language, though this, properly speaking, was not our set duty, writing as we do a biography of a humble man, yet it is excusable, for, General Whitlock's Satellite, Captain Clifton, in no disparaging or mean sense of the word, shone resplendently taking part in all the operations undertaken in Bundelkhand country . . . and within . . . the compass of the gallantry of the Captain existed the Subject of this Life serving his master with faithfulness and loyalty, with honesty and singleness of purpose combined with alacrity in moments of peril and safety. . . . We are not writing, and this is not possible for us, a history of the Indian Mutiny to replace those splendid authoritative volumes of Kaye and Malleson.[65]

This modest disclaimer performed, Venkataswami goes on, "Yet we would, embolden, to speak of General Whitlock, Banda and Toruha in as few words as possible, as we have heard it personally from our Father." The focus is now restored to the "Subject" (Nagaya), who reports gut-wrenching "harrowing scenes" of the battlefield. Through Nagaya's eyes we see the "large mound of parched Bengal gram and jaggery heaped up with potfuls of water" by desperate Indian soldiers who do not want to break for food while fighting the British. We witness Whitlock's "immediate and constant hanging on trees" of captured men, and his handling of men of importance such as an old raja and his son by tying them to the mouths of cannons and firing them. And we are moved with Nagaya as he recounts how women all over the country threw themselves into wells, preferring to die rather than be captured and raped by British soldiers. But it is the "Loot of Banda," the small kingdom in the Central Provinces, that Nagaya remembers "at length and with special stress." The nawab who had supported the rebels was overthrown and banished to Indore, his palace looted by the British, who took his rare and old books valued at "at 12 lakhs of rupees" and all the family's gold and silver and jewelry. The quantities were so large that it took the British "60 carts daily for three months for the removal to Bombay" to ship to England.[66] Thus, as events of fifty years earlier become experience-near for Venkataswami through his father's memories of witnessing them, John Kaye and George Malleson's one-sided account is thoroughly unsettled. Similarly, Venkataswami cites James Rennell's 1785 cartographic reconnaissance of Nagpur but shifts it out of focus through Nagaya's reminiscences about Nagpur's hills and streams and communities. Minutiae from the biography provide the texture that is absent in dominant narrations. Narrative justice is accomplished when the historical record is thus formed through many and textured tellings that complicate the moral resonance of places and events.

The Subject of Small Kingdoms: Venkataswami's *STORY OF BOBBILI*

Before Venkataswami produced the second edition of *Life of M. Nagloo*, he compiled an extraordinary account of the tragic battle in 1757 between the kings of Bobbili and Vijayanagaram (Vizianagaram) in the Andhra region of southern India. The story, with its dramatic episodes of war, mass suicide, political machinations, cockfights, wagers, and heroism, is popular in the imaginary of the Telugu-speaking world.[67] The story is likely to have gone into the oral tradition soon after the events of 1757 in the Andhra country, and there are several versions that vary significantly, although they share a common core.[68]

Venkataswami's version is the only version of the story in English, recorded and translated from the oral tradition. It is also probably unique in that it was narrated by itinerant Telugu singers who went from the nizam's state of Hyderabad to the Central Provinces in the late nineteenth century.[69] The version is extraordinary also for its explicit framing by Venkataswami and for its implicit dialogue between Venkataswami and Jadunath Sarkar—

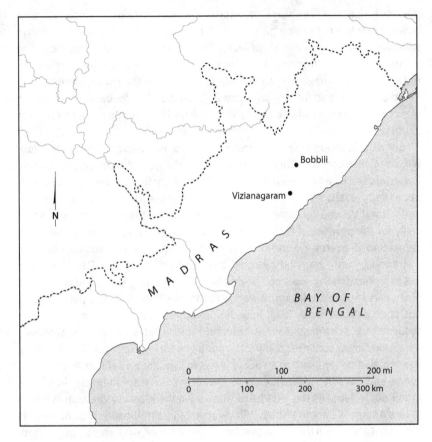

MAP 4. Bobbili and Vizianagaram
Source: Map by Bill Nelson. Based on information from J. G. Bartholomew, *The Imperial Gazetteer of India: Bombay Presidency*, Volume 18. (Oxford: Clarendon Press, 1909).

who wrote the foreword to the book—on the subject of history. We have here a different texturing of the question of truth in history, which, we have seen, was an intellectual and ethical question for both Sarkar and Venkataswami. Since Venkataswami's *Bobbili Story* is a rare book, perhaps available only in the library of the University of Cambridge, I provide a summary in the text that follows.

Bobbili is a small town in northern Andhra Pradesh, just south of the state's border with Odisha. The story recounted by Venkataswami's "minstrel" about the battle of 1757 begins in the early 1740s in Rajahmundry, about two hundred miles to the south. Two local chieftain brothers from Rajahmundry, Ranga Rao and Vengala Rao, on a rather unsuccessful hunting expedition with their two young nephews Papa Rao and Dharma Rao, come to a wild unpopulated land, where their hunting hounds at last spot a hare and give chase. To their surprise, the hare turns around and attacks the dogs, which run back whimpering to the hunting party. The chiefs learn of a local legend that says whoever lives here is unconquerable. They decide to build a fort here and establish a small kingdom. They thus become vassals of Vijayarama Raju, the ruler of Vijayanagaram, a kingdom forty miles to the south, under whose jurisdiction the land falls. Vijayarama Raju himself is a feudal king under the nizam of Hyderabad, whose capital is in Golconda, about three hundred miles southeast.

Soon the brothers build an impressive kingdom of twelve villages called Bobbili. Ranga Rao becomes king and lives in a colorful gem-studded palace. Bobbili is surrounded by an impregnable fort, and the deity Gopalaswami, whose temple already exists, now becomes Bobbili's protective god. The Bobbili people, agricultural Velama by caste, become renowned for their courage, and especially for the prowess of their thousand warriors. All is well for four years until Ranga Rao abdicates the throne to his nephew Papa Rao, who has now become a strapping young man and a strong, bold, and skilled warrior. Papa Rao turns out to be headstrong. He stops paying taxes to Vijayanagaram, and when after nine years the king, Vijayarama Raju, approaches Bobbili for the payment that has been delayed for so long, Papa Rao roughly rebuffs him. Ranga Rao, now reduced to a powerless elder statesman, remonstrates against his nephew's dangerous impetuousness, calling the nonpayment of taxes unethical. But Papa Rao remains defiant, and in an act of insult to Vijayarama Raju, he goes to Golconda and pays the taxes directly to the nizam. To heap on further insult, he gratuitously deposits the gifts he receives from the nizam in Vijayarama Raju's palace and goes back to Bobbili. Vijayarama Raju, a hotheaded man himself, is infuriated and sends three hundred troops, who cut off the water supply to Bobbili. Two Bobbili warriors discover the troops and, in a demonstration of Bobbili valor, they vanquish the troops and open up the water supply. These incidents set up the drama of lasting enmity between Bobbili and Vijayanagaram.

Vijayarama Raju hates Bobbili deeply but realizes that he does not have the strength to overcome Bobbili. His advisers come up with a plan to invite Papa Rao to a cockfight, in which he can get Papa Rao to wager and lose Bobbili. Cockfighting is Papa Rao's weakness. The wise Ranga Rao warns him that the cockfight is a trap, but he accepts the challenge on the condition that the event should take place in neutral territory. Vijayarama Raju agrees but, at the beginning of the cockfight, imposes another condition: that the winner not laugh at the loser. The Bobbili cock, after an initial setback, dramatically wins against many others and is ultimately declared the winner, but excited by the fighting, it flies at Vijayarama Raju himself, who runs away to avoid it. Papa Rao breaks into laughter. Immediately, Vijayarama Raju claims victory, holding Papa Rao in violation of the agreement. A fight ensues between the two parties, and they retreat to their own kingdoms, nursing wounds and grievances.

With his hatred fueled by humiliation after this defeat, Vijayarama Raju is now bent on destroying Bobbili. He bribes the nizam's officer Hyder Jung, who arrives with thousands of troops. Together they recruit Dubash ("accountant") Lakshmiah, a cunning multilingual feudal lord, who also demands a large bribe. He suggests that they recruit the powerful French general Bussy, who is in the French colony of Pondicherry, and demands a hefty fee to serve as translator between Vijayarama Raju and Bussy. The greedy Bussy agrees after a massive payment on the condition that he receive a separate huge amount for every stage of the journey. Making frequent stops in order to get more money, Bussy comes with the three warlords to Bobbili. They now have 100,000 troops together, and they lay siege to Bobbili.

Papa Rao meanwhile is away from Bobbili at the Durgammah fort, where his sister lives; he is attending the marriage of her son, having gone there against the strong warnings of Ranga Rao. He takes with him only one trusted friend. While at Durgammah, he is enticed by a cockfight challenge and forgets his promise to return to Bobbili within a day.

Ranga Rao sends a message to Papa Rao informing him of the siege and asking him to return immediately. The messenger, dressed as a *bairagi* (a wandering Hindu holy man), is trapped by Bussy's men. Bussy, ignorant of the culture, thinks the messenger is a Muslim fakir and asks him to read the Qur'an as a test. The messenger prays to Gopalaswami, the Bobbili kingdom's protective deity. Miraculously, he finds he is able to read the passages. Just as he is about to leave the camp area, he is discovered. Without the arms to fight, rather than surrender, in Bobbili warrior-style, he kills himself with a small knife. Vijayarama Raju and his men discover the message intended for Papa Rao and are thrilled to learn that the redoubtable Papa Rao is not in Bobbili.

Ranga Rao sends Papa Rao's brother, the more levelheaded Dharma Rao, to negotiate with Hyder Jung, the representative of the nizam. But the attempt fails and Dharma Rao returns after a fight. Ravanammah, Papa Rao's wife, sends a letter to Vijayarama Raju with an old maidservant requesting as his symbolic sister that he stay out of the war against Bobbili. But Vijayarama Raju laughs off the request, and the old maid and the soldiers accompanying her have to fight their way out of Vijayarama Raju's camp. When she returns and tells the story, Ranga Rao expresses sorrow and loudly wishes that the taxes had been paid and that Bobbili had not been in breach of ethics. At this, Ravanammah, who is Ranga Rao's daughter, chastises her father for not being a strong Velama. But there is not much time to quarrel, because Vijayarama Raju and his partners attack the Bobbili fort that very night, a moonless night.

The people of Bobbili put up a brave fight; even the women throw the French soldiers off the fort walls, arming themselves with mortars and pestles and paring knives and chili powder. But the enemy's numbers are too large for the people of Bobbili. Ranga Rao decides to leave the fort and fight the enemy. With him are his brother Vengala Rao, his nephew Dharma Rao, and a thousand Bobbili troops. He stops to pray at the Gopalaswami temple, where the signs are all inauspicious: the golden spires of the temple look worn and bent to one side, and all the lamps inside the temple have gone out. The Bobbili lords relight the lamps then beg Gopalaswami's permission to go to war and ask for his protection. The god, instead of giving permission or protection, tries to run here and there, and is in fact about to bolt altogether when Dharma Rao forcefully brings him back. Gopalaswami tells the lords that they have had enough time in Bobbili and should move on, and that he does not want to stay here either, especially now that foreigners have touched the fort walls. He reluctantly agrees to protect them for "seven *gadiyas*" (a *gadiya* is twenty-four minutes) in the battle.

Ranga Rao and the Bobbili army march out, and though outnumbered, they fight the enemy with astonishing valor. There is tremendous loss of life on both sides in the fierce fighting, and the remaining Bobbili men turn back to the fort to recoup. Just outside the fort walls, however, they are caught in a trap of gunpowder and mines laid by one of the nizam's commanders. Most of the remaining Bobbili warriors are killed. Ranga Rao and a few others manage to return to Bobbili. Ranga Rao decides that with defeat on their doorstep, all the women in the royal household have to be killed to avoid abduction and rape. He blindfolds his wife, Malammah, and kills her with his sword. He similarly kills his daughter Ravanammah (Papa Rao's wife) and all the other royal women. He also intends to kill his son, an infant, but an old maidservant escapes with the child in a basket. Most of the common women hang themselves from lime trees, and the remainder lock themselves in huts that they set ablaze. Ranga Rao, Vengala Rao, and Dharma Rao go to the Gopalaswami temple, where they pray to the god and then kill themselves with their own swords. Everybody in Bobbili is dead.

The servant who has tried to escape with the sole Bobbili royal child is captured by the enemy and brought to Bussy's tent. Bussy, however, melts and, telling the others that a child should not be killed, he lets her go with the infant. She rushes to the Durgammah fort, where Papa Rao is still engrossed in the cockfight, and tells him about Bobbili's destruction. Papa Rao comes out of his stupor and rushes to Bobbili. He is overcome upon seeing the destruction. In a furious rage, he charges into the enemy camp and kills Bussy, Dubash Lakshmiah, Vijayarama Raju, and Hyder Jung, one after another. Blaming himself for being so headstrong, and holding himself responsible for the destruction of Bobbili and all its families, he kills himself with his sword.

The story ends in the court of Golconda many years later, where the gracious nizam reunites the children of the Bobbili and the Vijayanagaram kings and gets the current Vijayanagaram king to pay for the rebuilding of Bobbili for the young Bobbili prince, who has survived the decimation.

How did Venkataswami encounter the story to begin with? Nagaya's house in Nagpur in his better days was a cultural center for the caste community. The Telugu-speaking diasporic community of Nagpur welcomed *daṇḍadāsaris* (traveling traditional storytellers) from the old Telugu lands of the Vanaparthi region who made the three-hundred-mile long journey from Golconda in the Deccan to Nagpur, crossing bandit-ridden ravines. But once they reached Nagpur, these *daṇḍadāsaris* were rewarded well by their nostalgic audiences. Venkataswami had heard the story of Bobbili many times in his youth in these contexts. The story itself, the performance, which took place typically after the midday meal, and the flows of sociality that marked these occasions—some people staying on and others leaving to attend to other work—made a formative and lasting impression on him. Perhaps the best way to understand Venkataswami's re-telling of this remembered story as a composite of many performances is to see him too as belonging to the tradition of storytellers who relate the Bobbili story. Forty years after he had heard the story, with its echoes still reverberating in his mind, he revisited it by writing it down into English. He does not tell us whether he wrote it down first in Telugu (or even in Marathi, given that he was raised in Nagpur). He then conducted research for "two years and a half," reading everything he could find on Bobbili history in "encyclopedias, manuals and magazines as also going through a Telugu History of Bobbili written by the present enlightened and cultured Ruler of the State himself."[70] He read the account of the Bobbili battle by the colonial historian Robert Orme.[71] He was familiar with the *Pedda Bobbili Raju Katha*, which was available in printed form,[72] and came to hold the view that it "seems to be an inferior production; a second-rate book, interspersed with Brahminical legends."[73]

With these experiences, Venkataswami has some insights into the role of the itinerant storyteller (*daṇḍadāsari*) as a narrator of the past, and consequently into the immense role of art and experience in the transmission of "history." The *daṇḍadāsari*, he says,

is a powerful narrator with a large fund of unfailing humour, telling the stories in a sing-song tone and explaining, his wife or an elderly female relative or his younger brother playing on a harp-like instrument, and holding the men sitting before him spell-bound. At one time, in the course of his story, he would rise high describing a scene of exceptional grandeur, at another time his voice falls to describe a sorrowful scene; once he becomes spirited to describe a war scene, at another time he breaks into a rapture to describe a laughable incident.

He is as ready to create laughter, as he is to create sorrow. . . . It is a rare pleasure to listen to him for 5 or 6 hours sitting on a comfortable chair after midday meals.[74]

The dramatic vigor of the telling enchants in another crucial way: it makes "history" relatable, opening possibilities for grounded aesthetic relationships with the past.

The creation of such relationships happens in a number of ways. First, the alliterative sounds and the regional multilingualism of everyday language appear throughout *The Story of Bobbili*. Take this example: When Dharma Rao goes to Hyder Jung's camp to negotiate, he is accosted by the Muslim guards, who challenge him, in spoken Urdu, "Kon janai walai? kon gaon walai? kidar janai walai?" (Who goes there? From which village? Where are you going?). Dharma Rao snaps back in a typical mix of Telugu and Urdu words in a nonsensical rhyme, "Kon ledu, meinu laidu" (There is no *kon*, there is no *mein*). Second, cultural metaphors that audiences know intimately are frequently employed by the *daṇḍadāsari*. To illustrate, Ravanammah's letter to Vijayarama Raju in her effort to preempt war calls up a resonant surrogate natal connection: "Consider me as your younger sister . . . and consider that Bobbili has been given to me in dowry or as a marriage-gift."[75] Third, descriptions are located in a materiality that directly connects to the everyday lives of listeners. When the mercenary armies of Bussy and Vijayanagaram attack the Bobbili fort, the Komati (merchant-caste) women spring into action. They quickly feed their infants and young children, tuck in their saris, and climb to the fort's ramparts. As cries of "deko, deko, banchote, aurath ko deko, acche hai, pukdo usko" (in Hindustani: look, look, sister-fucker, look at that woman, she's good, grab her) rend the air, they gather the measuring weights kept in their homes—"4 lbs, 2 lbs, 1lb and ½ lb"—tie them in cloth to make slings, and hit the clambering enemy soldiers with them.[76] Finally, an expansive religious imaginary connects the performed story to lived religion. We can imagine the audience in Nagaya's courtyard emoting along with the scene in which the Bobbili messenger, on his way to alert Papa Rao disguised as a Hindu mendicant, is trapped by Bussy, who puts him to the Qur'an test. The audience can sense his fear, they can understand the fervor of his prayer, and they can exult with him when the god helps him out:

The Rajah's courier was a Vellama [agriculturist] by caste and cowherd from early life, and as such was quite innocent of education, as well of arts as of sciences. Seeing the Koran, three-yards in length, put before him to read, his courage sank within him, and he meditated within himself, "O Rangesa, Ranganatha, life is departing, it is unquestionably departing; be kindly disposed towards me. O Knower of the four Vedas, Sri Ranganathaswami, Protector Lord Ranga O ye possessor of the bird (as a vehicle), do help me to tide over this difficulty." Soon after he contemplated on Gopalaswami who was existing before the fortress and earnestly entreated of Him not to fail in kindness. . . . [H]e contemplated on golden Mysammah and Hanumantharayudu . . . and the deities treating him indulgently, he read out the Koran fault-lessly for 3 *gadiyas* [seventy-two minutes].[77]

The same audiences probably also would have known, either through other stories or through life experiences, that divine protection is fragile. As the narration proceeds, they see that Bobbili's tutelary deity Gopalaswami pro-tects, but himself flees when cosmic signs portend the fall of Bobbili. In this manner, the *daṇḍadāsari*'s narration of the past provides what factual history cannot: evocations that generate relatability.

Interestingly, the structure of *The Story of Bobbili* adheres to the conception of a work of history as an objective enterprise. It has a preface, a summary of the story, an elaborate section called "Comments," and a glossary (and errata, thanks to the printing follies that dogged Venkataswami's publications). Ven-kataswami describes the comments as his "dissection" of the Bobbili narrative. With the dissection, he hopes, first, to set right "inaccuracies of statements" that are in "glaring contradiction of facts." (Bussy, for instance, was not killed by Papa Rao but died in Pondicherry.) It would prevent, he explains, "later genera-tions" from accepting the entire story as "true" or prevent skepticism that would altogether dismiss the story as invalid. Second, the dissection seeks to provide portraits of the main characters in the Bobbili drama, through "analyses of [the] working of their minds, grouping around them their objects and aims."[78] Venkataswami's from-the-inside analysis of characters—for example, what in Vijayarama Raju's nature does not let him forget his defeat at the cockfight, or why Ravanammah loses her temper at her father—anticipates the historian R. G. Collingwood's idea of historical study as "re-enactment." Collingwood, whose advocacy for anthropology is little known, said in an unpublished lecture in April 1928: "To write the history of a battle, we must re-think the thoughts which determined its various tactical phases: we must see the ground of the battlefield as the opposing commanders saw it, and draw from the topography the conclusions that they drew, and so forth. The past event, ideal though it is, must be actual in the historian's re-enactment of it."[79]

Yet this structure and rationale are less about asserting the infallibility of objective history than they are about taking seriously the knowledge con-tributions of itinerant, orally literate raconteurs. In Venkataswami's words:

The narrations are not histories, pure and simple, but are stories combined with truths and untruths, and devoid of dates to boot, yet they may go a long way to piece together the history of India—the blank portions of course—aided on by the rock edicts of the Buddhist Emperors of the Mauryan dynasty, and informations [sic] obtained from copper plates and researches of honorary archaeologists. . . . [All these] give [India's] history in a connected form.[80]

Sarkar's praise for the book needs to be appreciated in the light of his own "methodological obsessions" with fact = truth, consistent with the intellectual horizons of his time.[81] The comments and the glossary have brought "authentic history and modern topography" to the narration such that even the "critical historian will have no occasion to cavil at the Story as a mere story," Sarkar writes in the foreword.[82] And thus, Sarkar and Venkataswami agree on the necessity of "facts." But there is a revealing divergence between them. For Sarkar, the value is that the Bobbili story provides an *original* narrative that shows the true uncorrupted "heart" of the people, who have not been civilized, colonized, or converted. This heart has a specific geography: "For the purposes of such a study, the most favorable fields are the debatable land between the Aryan and Mongolian in the extreme north-eastern corner of Bengal, the arid jungly core of the Indian continent (viz., Telingana [sic] and Gondwana), and the last asylum of the Dravidians in the less advanced districts of Madras." Therefore, Sarkar concludes, *The Story of Bobbili* is a "very interesting 'human document.'"[83] For Venkataswami, the value of the Bobbili story and its narrative environment is that it helps construct a "connected form" of Indian history without bypassing a pervasive and vibrant oral record.

The Subject of Indian Folktales

"I have named it after my parents," says Venkataswami, referring to the title of his first collection, *Tulsemmah and Nagaya, or, Folk-Stories from India,*

the late Maidara Tulsemmah, that chaste and superstitious soul who had been reposing in the Nagpore Cemetery with the meandering Nagnuddi flowing by these seventeen years, and the late Maidara Nagaya, the head of "Sur Punch" [*sarpanch*: village council] and known amongst Europeans as "Nagloo," the hotel-proprietor of Nagpore and Central Provinces hotels' fame who had followed her in 1893 and reposing there. Parents' debts are very heavy and I see no other way of liquidating their [debt] partly except by naming the little book as I have audaciously done. . . . [T]erm it audacity if you please.[84]

The audacity is of course broader. One of the promised deliverables of scientific anthropology was the display of natives. It was epitomized in the eight-volume government-sponsored photo-ethnology *The People of India* (1868–1875), in which objectified "natives" could be classified and, more important, subjected to surveillance and regulation—and thus also contained.[85] It was the highlight of the India section of the "Great Exhibition of 1851" in London, in which handpicked natives were curated to depict "traditional" occupations (though some natives, we should however note, resisted).[86] Venkataswami's folktale collections, ethnographic and ethnological in every way, audaciously had no natives to display.

Instead, people are abundantly present. Venkataswami names and acknowledges members of his family, recounts his own experiences, modifies and uses family photographs to illustrate fairy stories, and openly pays homage to the family's dead. His collections emphatically make the point that Anna de Souza had made to Mary Frere fifty years earlier: stories circulate within communities and families, and are connected to particular moments and particular relationships. "Folk-stories of India" are ultimately about embodied tellers and listeners and their inventive narrations about places and other possibilities. India was indeed *peopled*. The French historian Pierre Nora may be right to disparage what he calls the "era of commemoration," by which he means the parades of display or "places of memory" (*les lieux de mémoire*) maintained by histories that triumph in the narration of the nation-state. What can we say, however, about commemoration that isn't merely in the service of nationalist history but that permeates a human subject's sense of personhood amidst a confluence of pasts? The philosopher Edward Casey's more expansive understanding of commemoration works better in Venkataswami's context. Drawing on the original meanings of commemoration as "intensified remembering" and participation in a formal eulogy, Casey writes: "In acts of commemoration remembering is intensified by taking place *through* the interposed agency of a text . . . and *in* the setting of a social ritual. The remembering is intensified still further by the fact that both ritual and text become efficacious only in the presence of others *with* whom we commemorate together in a public ceremony."[87] And as Ngũgĩ notes, "Names have everything to do with how we identify objects, classify them, and remember them."[88] As we will see, for Venkataswami, the recording of narratives is a commemorative effort that seeks to recognize a particular kind of peopling. In the sections that follow, I consider how he uses two modes of commemoration: inscription and photographs.

Inscriptions

The forty stories in *Tulsemmah and Nagaya* were collected, Venkataswami tells us, at Nagpur and at Hyderabad, beginning in 1899. The dedication of this book reads:

> To the Memory
> of
> **Those Chaste Souls**
> (the Author's Sisters)
> The Kind-hearted Puttem Huthoolummah
> The Gentle Kaki Chinammah
> The Upright Collum Polummah and
> The Loving Maidara Venkammah:
>
> *Residents of the Upper World.*
> THIS BOOK OF FOLK-STORIES, NAMED AFTER
> THEIR PARENTS,
> IS
> LOVINGLY INSCRIBED

By the time the book was published in 1918, Venkataswami's sisters had all died. The zeitgeist of the dedication comes from the biography, where the birth and death of each sister is recorded. Nagaya and Tulsemmah had celebrated the arrival of each baby girl, seeing each birth as mitigating their misfortunes. And each death left them in great sorrow. The year 1876 in particular was a year of loss, when smallpox took two sons and the daughter who appears in the dedication as Maidara Venkammah. Venkataswami, who witnessed these deaths from age nine, seems to have had a special relationship with his sisters, just as Nagaya had had with his sisters, who had rushed to rescue him when he was orphaned in Hyderabad. He remembers vividly how Pollummah, the oldest and Nagaya's "darling eldest daughter," named after the ancestor's tutelary deity, had once wrapped some chilies and salt in a small piece of fabric and waved it around her father, who was ailing with a fever. She lit it, and "when it was all ablaze and making a crackling noise, as the Chinese crackers do on a Diwali night," she made him step across it three times, believing it would cure him of the evil eye that had caused the illness. When Polummah's infant child died years later, Nagaya himself buried the baby in the hotel's compound, not sending it to the cemetery. Nagaya's second daughter, Huthoolummah, had assured her father that he would not lose his hotel even when the town crier had announced its auction, a reassurance that had kept Nagaya sane. (Huthoolummah and Polummah died within two months of each other in 1887.)[89] The youngest sister, Chinnammah, who died in 1912 in childbirth, is eulogized in the biography through a poem composed by Venkataswami's brother.

The titling of Venkataswami's folktale collections also breathes this aesthetic of evocation. With *Tulsemmah and Nagaya*, Venkataswami commemorates his parents' relationship. It was a companionship of thirty years, but it had not been easy on Tulsemmah in the later years. Married at twelve, Tulsemmah found life with Nagaya at first full of mutual affection. Then her life became full of cares as Nagaya took up with other women, incurred debts to attend to them, and lost his reputation and his business. Her censures and entreaties were ignored—and he began to beat her. From his narration of his mother's life in the biography, it is clear that Venkataswami felt immense empathy and admiration for her. "Her tone was [as] perfect as her features were comely, the limbs symmetrical and the figure tall and grand," writes Venkataswami. She came from a close-knit family in Nagpur, where she had been especially adored by her only brother. On Sundays, she took the children on outings in bullock carts to the Vaishnava temple of Lakshmi Narayana in Sakkardara in Nagpur.[90] She also loved visiting Ramtek, a Vaishnava pilgrimage town fifty miles from Nagpur, and its ancient temple of Rama, whose towers could be seen gleaming in the sunset from four miles away. I wondered whether the fact that Tulsemmah had been raised in a Vaishnava family was why she preferred these temples rather than praying like Nagaya at the shaiva temple of the village deity, Munaispurudu. Venkataswami reproduces three of the many Telugu songs she used to sing, for example, "*Vandanam ayya vasudeva hare, sundara murti sompu nike sare, balulam ayya, Balakrishna hare*" (which I translate as Respects to you, O Vasudeva, image of beauty, grace looks best on you, we are but children, little Krishna). The commemoration of the relationship between his parents in the title of the book, as I understand it, is not a refusal to acknowledge Tulsemmah's suffering as a result of Nagaya's excesses; it is rather the acknowledgment of their relationship, which, with its ups and downs, had provided Venkataswami and his siblings a home.

The case is similar with *Heeramma and Venkataswami; or, Folktales from India*, which Venkataswami self-published in 1923. He dedicates the book to his nephew, calling him "the only surviving son of a favourite sister of mine

[Huthoolumma]."[91] The nephew—also named Venkataswami—who was deputy auditor in the Posts and Telegraph Department in Nagpur, had followed Nagaya's footsteps, and had in addition become acting head of the *sarpanch*, the village council. The narrators of the 101 stories are mostly women from Venkataswami's family: his wife, Heeramma; sister Huthoolumma; and mother-in-law, Narayanamma, who he says had a "retentive memory and graphic powers of narration." Venkataswami had overheard some of the stories when they were being narrated in his childhood to his sisters by a paternal aunt, who he recalls was "a much-traveled woman."[92] We do not always know which of these women narrated which story (or when). Some stories were told in Nagpur and others in Secunderabad, in a variety of languages—Telugu, Hindustani, Marathi, and, to a lesser degree, Tamil.

The narrator that Venkataswami singles out is Heeramma. He explains:

> I have named [the book] after my deceased wife, the late M. Heeramma, that lodestar of my life for seven years, that thoughtful girl, that chaste soul, that close, almost Lubbock-like observer of ant's habits and ways, lying with her sweet first-born these five years in the Hindu necropolis at Nagpore, the Naganuddi flowing by. Without dissociating myself from one whose love was like that of a mother I have linked my name with that of my wife and this explanation will, I hope, absolve me from a charge of presumption in naming the book as I have done.[93]

Explaining why he dedicates his book to his nephew, Venkataswami writes, "As they [the folktales] are named, as elsewhere explained, after my departed consort and myself, I do not see the propriety of dedicating them [folktales] in this collective form to anyone outside of the family circle."[94] Again, from the biography we know that Heeramma was the oldest daughter of Majaity Surwiah, a Telugu scholar and calligrapher who was employed in the stores of the Great Indian Peninsula Railway at Jabalpur. Venkataswami married Heeramma in 1886, and, as we saw earlier, she died in 1893, six days before Nagaya, who had been in her care.

There is an extraordinary translation of Heeramma's presence into some stories in this collection. For instance, take the story "The Prince, His Wife, and the Fairies."[95] A prince is in despair because his young wife leaves him every day from six in the evening to six the next morning. He jumps into a well to end his life, but is rescued by an old man who endows him with the magical capability of turning into a fly so that he can follow his wife. The fly-prince finds her, dressed beautifully in a sari and a blouse of lilies, playing in a lake in the company of fairies (*kanyakulu*). He makes off with a pearl necklace belonging to the lead fairy, and in his palace, within earshot of the princess, narrates this adventure to his attendant as if it were a dream he had had the previous night. The princess pleads with him to return the pearl necklace to the fairies. He does. The fairies, understanding his plight and his desire for his wife, help him go through a transformation and test in the god Indra's court. It all ends with the prince happily regaining his wife for all time.

One of Venkataswami's notes to this story pushes the tale into another register. He writes: "There is a superstition that kannaikulu [fairies] select from human beings beautiful virgins or newly-married women of great personal attraction to keep company with them. I remember my wife, who is now no more, telling me of her having seen five water nymphs of unheard-of beauty in a konairoo [lake], where she went to bathe sometime after her marriage and that they had attracted her, one exhibiting her beautiful hands."[96] This note shifts the focus of the story to Heeramma and her untimely death. It displaces the fairy-tale ending with a suggestive "explanation" for a real loss in Venkataswami's life, turning the "happily ever after" mood of the story to a mood of pathos. We will see in the next section how Venkataswami transforms this particular loss through visual techniques.

Photographs

A photographic imaginary animates the inscriptional in Venkataswami's folktale collections. To contextualize his use of photographs, I begin with a thumbnail account of the early development of photography in India. Photography arrived in the subcontinent the 1840s almost immediately after the invention of the photographic process in Europe.[97] As anthropology came of age in the 1870s in Europe, photography was ready as an essential tool in the field. The rationale: subjective bias could assail the scientific self and make personal observation unreliable, and native testimony was either not trustworthy or dependent on the European anthropologist's shaky or nonexistent linguistic competence.[98] Trashing the prevalent practice of engravings of racial types, E. B. Tylor asserted, "Little ethnological value is added to any but photographic portraits, and the skill of the collector lies in choosing the right individuals as representative of their nations."[99] The photograph, it was imagined, could not lie; it assured incontrovertible and unchanging evidence. But as we know, anthropology was also the long arm of the colonial body politic. Photography saw a surge after the 1857–58 Indian Uprising, a surge that coincided with the growing conviction in colonial administration that ethnology was indispensable to colonial governance.[100] The first viceroy, Charles John Canning, urged officers to capture Indians photographically.

Army officer John W. Kaye (author of the three-volume *History of the Sepoy War in India*) systematized Canning's exhortation, and thus the vast *People of India* project was born.[101]

While photography was making its rounds in the circles of Company, Crown, and census, for members of the Indian aristocracy, photographic portraiture offered another medium to depict their princely identities and regal culture. Indians were noticeably productive in the Photographic Societies of Bombay and Bengal, and instruction in photography became part of the curriculum in technical colleges in Madras.[102] Some Indian photographers became famous. As early as 1855, Ahmed Ali Khan, a photographer from Lucknow, was commissioned by the nawab of Avadh to photograph the royal family and the court. Between 1860 and 1880 another Lucknow-based photographer, the former engineer Darogha Abbas Ali, published three photographic albums of Lucknow architecture and Avadhi culture. The work of both photographers can be seen as efforts to visually narrate Lucknow "before" and "after" the Uprising.[103] Around the same time, in the 1870s, Lala Deen Dayal, who would become British India's best-known Indian photographer, resigned from government service and set up studios in Bombay, Indore, Secunderabad, and Hyderabad. He also became the court photographer for the nizam of Hyderabad. His thirty thousand photographs of famous Indian and British personalities, durbars, landscapes, game hunts, and large infrastructural state projects mobilized new circuits of a visual India where "colonial administration, princely India, and the emergent cosmopolitan metropolis" intersected.[104] As photographic equipment became less unwieldy, studios in urban centers began to serve the photographic aspirations of upper-class and middle-class Indians. In addition, entrepreneurial Indians set up portable booths in bazaars across India taking photography to the common people.[105]

Venkataswami embraced this visual medium. Allusions in his writings to the "picturesque" and "cinematographic film" suggest that he was aware of established pictorial conventions and emerging visual technologies.[106] Although he includes a few line drawings in his folktale collections and an occasional painted plate like that of the Railway and Residency Hotel, his versatile use of the photograph is fascinating. Almost invariably, his dedicatory pages include photographic portraits of members of his family with elaborate captions. He clearly commissioned some of these but also went to some lengths to borrow other photographs from friends and relatives. Recall that for *Life of M. Nagloo*, he got photographs specially taken of his father's tomb, the tomb of George Forster in Nagpur, and that of the raja of Nagpur (the last from a painting hanging in the store of Messrs. Cursetjee & Co, wine merchants in Jabalpur). Friends supplied photographs of the Jumma tank, the Free Church Institution, and the temple at Sangam. These photographs are vital, not ancillary, in his construction of a visual narrative around the monuments and makers of Nagpur, among whom Nagaya the so-called pariah is prominent for his introduction of the hotel system into Nagpur. Thus, photographs serve to radically adjust the lens on untouchability, shifting "untouchable" from an invisible or gratuitous periphery to the center of transformative nation-making.

It is, however, in his folktale collections that we see Venkataswami's ingenious use of the photograph. Let us consider two stories, both from *Heeramma and Venkataswami*. The first story, called "The Seven Princes and the Fairies," recounts the high adventures of a young prince and his six brothers who go out hunting.[107] Unsuspecting, they find themselves beguiled by seven beautiful *kanyakulu* (fairies) and marry them. A life of luxury and merrymaking follows, with the odd exception that the youngest prince is confounded by his wife's constant weeping. Learning from his brothers that none of his wife's sisters weep, he gently pursues the matter with his wife. She tells him that the fairies are in truth *rakshasis* (ogresses), and that their father, a giant *rakshasa*, is counting on eating the princes upon his return. She herself is a princess from the land of humans. She advises the prince on an escape plan, and he and his brothers get away—but not without a tragedy. As they are escaping, the six *rakshasis* attack the prince, but his wife shouts and directs him to safety. She, however, is caught and turned to ashes by her "sisters." Years later, the prince and his brothers wander accidentally into the same area. Again they are rescued by the spirit of the prince's wife, who whispers, "Go hence or danger will befall."[108] Back in his kingdom, the prince builds a cenotaph to the memory of his dead wife with a loving inscription on it that reads:

SACRED
TO THE MEMORY OF
MY DEAR WIFE
WHO THOUGH DEAD IS STILL LIVING BY
THE REMEMBRANCE OF HER SIGNAL
KINDNESSES CARVED ON THE
TABLET OF MY HEART.
IN OUR SHORT CONJUGAL LIFE WE SAW
EACH OTHER AND OUR SOULS MET.
I SEE NO PORTRAIT OF HERS
YET THE PORTRAIT* IS EVER AND ANON

BEFORE THE MIND'S EYE
AND IS NOT LIKELY TO FADE OR CORRODE
TO THE END OF MY DAYS HERE
WHETHER THAT BE SHORT OR LONG.[109]

FIGURE 10.   The cenotaph. Reproduced from M. N. Venkataswami, *Heeramma and Venkataswami; or Folktales from India* (Madras: SPCK, 1923).

The illustration that accompanies the story is startling: it is neither a line drawing nor a painting as in most folktale collections but a photographic image. The photograph is of a cenotaph that bears signs of weathering. Whose cenotaph is it in real life?[110]

If we look closely, it emerges that the "inscription" on the photographic image of the cenotaph is handwritten. With ink smudges and rough edges, this handwritten note seems to have been superimposed on the photo of the cenotaph—and re-photographed to illustrate the story. The handwritten note is legible enough that, with magnification, one can make out that the text in the photographic image is exactly what the prince in the story inscribes on his wife's cenotaph. The asterisk in the inscription takes us to a footnote informing us that "she was not painted nor photographed in her lifetime,"[111] indexing a woman who is clearly *not* the fairy princess of the story but a real-life person.

I surmise that the allusion is to Heeramma and that the cenotaph illustrating the story is her tomb. To begin, Venkataswami had built her tomb next to Nagaya's in Nagpur,[112] and since Venkataswami had moved to Hyderabad, he had to rely on his nephew Ramaswamy, who lived in Nagpur, to provide the photograph.[113] Why was he keen on a picture of *that* tomb? After all, there were many graveyards with tombs in Hyderabad that he could have photographed. It is impossible not to see the autobiographical trace in the superimposed inscription that draws attention to the "short conjugal life" between the prince and the princess; Heeramma and Venkataswami's marriage, too, had been short-lived.

There are other signs of resemblance. Both Heeramma and the princess have shown themselves to be selfless women. Venkataswami tells us—in *Nagloo*—that despite being frail, Heeramma was "the only being that tended [to Nagaya], washed his face and hands and fed him."[114] Finally, the quality of augury fuses the ethereal and the real and creates hyperreal images in the text. As she was taking care of the dying Nagaya, Heeramma had told Venkataswami that before they tided over the crisis, either she or Venkataswami would die.[115] Her premonition resembles the whispering voice of the dead princess who also warns the prince of potential death. The element of augury is also visible in the dangerous presence of *kanyakulu* in the lives of both women. Heeramma had been alarmed to see them in a pond while bathing (recall the folktale I discussed earlier), and the princess in this story meets her end at their hands.

Still, there are some questions that are raised by this remarkably inventive use of the image of the tomb that I do not have answers for. Why was a photograph of a real-life tomb necessary? Did Venkataswami's inability to reproduce a photograph of Heeramma in a collection named after her—as he customarily did—prompt him to memorialize her instead through a picture of her tomb? What resemblance, if any, did the actual inscription on the tomb in Nagpur bear to the one in the story? Was it necessary to paper over the "original" inscription because it had Heeramma's name on it and would by its realism "falsify" the fairy story? (As with Nagaya's tomb, the inscription on her tomb would have been in English, with her name on it.) Did the princess's death strike a chord in Venkataswami when he heard the story, or did he invent the story (or part of it) to commemorate Heeramma? As a storyteller himself, he has, he says, "in some cases . . . added a touch to embellish a story or heighten its effect . . . and omitted what was obscure."[116]

The second folktale is "The Fakeer's Daughter and the Wicked Queen."[117] This story is about a girl who is born to a fakir through divine means and becomes the most beautiful woman in the kingdom as she grows up. The queen of the kingdom, on one of her sojourns, sees the girl and becomes afraid that the girl will compete with her for the king's affections. So before the king can see the girl, the queen steals a necklace of pearls that protects the fakir's daughter, and the girl dies. The poor fakir, grieving over his dead daughter, has a dream in which he is asked not to bury her body but to take it to the forest and leave it under a sandalwood tree. He does that, and soon the most fragrant flowers grow up around the corpse, which remains pristine. The fragrance of the flowers attracts the king, who is hunting nearby, and he is advised by the fairies guarding the body to fetch the pearl necklace from the queen. He brings the necklace, the girl is revived, and he marries her. The queen is punished for her evil act, and the fakir's daughter and the king live happily ever after.

Again, Venkataswami jolts us by illustrating the story with a photograph, fusing the otherworldly and fantastical events of the story with the real world. He uses a photograph of a woman who seems to have died young to depict the princess lying under the sandalwood tree among fragrant flowers. The woman in the photograph lies on her back on a raised bed; her arms are folded across her chest, and her eyes are closed. The upright fingers, stiff posture, and foot resting on a brick strongly suggest that her body is in rigor mortis. She is dressed in a brocaded sari, wears bangles and anklets, and has a *bottu* (vermillion dot) on her forehead, traditional markers of auspiciousness for a Hindu woman. The floral-printed sheet on which she lies mirrors the caption's odd description of the corpse as "fresh and blooming."[118] The image shows some obvious doctoring: the background of the photograph has been brushed over in uneven strokes in a light color, highlighting a still body amidst an absence of people or things.

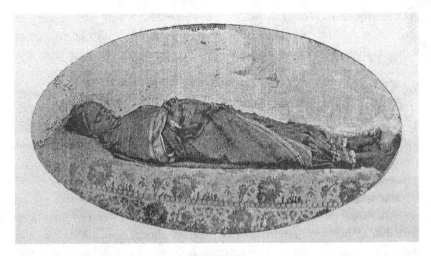

FIGURE 11. The fakir's daughter. Reproduced from M. N. Venkataswami, *Heeramma and Venka-taswami; or Folktales from India* (Madras: SPCK, 1923).

I am struck by Venkataswami's total silence about the details of this pho-tograph. With other photographs, he meticulously credits and thanks his sources—whether they are scholars or shopkeepers or friends—and explains the pictures. He identifies each photograph: Gaja his niece, or Chelli his daughter, or even Forster the historian, and so on. Even with the photograph of the cenotaph that he does not identify, he thanks his nephew for providing it. But this photograph of the young dead woman is the *only* picture in all his writings that remains both unacknowledged and unexplained. Was this unsettling image a photograph of Heeramma? Was he silent about attributing this photograph because it was, after all, *his*, something that perhaps he com-missioned just after Heeramma died? While I cannot be certain, the cryptic phrase "she was not photographed in her *lifetime*" that we encountered earlier hovers over this image. As with the grave of Anna de Souza that I could never trace, like the portrait of Ramaswami Raju that I could never find, I have had to reconcile myself to the fact that some trails are impassably overgrown.

I am strongly inclined to believe that the dead woman in the photograph is indeed Heeramma. I am therefore compelled to wonder: By using an image of Heeramma's dead body to signify a dead princess who returns to life, was Venkataswami trying representationally to transform the permanence of his loss? Walter Benjamin has famously reflected on the destiny of the "aura" of the phenomenal world amidst the technology of image production. He writes: "In the cult of remembrance of dead or absent loved ones, the cult value of the image finds its last refuge. In the fleeting expression of a human face, the aura beckons from early photographs for the last time. This is what gives them their melancholy and incomparable beauty."[119] Here we might also borrow from Ranjana Khanna and adapt her term "critical melancholy," an affect that "has a critical relation to the lost and to the buried."[120] Such a melancholy manifests loss but simultaneously demands that the imagination of a new future be cognizant of specters of the past. While Khanna's context is the conflicted interiority of the new postcolonial nation-state, which has to contend with both loss and recovery, "critical melancholy" can also help us see how Venkataswami preserves personal loss and intimacy from being anthropologized by colonial science. He remains sovereign over the intimate world between himself and Heeramma, free to represent and transform that world as he chooses.

With Benjamin's thinking, we can appreciate Venkataswami's innovations with the "technological reproducibility" of the photograph, which "place[s] the copy of the original in situations which the original itself cannot attain. Above all, it enables the original to meet the recipient halfway."[121] And it is at this halfway point that Venkataswami's sepulchral fusions occur. Aura is not lost but is mythically transposed onto story texts. Evoking sepulchral fusions, Venkataswami renders the photographic surface as a porous boundary between the imaginary and the real, between the living and the dead. Indeed, his writings, with their visual and other narrations, had pushed me to think about how family memory is not archival but alluvial, and how things we call "texts" are also fusions provoked by the flux of life.

After finding Venkataswami's autographed copy of *Life of M. Nagloo* in a London used book store, I tried to trace the family. What happened to Venkataswami after Nagaya died? Where were "The Retreat" in Hyderabad and "The Hermitage" in Secunderabad, names he mentions in all his prefaces as those of his residences? Each question seemed more enigmatic than the next. I began to explore both Nagpur and Hyderabad in parallel. Through the Internet I found Harshawardhan Nimkhedkar, a volunteer in Nagpur with the international organization called Random Acts of Genealogical Kindness, which aimed to help people searching for past monuments. I wrote to him—in 2004—listing all the places mentioned in the biography: family names, the hotel site, the tanks, the temples, and the graveyards and cenotaphs. Mr. Nimkhedkar wrote back promptly. He was, he said, a lawyer by profession, a former English lecturer, a P. G. Wodehouse fan, a "confirmed bibliophile," and an ardent student of British Indian history. Two emails later, we discovered to our astonishment that he was a close friend of a former student of my father's who also lived in Nagpur. After a couple of weeks and considerable scouting on my behalf—including following my request to check out a masala shop by the name of Kaki Masala (one of Venkataswami's sisters had married into a Kaki family in Nagpur)— Harshawardhan wrote back with disappointing news:

> I personally went to the only cemetery that's on the banks of the river Nag—it's old, big, and the only place for those monuments. It's called "Mokshadham" these days (formerly Tikekar ghat). UNFORTUNATELY— nothing of the past is preserved there. The whole big plot of land is now being used to build re-modelled and re-designed crematoria and also, to accommodate new burials. They have simply demolished the entire old structures, razed to ground and bulldozed every structure standing there, including chabutaras, chhataris, samadhis, tombstones, monuments, inscriptions, memorial pillars—and there is nary a thing that can tell you about the past burials.[122]

The Nagpur trails of the Nagaya family—the tombs, the hotels, and the neighborhoods—had all vanished.

In 2003, trying to follow Venkataswami's Hyderabad connections, I called Mr. Narendra Luther, a retired Indian Administrative Service officer and historian of Hyderabad. He did not know about Venkataswami but agreed to publish my inquiry in the column he wrote for the Hyderabad edition of *The Hindu*. There were exactly two responses. One was from a librarian at the State Central Library, who said that the library was in possession of a book of essays by Venkataswami—a publication I had not known about and which turned out to be crucial later on.[123] The second was from an army officer who said that one of the buildings in the Secunderabad cantonment could have been Venkataswami's home "The Retreat." I remember visiting the state library with my leg in a cast, having broken it, to photocopy the book. A few weeks later I met the generous army major in the cantonment area. "Fortunately, you caught me on the day my leave for a week has started," he had written in his email. He took me to the building identified in military records as "The Retreat." Despite its promising colonial allure, there was no likelihood of Venkataswami's ever having lived there; British officers had always occupied it. I found out later that Winston Churchill had stayed here briefly as a subaltern in 1896.[124] The army officer offered to scout out another building in the city that he knew was called the Hermitage Complex; it, too, did not take us to Venkataswami. So in both Nagpur and Hyderabad, I had failed to locate any trace of the man who had written in such photographic vividness about monuments, places, and people.

In 2010, preparing to teach a course, I wanted to gather stories about Indian-English interactions in everyday spaces in India. I recalled a striking essay in

Venkataswami's book of short essays (the book that the state librarian had drawn to my attention) that made a distinction between relations that the early Englishmen in India had with Indians and the ways in which post–World War I officialdom treated Indians. "Despite the fact that India has been under British rule for well-nigh four centuries," Venkataswami writes, "the Englishman is still a tyro in his manners towards Indians. He does not even try to understand the ways and manners of Indians or even to learn their language. . . . Indians sometimes go to an Englishman's bungalow and after a long wait an audience is granted but they are half-heartedly listened to and sent away not a bit wiser for all the trouble taken."[125] I continued to leaf through the essays, marveling again at how he acknowledged people without hesitation. An essay titled "Hospitals and Doctors" ends with him thanking "Russool, Jamal, and Babiah, the sweepers" and "telephone callers, Messrs. Barnabas and Joachim," who helped during the hospital stay of his son Abhimanyu.

As had become something of a wistful habit, I started searching for Abhimanyu on the Internet. Playing around with the fact that Venkataswami used the initials M. N., in which N. stood for his father's name, I googled "M. V. Abhimanyu" (that is, Medara Venkataswami Abhimanyu). Suddenly an electoral record from Hyderabad popped up. It gave the name Shravan Kumar as the son of a deceased M. V. Abhimanyu. Shravan Kumar's wife and two sons and a daughter were also listed as registered voters. I located one of the sons, Karan Kumar, on Facebook, which, in addition to displaying a picture of him working on a laptop with a beautiful German shepherd beside him and a Pink Floyd poster behind him, listed his phone number. Encouraged by these "signs" that somehow in my eyes lessened the absurdity of my mission, I waited for the day to break in Hyderabad (it was late evening in North Carolina) to call him. "Sorry to call out of the blue," I said, identifying myself. "Would you happen to be related to M. N. Venkataswami?" I hesitated, embarrassed and hopeful. Karan was indeed a great-grandson of M. N. Venkataswami. An exciting conversation followed. And thus, in early April 2010, after a seven-year search, I had connected to Venkataswami's family. By the time I went to Hyderabad that summer, we had exchanged several emails. Karan took me to meet the only surviving son of Venkataswami, Lakshman Rao, who lived, as grand coincidence would have it, twenty minutes away by car from my parents' house.

Lakshman Rao was in his eighties, retired from the police force. The conversations with him and Padmamma, his wife, during several visits to their home over the next few years, a few of which I audio-recorded, answered some questions that had nagged me for many years. We spoke in Telugu, English, and "Hyderabadi Hindi," a unique variation that seamlessly blends Hindi, Telugu, and Urdu. As I had guessed, after Heeramma's and Nagaya's deaths, Venkataswami had moved away to Hyderabad. Initially, before he found a job as a librarian, he stayed with a relative in the present-day Osmania University area. Later he built a small house in Bogulkunta, near King Koti—today these areas of Hyderabad would be among its oldest neighborhoods—and called this house "The Hermitage." Later he renamed it "The Retreat." Although Venkataswami lists "The Hermitage" as being in Secunderabad and "The Retreat" as being in Hyderabad, Lakshman Rao was quite certain they referred to the same house. I continue to wonder, though, whether he called his first home with relatives in the Secunderabad area "The Hermitage" because it had been a refuge after the tribulations of Nagpur. *Heeramma and Venkataswami*, dated 1898, his only book that bears this address, was written just after his move to Hyderabad. All his other books, written later, mention "The Retreat, Hyderabad" as his home.

In an alcove in the living room, a picture frame that held three photographs intrigued me. I recognized Venkataswami. "Who are the two women?" I asked. There was a picture of an older woman and another of a considerably younger one on either side of Venkataswami's picture. I learned that after he had moved to Hyderabad, Venkataswami had married twice. The older of the two women was Lakshmamma, with whom he had two sons, Nagabhushanam and Govindaraju. The younger wife was Ramanujam, whose children were her sons Abhimanyu and Lakshman Rao and a daughter, Sumitra. "I loved both my *attalu* [mothers-in-law] and all the children loved them both. Twelve of us were very happy in that small house," Padmamma told me, speaking in Telugu.[126]

A conversation in 2013 turned to Venkataswami's second son, Govindaraju. "Whatever we are today, we owe it to him. . . . He used to tell us: 'Work hard. That's the only way to do it. Even if you earn two *paisa*, get it through hard work.'" Lakshman Rao said then, continuing in the spirit of the living truths that had so engrossed Venkataswami in his writings, "Our grandmother used to visit him." I asked, *"Yevaru?"* Who? Padmamma answered, *"Ayana anevaru, 'Avva vachindi, kalalo avva vachindi.'"* (He used to say, "Grandmother came, she came in a dream)." Lakshman Rao elaborated: "She used to come often. We now have a belief about it. The old lady, god knows where she is, but if we had any problem, she used to come. Someone wasn't well, she'd come to ask, 'How are you? I'm still there looking after you.'" In the back-and-forth of clarifications, I learned this "old lady" was Tulsemmah, Nagaya's wife, who had predeceased him. She was known not as Tulsemmah, a name I knew from the biography, but as *"Nagulu-tata bharya,"* or Grandpa Nagulu's wife. When I said, "So Govindaraju would see her in his dream?" Lakshman Rao corrected me: *"Kanipicchedi kaadu. Vachedi."* (He would not *see* her. She would *be* here.) "It was a trance."[127]

FIGURE 12. Venkataswami with his two wives, Lakshmamma (far left) and Ramanujam (far right). Photograph by Leela Prasad, May 2010.

Other family stories about Venkataswami recall his obsession with books and writing. His personal collection included gilt-edged copies of *Aesop's Fables* and the *Arabian Nights Entertainments*. Once, I asked Lakshman Rao if there were stories about Venkataswami's routine or his daily life. "I've heard that he used to come home—he had a job as a librarian—and after a while, dust his desk, and his books in that almirah [cabinet], and sitting on the floor he would begin to write," said Lakshman Rao. I saw the small, sturdy, well-used desk and the walnut-colored wooden almirah. Apparently Venkataswami's books had been donated or sold. "People can pay me anything, but I can't part with this. This is our inheritance. It will at least help me tell my children who we are," he added, pointing to the furniture.[128]

It seems perfectly befitting Venkataswami's imaginative fusion of the living and the dead that I close this chapter with Venkataswami's death. "I don't know how he died; I was only eight or nine months old when he died in 1931," Lakshman Rao told me. "But we have a tradition in the family of paying our respects at his grave every year at Diwali."[129] Lakshman Rao's health did not allow him to take me to Venkataswami's tomb in the Himayatnagar neighborhood, close to where he had once lived. Lakshman Rao died in January 2016. His son Devender invited me to join the family on the traditional visit to the gravesite on Diwali in 2018 (November 8), remembering that his father had been awaiting this book. Continents away, I could not join them.

FIGURE 13A.   Venkataswami's desk. Photograph by Leela Prasad, June 2014.

FIGURE 13B.   Venkataswami's cupboard. Photograph by Leela Prasad, June 2014.

FIGURE 14.   Venkataswami's gravesite, Hyderabad. Photograph by Leela Prasad, May 2016.

I visited Venkataswami's grave on my own. The afternoon sun was so bright that it projected my reflection in the phone's camera viewfinder, and I was unsure if I captured the grave in the blinding light. Yet when I later viewed the picture I had taken, much to my delight, it showed three graves, newly painted in white. Devender, Venkataswami's grandson, identified these for me later: "That is Tata-garu's in the middle, between my two grandmothers."

CHAPTER 4

The Irony of the "Native Scholar"

S. M. Natesa Sastri

November 18, 2001.

"Two months back," Mr. Gopalakrishnan began his speech to his extended family, looking around at about twenty-five people seated on chairs and sofas or standing in his home in Sayeenagar, Chennai, "a small article appeared in *The Hindu*, talking about Natesa Sastri as a scholar, his works, and it ended with a small plea." He was referring to the letter I had written to Mr. Muthaiah in which I asked if he knew anything about the family of Pandit Natesa Sastri.[1] Sangendi Mahalinga Natesa Sastri intrigued me. He was born in a Brahman family in Tiruchirapalli district of present-day Tamil Nadu in 1859 and graduated from Madras University in 1881. Immediately after graduating, he joined the Government Archaeological Survey and over the years held positions in a variety of colonial departments—the Board of Revenue, the Office of the Inspector-General of Jails, the Local and Municipal Secretariat, and the Registration Department, where he was a manager when he died, just forty-seven years old.[2] I later learned that the circumstances of his death were sudden and tragic. A panic-stricken horse in a temple procession in Triplicane in Chennai knocked him down, and he died of his injuries. Like Ramaswami Raju, Natesa Sastri published on a variety of literary, religious, and philosophical subjects. A polyglot and a nimble translator, he had translated countless inscriptions and literary works from Sanskrit,

FIGURE 15. Natesa Sastri. Reproduced from S. M. Natesa Sastri, *Hindu Feasts, Fasts and Ceremonies* (Madras: M. E. Publication House, 1903).

Urdu, and English into Tamil and from Tamil into English. He was the first to publish Tamil folktales in English and was among the first to write novels in Tamil. He published also on Telugu and Kannada folklore in a number of leading journals of that time, drawing on his travels through the Madras and Bombay Presidencies. The scholar of Tamil literature Kamil Zvelebil writes:

Natesa Sastri's rich and many-sided work would require a full-fledged monograph of its own, so amazing are his activities and so remarkably diversified is his output: administrator, archaeologist, linguist, translator, folklorist and, above all, novelist, he went from one activity to another. The most prolific of all early Tamil prose-writers, driven by thirst after ever new achievements, he wished to demonstrate that what could be done in English could equally well be done in Tamil.[3]

The letter to Mr. Muthaiah was precipitated by a meeting I'd had with the literary critic P. G. Sundararajan, well-known as "Chitti," in Chennai in September 2001, when I visited libraries in Chennai in search of Natesa Sastri's materials. Chitti also described Natesa Sastri as a pioneering scholar. Although Chitti did not know anything about Natesa Sastri's family, he had a mysterious clue. About twenty years earlier, he said, he had heard that somebody in Natesa Sastri's family had his manuscripts. So I wrote to Mr. Muthaiah. I was expecting a reply from him, but instead he published parts of my letter in his column "Madras Miscellany" in *The Hindu*.[4] It worked like magic. Within hours of the morning newspaper's arriving on readers' doorsteps, he telephoned to give me the contact details of several people who had responded. And soon Natesa Sastri's grandson Gopalakrishnan, a partner in a consulting firm in Chennai, and I, in Hyderabad at that time, had connected. Now I was at the family lunch that Gopalakrishnan had organized, with cousins and other relatives gathering from all parts of Chennai. A Coimbatore family had planned to be there but were unable to arrive in time.

Gopalakrishnan continued his speech, indicating me: "This author who has been researching Natesa Sastri has not been able to come across any of his descendants. Jambu [a relative] saw the article and called me, and immediately also called Pattabhi [another relative] and some of you. The moment I got the message I contacted Mr. Muthaiah just as many of you called *The Hindu* and gave our contact information. Subsequently she contacted us." I had left my recorder on a coffee table that had been moved to the middle of the room; the little red lights on the recorder were flickering synchronously with the excitement in the room. I reproduce part of that conversation here. It was in English. (I have only keyword comprehension of spoken Tamil.)

GOPALAKRISHNAN: Dr. Leela Prasad is a professor of religion, interested in folklore and folklife, Hindu arts, and so on. As part of her research, she happened to come across Natesa Sastri's works. There are a lot of English publications by him on the folklore of south India, in various places, like the Archaeological Survey of India.

After she called me, I also started visiting Connemara Library, the Maraimalai Nagar library, and other libraries.

Someone mentioned another library's name.[5]

And that is the first time I started to ask, Who is my grandfather?

I think none of us knows him—due to design, or ignorance, or innocence, or failure of some sort, I do not know. I would like all of us to know that a great scholar has been forgotten by the family. Forgotten in Tamil Nadu, forgotten in the country.

Everybody was silent as he paused.

From today, let us try and learn who he was. He passed away in 1906 at the age of forty-seven. My father was at that time two years old. Maybe that is why we did not discuss him in the family.

Some people began to discuss how old their own parents might have been when Natesa Sastri, who had eleven children, passed away.

A RELATIVE: My father was the first person who republished *Dinadayalu* in 1971 [Natesa Sastri's first novel; second edition 1902].

GOPALAKRISHNAN: Let me finish, one second.

Forget about my generation. I want the younger generation, folks in their twenties and thirties, to get together and form a Natesa Sastri Trust, anybody among them, through a daughter or daughter-in-law—whoever has got even a streak of Natesa Sastri's blood running in their veins—let us find a way to honor him.

Tata [Grandfather] was many men rolled into one—an archaeologist, [someone interjected "an epigraphist"], novelist, folklorist, translator . . .

LEELA: His bibliography runs into several pages.

GOPALAKRISHNAN: So I hope the youngsters will do something.

Let's perhaps start with a library—some of his works are in Connemara Library, some in Tamil Nadu State Archive, some in Maraimalai Nagar library . . . we can do it. Just in two weeks, I have collected five Tamil novels by him.

Hey, Shyam!

Gopalakrishnan called out to his son Shyam, whose official name is Chandrachoodan; he had collected some of Natesa Sastri's works.

Shyam has visited the Tamil Nadu archives and already introduced himself [to librarians].

There are—um—a certain number of "statutory requirements," because he is not a research scholar . . . right? So getting access to the documents is difficult.

I spoke to the Special Commissioner and she has now said being a family researcher, personal research, it is harder.

[But] we have just overcome the difficulty.

For a while the family discussed Natesa Sastri's works, listing titles they had come across.

In closing, I want to say—

See, I see you somewhere at a marriage event, I have seen Pattabhi somewhere, I see Jambu at some other event—

But all of us have not met for one purpose together. . . .

So I say, let us rediscover Natesa Sastri.

He was our grandfather. Why not claim him?

For a while the family shared, in piecemeal fashion, stories of ancestors nobody had met and details of where Natesa Sastri had worked.

JAMBU [another of Natesa Sastri's great-grandsons asks in Tamil]: What was Tata's first job?

SHYAM: He was assistant to Robert Sewell, Archaeology Department.

GOPALAKRISHNAN: Yes, he was in the Archaeological Survey; he was epigraphist there. From there, he was transferred to Mysore. Then he came back and worked as a jail warden for two years. After working there, he joined Inspector General of Registrars in Madras as a manager. Then went to Padalur as registrar himself, then came back to Madras. He was founder-director of the Triplicane Urban Co-operative Society.

Somebody mentioned the names of other founders.

GEETHA SUNDAR [Natesa Sastri's grand daughter-in-law]: How did he get called "pandit"?

GOPALAKRISHNAN: Robert Sewell, who was his boss in the Archaeological Survey, looking at his scholarly ability in Tamil, English, and Sanskrit, named him "pandit."

SHYAM: He knew eighteen languages. He translated all of the inscriptions of the first Archaeological Survey of Western India. He translated all the Dravidian inscriptions—and he was given the title of "pandit."

LEELA: I tried to follow this lead because I also got the same information. I went to the library at Fort Saint George, and I spoke to the superintending epigraphist here about Natesa Sastri. The other thing is, in his prefaces, Natesa Sastri mentions Brodie's Road as his residential address.[6] Now, I don't know what that means. . .

GOPALAKRISHNAN: As soon as *I* learned of this, I called [mentions a relative's name, unclear on my tape]. He is one of the oldest around—

and he told me Natesa Sastri had never lived on that road. He lived
only in Triplicane on Parthasarathy Swamy Road.

LEELA: I looked up the English almanacs, and there, the address that
was given, under "Native Residents," they list all the native residents
for eighteen ninety-three, and the exact address that was given was
10 Veeraraghava Mudaliar Street.

Animated discussion followed. Should we trace old addresses—like the one
on Brodie's Road? Look up records of the Triplicane Urban Co-operative
Society? Who had family portraits? If we visited Sangendi, would we find
anybody still there from the family? (Gopalakrishnan later did visit Sangendi.) Which libraries seemed promising? Should we try old printers and
publishers in Chennai? The discussion also mapped the family tree: Natesa
Sastri had eleven children, and soon I was writing down the names of each
one of them, notating them with the occasional glosses that family stories
came up with. Natesa Sastri's daughter-in-law, Gopalakrishnan's eighty-
four-year-old mother, who had married Natesa Sastri's youngest son at age
thirteen, shared memories of the family she had virtually grown up in,
especially of the friendship she had with her much older "co-sister" (Indian
English for sister-in-law). She sang a couple of Tamil songs that ran in the
family. My recording became precious to the family after she passed away a
few months later.

I handed around my fragile copy of Natesa Sastri's *Folk-Lore in Southern
India*. As the four small volumes circulated, their faded green covers and
threads of the binding showing, somebody recognized the story of "Why
Brahmans Cannot Eat in the Dark." In the tale, two gutsy sisters nab and get
rid of a demon that has been stealthily finishing their meal as they eat in the
dark. Somebody else in the gathering began to narrate the story enthusiastically from memory, and the narration was collectively completed—in a mix-
ture of Tamil and English—amid laughter. A few more stories were narrated
that I recognized as part of Natesa Sastri's collection. People remembered
who had told stories and when they had been heard, but most palpable of all
was the shared excitement in discovering that stories in Natesa Sastri's collection had persisted and circulated across the dispersed family for more than a
hundred years. The folklorist, poet, and translator A. K. Ramanujan's remark
about Natesa Sastri in his *Folktales from India* made renewed sense to me. He
writes: "My grandmother, who was in her sixties when I was a boy fifty years
ago, told me stories that she had heard from her grandmother. S. M. Natesa
Sastri, who came from the same part of Tamil Nadu (Trichinopoly [now
Tiruchirappalli]), heard the same tales in his childhood and published them

in Tamil and in English in the 1870s. This kind of corroboration inspires trust in many of these early recordings."[7] The last line is especially revealing: storytelling is ratified by a tradition of storytelling. It dawned on me that afternoon that Natesa Sastri had not been lost to the family. He was, just as Gopalakrishnan had hoped, being rediscovered and reclaimed by the family through their repertoire of stories. In my earlier writing on Natesa Sastri in 2003, I had echoed what Gopalakrishnan had said to his family: "Tata was many men rolled into one."[8]

As familial and archival reflections came together, and as I interacted with Gopalakrishnan over the years and understood deeper identifications, I began to see Natesa Sastri not as a "native scholar," the supposedly subordinate figure that colonialism created to expand its empire of information, but as a sovereign raconteur. As an epigraphist, he deciphered inscriptions that spanned several south Indian empires; as a folklorist and translator, he drew on oral and written traditions that ranged from Persia and England to Sangendi and Kashmir; and as a novelist, he crafted stories that reached into interior landscapes of memory and emotion. Natesa Sastri's authorial self is kaleidoscopic, as we will see more fully in the sections that follow, where I trace his creativity as an epigraphist, folklorist, and novelist. When Kirin Narayan observes, "Acknowledging ourselves within multiple creative domains, I think, allows for a cross-fertilizing of insights," she could well be speaking of Natesa Sastri.[9] My larger argument is that this kaleidoscopic authorship articulates an epistemic sovereignty, a sovereignty that could never be reined in by the rule of empire. Such a sovereignty sets a limit on the native subordination that can be claimed by disciplines such as archaeology and folklore, or on the exclusivity that can be claimed by genres such as the novel that were colonial or "Western" in conception. Instead, it redirects our attention to the paradox that the content of these disciplines depended on indigenous learning, concepts, experiences, and, ultimately, individual creativity. This is not the kind of epistemic sovereignty that troubled Foucault, the kind in which a regime of knowledge legitimizes its power by making itself exempt from error. As Joseph Rouse puts it, "This legitimation does not produce knowledge, in the sense of producing new possibilities for truth."[10] It merely promotes a singular "truth" by suppressing conflicting truth claims, dismissing them as irrational. As we will soon see, the epistemic sovereignty that Natesa Sastri exemplifies comes from his vast erudition, from his creative faculties, and from his unassailable dignity as a scholar in fields that routinely exploited native knowledge.

Neither could Natesa Sastri's outspokenness be reined in. Although a Tamil imaginary predominated in his literary efforts, it was a larger nationalist imaginary that informed his political vision, and on at least one occasion it brought him controversy. In an article in the *Madras Mail* (October 29, 1902), for instance, he advocated the teaching of Sanskrit as a compulsory subject in the schools of Madras Presidency and drew the ire of many who felt he was making the case for Sanskrit—a pan-Indian language—at the expense of Tamil.[11] In another instance, in 1887, when a committee was constituted to evaluate the performance of the Archaeological Survey of India, he told the committee that unless the department hired more epigraphists, "it would take a hundred years to complete the task of collecting, deciphering, and translating all the South Indian inscriptions."[12] The anonymous biographical sketch published after his death suggests that he may have been advocating for the hiring of *Indian* epigraphists. The author writes, "[Natesa Sastri's] evidence before the Public Service Commission advocating the claims of educated Indians and their special aptitude for archaeological research, was marked by an independence which was a notable trait in his character; but it served ever after as a bar to that official preferment and personal recognition to which his scholarship and great abilities fully qualified him."[13]

Natesa Sastri's argument for more Indian representation echoes the sentiment expressed in the first resolution of the Indian National Congress, which was formed in 1885; it demanded an inquiry "into the working of Indian administration and adequate representation for our countrymen."[14] The resolution was tabled by the Indian freedom fighter and social reformer G. Subramania Iyer, who founded the English-language newspaper *The Hindu*—and also the Tamil daily *Swadesamitran*. It is not coincidental that Natesa Sastri chose the pen name of "Swadesamitran" for his first novel, *Dinadayalu*. Swadesamitran literally means "friend of self-rule," and the pen name carried all the overtones of the politically assertive newspaper. Avowedly committed to promoting the idea of home rule, *Swadesamitran*, started in 1882, quickly acquired a vast Tamil readership. The weekly publication (which became a daily from 1899) reported on the growing political discontent toward the end of the nineteenth century in India and in Britain's colonies in general. It exposed Tamil readers to national and world events such as Bal Gangadhar Tilak's imprisonment in 1897, the ruthless administrative policies during the Bombay plague of 1897, and the Boer War of 1899–1902. It enlightened Tamil readers about the failings of British policy and stoked a national spirit. When Russia lost to Japan in the Russo-Japanese War of 1904–5, *Swadesamitran* pointed out how the idea of Western superiority was a myth.[15] The sensibility of the *Swadesamitran* would have appealed to Natesa Sastri. Its nationalist tone was "sober and its articles were characterized by cogency of argument and a thorough grasp of facts,"[16] qualities that Natesa Sastri valued.[17] Natesa Sastri's adoption of Swadesamitran as a pen name is remarkably audacious, considering he was employed by the government. If outspokenness had barred his professional advancement in the colonial administration, he stood to lose a lot more by aligning himself with an emerging, vocal freedom movement. Yet he did. The editor of *Swadesamitran*, G. Subramania Iyer, it must be noted, was later accused of sedition by the British; he died at sixty-one, his health broken by repeated jail terms.[18]

The Construct of "Native Scholar"

The expertise of Indians—of pandits, *maulvis*, *munshis*, and *kazis*, for instance—came to seen by the East India Company and the colonial government as pivotal to the success of their expansionist programs.[19] The need crystallized into the constructs of "native scholars" and "native assistants," constructs that say as much about colonial tactics of subordination and demoralization as they do about colonial dependence on Indian erudition and lived experiences. Archaeological studies, as the art historian Tapati Guha-Thakurta shows, could hardly have progressed without four key Indian figures: "the site laborer, the informant, the trained draftsman and the Sanskrit *pandit*: those who dug mounds, prepared drawings and plans for the *sahib*, identified sculptures, coins, or inscriptions, and most important, helped decipher scripts and legends."[20] From the 1770s, when Warren Hastings was governor, the fields of orientalism and Anglo-Indian law turned to "pandits" to build their knowledge bases. One can always discuss the reciprocity of knowledge exchange between pandits and British scholars, but this reciprocity is subsequent to the fact that the "pandit" in colonial discourse (different from indigenous understandings) was positioned lower in an asymmetric relationship of power. Relationships between pandits and British scholars were not always cordial, and at times they devolved into outright suspicion over cultural and intellectual appropriations.[21] A peculiar distancing from the contemporary is intrinsic to the construct of the "native scholar": orientalists often, in Brian Hatcher's words, "tended to view their pandit associates more as the embodiment of an ancient ideal than as living collaborators," although they viewed themselves as scholars in the present, a contrast consistent with the notion of civilizational advancement embedded in nineteenth-century racism. Hatcher incisively remarks that when the orientalist H. H. Wilson worked with Sanskrit scholars, he remained "the pandit's superior, both as the man who would arrange for their employment and as the man who would estimate the worth of their learning. Despite his respect for his pandit collaborators, he was not about to advocate sympathy for the 'tastes' and even the 'talents' of the pandit. What he did advocate was patronage: 'we can give them bread.' "[22] Orientalists like Wilson would have been surprised to discover that, ironically, "native scholars" reciprocated his sentiment. Many scholars who collaborated with C. P. Brown, best known for his dictionary of the Telugu language, did not consider him worthy of being called a pandit. They held the opinion that Brown "paṇḍituḍu kādu, āyana poṣakuḍu" (He is not a pandit, he is a "bread" provider).[23]

It is hardly surprising, then, that colonial praise for the "native scholar" was always a discourse of equivocation. In this discourse, the "native scholar"—like the modernizing ancient who was always close to modernity but never close enough to be called modern—could be an accomplished scholar, a raw repository of native knowledge, but not capable of sophisticated analysis. For instance, Henry K. Beauchamp, introducing Natesa Sastri's *Hindu Feasts, Fasts and Ceremonies* (1903), says:

> Pandit Natesa Sastri is doing most excellent work in collecting, arranging, and recording in concise and easily assimilable form some of the more noticeable tales, traditions, customs, beliefs, and ceremonies of the Hindus. And it is to be hoped that many others of his educated countrymen will follow his good example. For there are mines of wealth to be exploited in this manner, and there is work for many scores of writers, compilers and translators.[24]

(Beauchamp was of course talking about an Indian workforce.)[25] Despite noting, "It is one of the excellent characteristics of Pandit Natesa Sastri that he particularizes where necessary and generalizes only where it is safe to do so"—an observation I would imagine is crucial to the work of theorizing—the bulk of Beauchamp's introduction quotes at length generalized observations about Hindu practice from an 1887 book by the orientalist William Wilkins (whom he does not name).[26] Similarly, A. G. Cardew, acting secretary in the Revenue Department, writes:

> [Natesa Sastri] also possessed a facility of invention which left him at no loss to supply deficiencies when his memory failed. Like Sir Walter Scott, he united the talents of a *raconteur*[27] and the tastes of an antiquarian. . . . It is on the rescue of these popular tales from oblivion that pandit Natesa Sastri's claim to recollection will chiefly rest. His own avowed romances are meritorious productions, but they hardly possess permanent value. But his reproduction of the stories he learned at his mother's knee will always retain an interest proportionate to their faithfulness.[28]

Perhaps the best example of arrogant equivocation is by the well-known theosophist Henry Steel Olcott, who pronounces:

> The progress of modern scholarship has enabled us to trace back to Aryan sources our popular legends and nursery tales. The appearance, then, of a competent Indian pandit, who can give us, in a Western vernacular, the folklore of the Dravidians or Aryans, is a very fortunate event. And fortunate the pandit if he can find so able an editor and competent a specialist as Pandit Natesa Sastri has found in Captain R. C. Temple. The advantage of such collaboration could not be more strikingly proven than it has been in the instance of the three books under notice. The two Parts of "Folklore of Southern India," while no more interesting as to subject matter, are infinitely superior to the "Dravidian Nights' Entertainments" in being faultless in English idiom, while the latter bristles with errors and is, in fact, a bad example of the faulty style too common among our "educated" class. It is a great pity, for we have no doubt that in his own vernacular the Pandit would have made it as charming in style as it is valuable in material. The severity of criticism is, however, quite disarmed by the frank apology offered in the Author's Preface. Certainly the amateurs of this class of literature will be ready to forgive him the worst of grammatical and idiomatic mistakes, in gratitude for the pleasure and instruction to be derived from his charming stories.[29]

Olcott was oblivious to Natesa Sastri's intent and mindfulness in translating Tamil narrative experience. Explaining why he chooses to do a more literal translation of the Tamil *Madanakamaraja Kadai* (*Dravidian Nights Entertainments*), Natesa Sastri writes in the preface:

> Every original story must be read and appreciated in its original language. And Tamil stories have so many peculiarities and beauties that is almost impossible to produce a translation which, while retaining the many idioms particular to the Tamil, shall, nevertheless, be in strict grammatical accord with the language in which I have written it. . . . My principal object in publishing these translations is not to show that I am any bit of an author or translator, but that stories in Tamil are in no way inferior in their richness of thought, soundness of morality and luxuriance of imagination, to the other stories of Oriental romance.[30]

Sift through the curmudgeonly praise for a "native scholar" by reviewers such as Olcott, and we see Natesa Sastri as a critical translator, a natural ethnographer, and an inventive raconteur in at least two languages.

The Epigraphist

In 1881, twenty-two-year-old Natesa Sastri joined the Archaeological Survey of India (ASI) in Mysore (now Mysuru) for his first job as epigraphist. He quickly became recognized as a "native scholar." The ASI had been founded in 1861 by Alexander Cunningham, a military engineer and employee of the East India Company, with the intent of launching "a careful and systematic investigation of all the existing monuments of ancient India." Epigraphy, the deciphering of old inscriptions and scripts, was "identified as one area of archaeological research with maximum potential for roping in and training native scholars."[31] The south Indian branch in Mysore was only seven years old under the directorship of Robert Sewell when Natesa Sastri joined it at a salary of thirty rupees a year. As an epigraphist, he would have visited historic sites that were either decaying or active centers of worship. At these sites he would have located inscriptions and studied architectural features and archaeological relics. Sometimes he would have traced copper plates containing historical information about families and their lore to private individuals. He would have described all findings in technical terms specifying location, dimensions, and material, for example. He would have identified languages and scripts and translated inscriptions with attention to narrative, orthography, and dating. The process, it is easy to imagine, is riddled with interpretive challenges. Indeed, Natesa Sastri's grounded knowledge of language and culture would have been essential to the survey. For example, the epigraphs of the Vijayanagara kingdom were in Kannada, Telugu, Tamil, and Hindustani, languages he clearly knew in addition to Sanskrit. Translation and contextualization depended not on "native assistance," a euphemism for mechanical labor, but on a scholarly understanding of how language worked across historical contexts and culture.

His article on two land grants made by Eastern Chalukya kings is an excellent illustration of his erudition and skill. The copper plates conferring the grants, he tells us, were discovered by a farmer in the Krishna District (in present-day Andhra Pradesh) while plowing his field. The rectangular plates, we are told, had their "edges turned up to preserve the inscription" and were "beautifully-preserved" with Chalukyan seals of boars and lotuses. Then follows a line-by-line transliteration and translation of the Sanskrit inscription, which is replete with legend, praise, and genealogy. Glosses explicate metaphors: "That lord of Ganga, after ruling the kingdom for 44 years, acquired the friendship of the husband of Sachi (Indra, i.e. he died)."[32] Ancient sites brimming with *sthala puranas* (place narratives) evoke Natesa Sastri's sense of history. For instance, his "Notes on the Tiruvellarai Inscriptions" begins: "Tiruvellarai is an ancient village 8 miles north of Trichinopoly [modern Tiruchirapalli in Tamil Nadu]. It is in a rocky situation and reminds one of the ancient Jaina settlements." Two saints of the eighth and ninth centuries, Tirumangai Alvar and Periyalvar, he continues, composed songs and sang to Pundarikaksha, the Vaishnava deity of the temple. "This temple is built upon a small rock, below which is a cave temple, with no god, however, placed in it." Lines of religious poetry must have come to Natesa Sastri's mind as he looked at the stacked temples: "The saint Tirumangai Alvar, when extolling Pundarikaksha, must refer to this cave in his expression 'Kallarai mel Vellarai yay,' which means 'The white chamber over the rock chamber.'" A fuller description of the site follows. Of the three wall enclosures around the temple, two are "studded with inscriptions." Yet, he observes, the inscriptions seemed to have suffered wanton erasure and become illegible. Nearby was a neglected Shiva temple, and to the south of it a shrine in ruins. The inscriptions were in Sanskrit and in Tamil, which he then translates in the article.[33] For readers, the site is rendered resonant with stories and poetry and indecipherable trails that are layered in the histories of sacred structures.

When Sewell discovered Natesa Sastri's ability with Sanskrit, he raised his salary to seventy-five rupees a year and conferred on him the title of "pandit"— something that Gopalakrishnan and his son had mentioned in the family meeting in 2001.[34] But more than the increases in salary and the title that the colonial administration conferred, it is Natesa Sastri's intellectual contributions that evoke his authorial primacy. Doubtless, Sewell says in thanking his "young fellow-laborer" Natesa Sastri, his "industry and zealous co-operation have most materially contributed to the completion of this work."[35] In another volume of the survey he writes, "Dr. Burgess [Cunningham's successor] informs me that he has a very considerable number of the copper-plate inscriptions, besides others from temples, from the Madura District, and the whole of the Tamil inscriptions in the Madras Museum, already translated by Mr. S. M. Natesa Sastri and others."[36] Robust author credits, rather than one-line acknowledgments, would have been more in order.

Equitable acknowledgment was certainly on Natesa Sastri's mind. On the one hand, we could say that Natesa Sastri signals his acceptance of "pandit" as part of his authorial identity; the title "Pandit" appears on every one of his major publications. But there is more to it. As we saw earlier, his evidence given before the Public Service Commission makes it clear that even at the risk of losing promotions, he had argued that the experience and erudition of Indians deserved to be tangibly recognized. Regardless of his own promotion and position, however, Natesa Sastri's high standing in the field of epigraphy is summed up in the words of the superintendent of archaeology of Travancore State, A. Gopinatha Rao, who writes:

> While editing the paper on the Sorraikkavur Plates of the Vijayanagara king Virupaksha in *Epigrahica Indica,* Vol. VIII, I happened to show a transcript of the inscription to the late Mr. S. M. Natesa Sastri, B.A., who, struck by the identity of the introduction of this record with another of which he had a transcript, placed that transcript at my disposal. I now edit the inscription from the transcript kindly lent to me by him. He added that the plates were discovered by one Sankara Sastri of Ariyur, while digging in a portion of his house for a foundation. The plates were made over to Mr. Natesa Sastri, who did not remember what he did with them, but thought he might have sent them to Dr. [John] Fleet [epigraphist of the government of India].[37]

The Folklorist

From Natesa Sastri's epigraphical descriptions of sites across south India, it would not be hard to imagine how the epigraphist in him was already steeped in the world of narrative. As in his notes on the Tiruvellarai inscriptions, Natesa Sastri imagined folklore expansively. Showing little interest in primitive theory or scientific typology, he recognized "folklore" in the everyday practices and orally circulating stories of a community. Folklore, for him, was the expression of a living culture. Consequently, the oral and the literary crisscrossed each other on his narrative canvas. As R. E. Asher, Kamil Zvelebil, and Stuart Blackburn have all noted, he adapted the popular stories of Tenali Raman, the famous jester in the court of the Vijayanagara emperor Krishnadevaraya; he translated the cycle of twelve Tamil stories known as *Madanakamarajan Kadai,* or *Dravidian Nights Entertainments*; and he wrote a Tamil version of the Delhi poet Mir Amman's *Bagh-o-Bahar,* itself a classic Urdu translation of Amir Khusro's Persian *Qissa-ye Chahar Darvesh* (Tale of the Four Dervishes). Natesa Sastri's twenty essays in his *Hindu Feasts, Fasts and Ceremonies* sparkle with ethnographic observations and his knowledge of Hindu texts. But it is his spirited engagement with the tradition that makes "Hinduism" come alive. For instance, in a chapter titled "Hindu Funeral Rites," he comments wryly on the practice in which relatives provide food to a mourning family:

> So far as the rule goes, it is a wise provision, for when the house goes into mourning, its comforts in the direction of feeding will be neglected unless some outside relation is chosen for the occasion. This

duty of supply is called *sar vaikkiradu*, which means the supplying of food with pepper water; only simple food is meant, and that was the rule in ancient days. But the modern Hindu custom is to supply a grand feast with all the modern art of which Hindu cookery is capable. All kinds of fruits, sweets and varieties of rice-preparations are offered to the mourners. One father-in-law vies with another in his competition to give grander and grander dinners on the successive days, and to crown the horror, quarrels sometimes spring up among some of these idiotic relations that due and proper invitation was not sent to such and such a party to be present at the dinner. Did the sages ever mean that their simple ruling should be thus abused by modern civilization? The sooner the old and orthodox custom is resumed the better.[38]

The corruption of traditional practices by modernity frequently draws sharp criticism from Natesa Sastri, but it does not dampen his appreciation of other aspects of lived Hindu traditions. Sensory images pervade his descriptions. He evokes the light cast by cauldrons of oil that are turned into huge lamps at hilltop temples to Shiva during the Krittika festival and the flowers, fruits, and sweets that create the auspicious ambience of the Varalakshmi Vrata (women's worship of Lakshmi, the goddess of prosperity). The aural and the visual blend in his portrait of the temple town of Chidambaram (about 150 miles south of the modern metropolis of Chennai). Here, he notes, "several hundred of Sudra mendicants are taught Sanskrit. A Brahman visitor to this sacred town will be surprised to see the number of Sudras repeating the Upanishads in the early morning in these monasteries. To add to his wonder, he will find that they have not only got by heart these sacred writings but that they understand their meaning and possess a perfect knowledge of the subject-matter which is a rare thing even with Brahmans."[39]

It was Natesa Sastri's four-part *Folklore in Southern India* (1884–1893), with its thirty-seven tales, that established him as the most prolific of Indian folklorists. While he was drawn to the riches of Sanskrit drama,[40] he writes that as he engrossed himself in the *Indian Antiquary* (the flagship journal of archaeology founded in 1872 by James Burgess, with whom Natesa Sastri worked), he "felt for the first time that [he] could utilize [his] early knowledge of folktales in the advancement of folklore literature."[41] The proliferating debates in archaeology and anthropology stirred his own sense of the vast resources all around him, and indeed within himself. He remembered the oral stories of his childhood and wrote them down in Tamil. Then, encouraged by Richard Carnac Temple, the editor of the *Indian Antiquary*, he translated them into English and published them between 1884 and 1893 in that journal.[42]

But it is not until part three of the collection (published in 1888) that Natesa
Sastri provides the context:

> I am a native of the Trichinopoly District and was in my early days
> brought up in the villages of Lalgudi and Kulitalai, where my parents
> lived. From my childhood, stories and tales had a great fascination for
> me, and I was therefore a favorite with every old dame in my family
> who, being disabled by age from doing any household work, was glad
> to beguile her hours by playing my sense of the marvelous. Moreover,
> having had the misfortune to lose my mother at a very early age, I was
> probably regarded as a fit object of compassion, and every story-teller
> in the village would readily comply with the poor orphan's request for a
> story. I, thus, early acquired an aptitude for tales and this was consider-
> ably improved from the fact that my father's second wife happened to
> be a great repository of this kind of learning. Unlike the stepmother of
> fiction, she was very kind to me, and spent all her leisure moments in
> amusing her step-son. So, before I had reached the age of ten my taste
> for stories had become largely developed, and I had heard almost all
> that any man or woman in the village had to tell. By constant repetition
> and narration, these tales became firmly rooted in my memory, and
> it was the greatest pleasure of my boyhood to amuse knots of eager
> listeners of about the same age as myself with side-splitting tales.[43]

The memory and innocent vanities of childhood performances and the
affection of childhood ties ensured that the stories, dormant during Natesa
Sastri's English-based education in college, resurged with new energy into a
scholarly pursuit. His ethnographic sensibility is apparent in his reproduction of a conversation with his grandfather about the origins of the Vaishnava sect in the Madras Presidency. The long conversation, reported in the
first person, displays an ethnographic transparency. Documenting prevalent
stories about origins, Natesa Sastri does not hesitate to report opinions that
could reveal his grandfather's biases. "Here ends my grandfather's story," he
concludes. "I have given his views in the hope that someone more learned
may take it up, and do more justice to the subject."[44] Writing about print and
the emergence of Tamil nationalism in the nineteenth century, Blackburn
argues that "anglicising forces had been displacing folklore" and that Natesa
Sastri, like his European counterparts, was motivated by the loss of the "vanishing village."[45] Yet as we follow Natesa Sastri's poetic descriptions of some
of the temple ruins he visited, and as we read his colorful re-creations of oral
stories and his novelistic fictions, we see also that a "sense of the marvelous"
animates his creative spirit. Natesa Sastri's reminiscent inventiveness is more

like the "remembered village" of the anthropologist M. N. Srinivas, whose brilliant 1976 ethnography of the south Indian village of Rampura was written from memory and reflection.[46]

Natesa Sastri's stories from the *Indian Antiquary* and *Folklore of Southern India* took an enigmatic turn when they appeared in *Tales of the Sun: Or Folklore of Southern India*, a collection whose authorship is attributed to a "Mrs. Howard Kingscote," with the title page reading "collected by Mrs. Howard Kingscote and Pandit Natesa Sastri." Mrs. Howard Kingscote, or Adeline Georgiana Kingscote, was the wife of a Colonel Howard Kingscote who was posted to Bangalore and Mysore in the late 1880s with the Oxfordshire Light Infantry. The Kingscotes lived in India for more than two decades. Our knowledge of Georgiana Kingscote's years in India comes mostly from her roughly two-hundred-page manual titled *The English Baby in India and How to Rear It* (1893). Belonging to the genre of writings by other Anglo-Indian women on domestic life and Indian servants—which we encountered in chapter 1—the racist manual catalogues the ailments that can afflict an English child in India and provides details of home remedies. The manual makes it clear that Kingscote despises ayahs. She says: "[Ayahs] marry and intermarry till they do not themselves know what relation they are to each other; they lie so readily and so craftily that the sharpest of detectives find it difficult to cope with them. . . . When we first took India we could have insisted on our own rules and regulations, and only employed those who fell in with them, and the native's love for money would have made him conform." And she concludes, "It is almost, if not quite, impossible ever to fathom the depths of native deceit."[47] Nonetheless, as we see from her preface, Kingscote needs ayahs and of course pandits:

> When I began writing down these tales, my only means of collecting them was through my native servants, who used to get them from the old women in the bazaars; but the fables they brought me were as full of corruption and foreign adaptions as the miscellaneous ingredients that find their way into a dish of their own curry and rice, and had it not been for Mr. Sastri's timely aid, my small work would have gone forth to the world laden with inaccuracies. Mr. Sastri not only corrected the errors of my own tales, but allowed me to add to them many that he had himself collected, and that had already been published, either in small volumes or in numbers of the *Indian Antiquary*.[48]

Kingscote's contextualization may have been relevant to the single story she seems to have collected ("Keep It for the Beggar"), because we discover that Natesa Sastri had already published elsewhere all the other stories in this collection. Five tales in *Tales of the Sun* are taken from part one of Natesa Sastri's *Folklore in Southern India* (1884), seven from part two (1886), and eight from part three (1888). One long story is from his collection *The King and His Four Ministers* (1889), and two appear in the *Indian Antiquary* (1888). Two tales and their notes refer to a stepmother as a narrator, suggesting these too may have been his. In sum, out of twenty-six stories in *Tales of the Sun*, Kingscote seems to have contributed precisely one. Further, for the most part, Natesa Sastri's stories were reproduced verbatim in *Tales of the Sun*, with only small changes accommodating Victorian readers. (For instance, "courtesan" and "prostitute" are replaced by "frivolous woman.")[49] The appropriation implies that Natesa Sastri is depicted in *Tales of the Sun* as the native assistant, the pandit who gave generous and timely assistance to Kingscote, and not as the contributor of twenty-five of the collection's twenty-six tales. The brazenness did not go unnoticed. The comparative folklorist Joseph Jacobs remarked, if somewhat mildly, "It would have been well if the identity of the two works [*Folklore in Southern India* and *Tales of the Sun*] had been clearly explained."[50] Sidney Hartland, president of the British Folk-Lore Society (1900–1901), said that Kingscote "carefully refrains from telling us" where she gathered the stories.[51]

We do not know when and whether Natesa Sastri and Georgiana Kingscote met. Perhaps they had become acquainted in Mysore, when Natesa Sastri was posted to Mysore's Archaeological Survey branch and Howard Kingscote was with the infantry in those parts. Intrigued by this "collaboration," I tried to unravel Georgiana Kingscote's life story. She was born in 1862 to the well-known diplomat and MP for Christchurch (and later Portsmouth) Henry Drummond Wolff and his wife, Adeline Wolff.[52] After their return to England, the Kingscotes lived in Dover, where Howard Kingscote was assistant adjutant general from 1890 to 1895,[53] and then in Headington, Oxford, in a house called Bury Knowle House, which now hosts the Headington Public Library.[54] I sat up when I found that a biography of an Oxford MP, Frank Gray, by Charles Fenby mentioned "the notorious Mrs. Kingscote." Gray, a former solicitor's clerk, who apparently served several writs on her, described her as "the finest adventuress [he] ever met."[55] According to Fenby, Georgiana Kingscote caused several men who stood surety for her to go bankrupt, and even obtained loans by claiming as hers property she did not own. Her obituary, excerpted from "The Daily News" in the *Bournemouth Visitor's Directory*, remarks: "She had an almost hypnotic influence over men and women, as is shown by the way in which she induced a British officer to marry her sister-in-law because she was in financial straits. The officer did as he was asked, but never lived with the lady, and five years later, obtained a divorce."[56] Bankruptcy seems to have spurred Kingscote into fiction writing. From 1900 until she died in 1908, she wrote over sixty novels under the pseudonym Lucas Cleeve. The titles reveal her feminist leanings: *The Double Marriage* (1906), *The Confessions of a Widow* (1907), *What Woman Wills* (1908), and *The Love Letters of a Faithless Wife* (which was published posthumously in 1911). In these, Kingscote took on themes of love and loyalty in marital relationships (which her iconoclastic heroines usually tested) and what she saw as double standards for women in nineteenth-century English society. And finally, she had fled from her creditors to Switzerland. My search took me to the library of the University of Lausanne in Switzerland, whose staff contacted the city administration of the town of Château-d'Œx. From the city's registers I learned that Georgiana Kingscote had died in Hôtel Berthod in Château-d'Œx on the thirteenth of September 1908.

The barely camouflaged *Tales of the Sun* presents an illusion of collaboration. Did Natesa Sastri consent to the reproduction of his stories? Was he assured that *Tales of the Sun* would help his work reach new audiences in England and other parts of Europe? Was he promised a joint authorship credit that did not materialize? Kingscote's crafty preface certainly presents an "illusion of consent," to use Gloria Raheja's characterization of the ethnographic construction of consent in colonial India. Raheja finds that British administrators in north India collected proverbs and severed them from their lived contexts so as to use them expediently in administrative discourse. These "entextualized" proverbs were then exploited to "prove" native consent to colonial governance, and "to foster the illusion that native opinion on caste and caste identities was unambiguously congruent with these colonial representations."[57] But the illusion of consent is also countered, Raheja says. In Survey of India reports, she sees a revealing shift in the British characterization of locals after the initial reports of the 1830s. George Everest, the surveyor general of India and the superintendent of the Great Trigonometrical Survey from 1830 to 1943, plainly records his frustrations with locals who evidently resisted his survey operations; they removed station markers or did not allow theodolites to be mounted on sacred structures. Later survey reports, however, dis-acknowledge such acts of resistance, reinscribing them falsely as acts of a superstitious disposition. With the "consent" of natives thus discursively secured, political opposition gets erased from the report. A rare but rousing Bengali song that Raheja finds recorded in a volume of George Grierson's *Linguistic Survey of India* (1903–1928) shows that opposition to the survey was robust and built into everyday activity and community organizing.[58]

Natesa Sastri's silence about the book leaves us without answers to questions of consent while also leaving us to surmise instead that perhaps just as Kingscote sold other people's property as her own, she did the same with *Tales of the Sun*. Kingscote's usurpation of authorial space is no worse than the claim to authorship that William Crooke made for a landmark collection of north Indian folktales. Sadhana Naithani's groundbreaking work has brought to light the hidden truths of a long-term "collaboration" between the well-known colonial administrator Crooke and the Indian scholar and interpreter Pandit Ram Gharib Chaube of Uttar Pradesh, who was behind most of the contributions made to the journal *North Indian Notes & Queries*, which Crooke edited. Discovering an unpublished manuscript of folktales in Chaube's handwriting in the Crooke collection in the archives of the Folk-Lore Society in London, Naithani published it, crediting Chaube as primary author. In doing so, she reversed a historical hierarchy in which the Crookes are upheld as authors and the Chaubes as "native assistants."[59] Perhaps the way to restore authorial credit to Natesa Sastri is to recognize that he remains sovereign over the storyscape. It is *his* remembering self, entwined with storytellers in Lalgudi and Kulitalai and elsewhere, that runs through the four parts of *Folklore of Southern India* and *Tales of the Sun*.

The Novelist

Natesa Sastri's entry into prose fiction began rather dramatically. In 1894 Inspector General Charles A. Porteous asked Natesa Sastri to write some detective stories in Tamil so that the Madras police force could be inspired by Western practices of crime solving.[60] Within six weeks, Natesa Sastri came up with a collection of five detective stories based on a character called Danavan, loosely constructed on James Muddock's popular Scottish detective character Dick Donovan.[61] *Dinadayalu* was Natesa Sastri's first full-length novel, the first of six that he wrote between 1900 and 1903, all in Tamil.[62] In the preface, he tells us that India was, after all, the cradle of storytelling; the *Panchatantra*, he notes, has seen global translation, and

> thousands of stories have been written [in Tamil] in the form "once upon a time there was. . ." Our country is a treasure-hold or a repository of stories. There is no comparable work to our *Kathasaritasagaram* . . . . And so people may criticize my current attempt to publish a new story as somewhat like "selling coal to Newcastle." My venture is not presenting a story to the Tamil folk. Thousands of stories are being published in English in the form of "novels." Our Tamil people con-

stantly ask, What exactly is this "novel?" They are unclear what is great
about a novel, as it is also about storytelling. Hence, for the benefit of
those who are not exposed to English or novels, I have written a novel
so that the people can understand the nature and the type of storytelling in the novel form. The word "novel" means "new."[63]

Here was a writer who had decoded genealogical histories and praise stories
from ancient rock scripts, translated popular Tamil narrative, collected and
re-created oral stories, telling his readers that the "English novel form" is
not novel because it tells a story; it is novel because it tells a *new* story. A *new
story*—distinct from a *re-telling*.

As it turns out, *Dinadayalu* is a story that has not been told before because
it is about Natesa Sastri himself. Let us trace the resemblances first with
a summary of the plot.[64] We meet the Brahman protagonist, Dinadayalu,
when he is twenty-five years old and employed in government service. He is
married with four children. His childhood was difficult. He lost his mother
in childhood, and his stepmother, Kanthi, was partial to her own son Sanku
and daughter Manti. He was sent away from his hometown to Kumbakonam
where he lived with his aunt Thayu and studied. He did brilliantly in his
examinations and landed a government job immediately after graduating,
with a salary of twenty-five rupees.

The story begins with a dramatic telegram notifying Dinadayalu of his
father's sudden illness. Dinadayalu manages to get five days' leave sanctioned
by a prejudiced and reluctant superior, and he and Thayu set out. It takes
two days for them to reach the village of Kshanakkal, where Dinadayalu's
father, Mahadeva Iyer (Mahadevar), lives. This initial setting then takes us
into the interior of Dinadayalu's family life. Mahadevar has great faith in his
son's intellectual abilities and in his sense of responsibility toward the family.

In Kshanakkal, Dinadayalu consults Ayurvedic and allopathic doctors and
provides great personal care. But Mahadevar dies. As soon as the crema-
tion rites end, and while the last of the Vedic chants are still echoing in the
house, Dinadayalu is besieged by lenders: Mahadevar had incurred monu-
mental debts. Relatives begin to loot the family's silver and other valuables,
and Kanthi—consumed by uncertainty for her son Sanku—gives Dinadayalu
a hard time over finances. Dinadayalu promises to repay the lenders and to
continue caring for his stepmother and her children. Sanku, a wastrel and
ingrate, cannot keep a job. Dinadayalu is forced to sell a major portion of the
family's agricultural lands to pay off the creditors and feed a large family of
twelve, who have by now become completely dependent on him. He takes
on the task of mastering land valuation, an area he knows nothing about.

But since he is gifted with the ability to learn quickly, he gets the best prices for the lands. After settling the family's finances, Dinadayalu returns to his home in Bagasuragiri with his family, Thayu, and Sanku. Kanthi and her daughter, Manti, and his father's elderly sisters all remain in Kshanakkal, living on Dinadayalu's monthly remittances to them from his salary. As his financial burdens mount, Dinadayalu becomes frustrated by the limited opportunities in Bagasuragiri. Sanku's continuous carping disrupts the peace in the family. Dinadayalu dreams of relocating to the metropolitan city of Punnai, where there are many opportunities to earn some extra money. To his luck, a senior officer who is on an official visit to Bagasuragiri is amazed by Dinadayalu's knowledge and arranges to have him transferred to Punnai as an epigraphist in the government's Archaeological Department—with his salary raised to fifty rupees per month. A year after his father's death, Dinadayalu goes back to Kshanakkal to perform the annual rites. His two elderly aunts return with Dinadayalu to Punnai, while Kanthi, fed by Sanku's lies and lured by the possibility of an extra allowance, stays in Kshanakkal.

Life in Punnai starts well, but troubles begin after Dinadayalu's boss is transferred. A detailed section describes the intrigue and the pettiness of the office under his new boss, Yenivalagan, who is given to nepotism and tactics of humiliation. Yenivalagan makes Dinadayalu the target of his vilification. Dinadayalu suspects that the animosity has its roots in one of Dinadayalu's ethnographic writings on Yenivalagan's community. His travails at work are compounded by the arrival in Punnai of Kanthi with Sanku and Manti, along with Kanthi's scheming and manipulative brother-in-law. He encourages Kanthi to impose unending extortions on Dinadayalu, who is also forced to take on the expenses for Manti's marriage. Dinadayalu is forced to sign the palatial ancestral home in Kshanakkal over to Sanku. Finally, as his aunts age, they wish to be back in Kshanakkal too, close to the village temple, so he arranges for their stay and food.

Brought to the brink of poverty, Dinadayalu sells off rare books and original manuscripts from his personal library. Kanthi and Sanku go back to Kshanakkal, where Sanku marries but begins to patronize a prostitute and to physically abuse his mother. The abuse induces a change of heart in Kanthi, who begins to appreciate Dinadayalu's goodness and generosity. She goes back to live with Dinadayalu's family in Punnai. Sanku, meanwhile, loses the house to the prostitute and falls ill. Dinadayalu's fortunes begin to change with another transfer, and an increase in salary, to the city of Pudhuverkadu, two hundred miles from Punnai. Pudhuverkadu, once a fertile city, has been hit by a severe famine, and corrupt officials have not been distributing famine relief funds. Dinadayalu excels in managing the relief effort, and within two years he restores prosperity to Pudhuverkadu. The novel ends with Dina-dayalu becoming commissioner of Cochin at a salary of a thousand rupees per month. He buys back the lost ancestral home, has Sanku restored to good health, and all ends well.

Critics and Natesa Sastri's relatives believe that the novel has autobio-graphical overtones. The allusions to his life are indeed resonant. Jambu, Natesa Sastri's great-grandson, said that in real life, Natesa Sastri's stepbrother was called Sanku (short for Sankaran), and his personality matched that of the Sanku of the novel. There are other parallels. Like Dinadayalu, Natesa Sastri lost his mother when he was very young and was raised by his step-mother and his aunt, although the portrayal of Kanthi is quite unlike Natesa Sastri's description of his own stepmother, who he says was kind and patient toward him. Perhaps Natesa Sastri thought that the fictional trope of the stepmother would appeal readily to his readers, but he made the stepmother reform at the end of the novel to more closely resemble the stepmother in his own life. Most important, it is hard to miss the resemblance between Natesa Sastri and the portrait of his protagonist. Dinadayalu works in the epigraphy section; he is recognized for his knowledge, intelligence, and diligence; and he takes up writing as a profession. Pressed for money, Dinadayalu muses, "One can pen a few articles or even creative writings for commercial maga-zines and periodicals during one's spare time; one can even write in English dailies on a variety of subjects like culture, language, history or on our epics to earn not less than Rs.15/-per month." Dinadayalu is also aware of the repercussions of writing. On one occasion he wonders if the grim politics of the office are the consequences of opinions expressed in his article on the ethnic community to which his boss belongs. "He was also aware that one should avoid getting involved in writing political issues, he being a govern-ment servant."[65]

Resemblances provoke questions—questions about the relationship between the self and the past, and between the self and its dreams. They create an alluring interpretive space where authors and readers can fill in the gaps between fiction and reality, asking questions that neither history nor fiction can answer singly; together, however, history and fiction suggest possibilities for a more imaginative being and becoming than our everyday lives can muster. The audacious promotion of Dinadayalu to commissioner of Cochin with the salary of a thousand rupees per month (exceptional for a "native" government employee) makes us wonder if Natesa Sastri lets Dina-dayalu index the professional recognition that would have been appropriate to his stature and experience rather than the one he was granted. As Dina-dayalu's story unfolds through the journeys of a young and aspiring Indian scholar who is attentive to the responsibilities and politics of an extended family, who overcomes the limits of colonial officialdom, it becomes clear that *Dinadayalu* is a novel about self-expression and not the self-erasure associated with a "native scholar." Through this story, Natesa Sastri exposes the absolute limitation of colonial power: it could curb native freedom of speech through policy and policing, but it could not stop the rambunctious creativity of raconteurs.

In 2002, when Gopalakrishnan decided to translate *Dinadayalu*, he was going through a challenging time in his life. He wrote to me, "I wonder whether I am also undergoing the ordeals faced by my grandfather Natesa Sastri—in fact as I read his biography *Deenadayalu*, I am reminded of myself, my traits and my life."[66] The translation seemed to help him tap into innate "wellsprings of creativity, resilience, and well-being" in adverse times.[67] His remarks over the years shaped my understanding that as resonances occur, translation can be an imperceptible entanglement with an ancestral past that stirs self-recognition.[68] Before long he had translated twelve of the fifteen chapters of *Dinadayalu* and emailed them to me. "I would like to get this translation published in English and I would love to have you as the co-author as it was 100% your motivation that made me to undertake this work," he told me. "The context and the dramatization of the novel are exactly as rendered by my grandfather and I have not altered them."[69] The note illustrated Gopalakrishnan's characteristic generosity.

He continued to work on a polished version, which he completed in July 2016. I visited him and his wife, Anandha, in their home in Chennai. They had made a meal that included dishes I had told them I liked: *vattal kuzhambu* and *paruppu thogaiyal* (spicy soups). As we went over his translation, I asked Gopalakrishnan what his resemblance to Natesa Sastri meant to him. "Let me tell you this," he said. "When I do the *tarpanam* [ritual water-offering to forefathers], I instantly feel connected to Mahalinga Shastri."[70] It would have been a strange response to my question, as Mahalinga Shastri was Natesa Sastri's father. But then I remembered the scene in which Dinadayalu sees his father, Mahadeva Iyer, die. Gopalakrishnan had translated the passage: "Every human being born on this earth has to endure the pangs of death. There was no escape from this. But, the way in which Dinadayalu was sitting close to his father's head and chanting the Karna Mantra, it looked as if he would protect his father at any cost from this pain. As he was chanting these scriptures intently, Mahadevar breathed his last."[71] Translation turned the kaleidoscope, connecting Natesa Sastri, Mahalinga Shastri, Dinadayalu, Mahadeva Iyer, and Gopalakrishnan.

The date was November 18, 2018. It was exactly seventeen years to the day since Gopalakrishnan had organized the family get-together about Natesa Sastri in his Chennai home. We had been steadily talking during the last few months as I was writing this chapter. I messaged him to say that I would be taking a break from writing. I told him that my mother had suddenly died on November 14 and that my world had been flung out of its orbit. He instantly video-called me to offer his sympathy. Two weeks later his son Shyam texted me to say that Gopalakrishnan had passed away on December 3, 2018. He was only seventy-three. In my phone, Gopalakrishnan's messages were still fresh.

Conclusion

The Sovereign Self

Audacious narrations represent an encounter with colonialism that goes well beyond the model of subaltern resistance. The insubordinate stances of the four raconteurs of this study have confirmed to me something rather fundamental about oppressive power: its limits are finite, and its claim to omnipotent sovereignty is at best presumptive. Undeniably, oppressive power performs various kinds of coercions, inflicts injury, denies economic well-being, and makes "others" out of fellow beings. But we have always known this about hegemonies. Audacious narrations, as I have argued in this book, project a counter-hegemonic sovereignty that is at once epistemic and resilient. Subjects of empire—or, for that matter, of any structure of domination—are not subjugated beings. They are instead sovereigns exercising power over territories of knowledge and experience that the oppressor may be able to enter but is never able to erase or conquer. The raconteurs exercise power in a variety of ways. They reject the supposed goods offered by the oppressor; they express perspectives that undercut the oppressor's views; and they refuse, either implicitly or explicitly, labels and paradigms that belittle. They speak as critical insiders to their traditions: to imagine, to innovate, and to narrate is their crucial resource; it is their inalienable right. Thus colonial power could succeed in curtailing freedom of speech through policy and policing, but it could not contain the rambunctious imagination of Indian raconteurs. Such a freedom cannot be taken away. Nowhere is this more apparent than in the encounter between the raconteurs' multilingual imaginations and the English language and its expressive genres. Anna Liberata de Souza dismissed outright the supposed superiority of English; P. V. Ramaswami Raju turned it upon itself through his literary ventriloquism; M. N. Venkataswami infused it with Indian languages and cultural imagery; and S. M. Natesa Sastri nimbly wove paths between English and a multitude of Indian languages. The brown sahib's story, itself a checkered one about the adoption of English by bourgeois Indians ("Babu-log"), is not the only one about the arrival of English in India. Indeed, Indian writing in English from the early nineteenth century, with its layered maps and unmappable terrains, is an empire by itself.[1]

And so, to look back, Anna Liberata de Souza chose not to go to England to serve English families, so that when she died, she could be buried beside her parents in Poona. For her, the modernity of colonialism was hollow, since it knew neither how to tell an oral story nor how to run an economy. Though Anna's life was difficult, she was not destitute, because even in our last sighting of her, she "still" had her riches of stories and her dreams of travel. Sense reading gives us Anna on her own terms, as "a girl who can do anything." P. V. Ramaswami Raju experienced a different sense of colonial alienation. He received a Western education in Madras, studied and worked in England, knew English etiquette and English versions of history. And yet these elicited from him the stories, the histories, and the gods of an Asiatic imaginary. Ramaswami Raju's questions are the questions that his Jahangir asks Thomas Roe: "Sahib Roe, what kind of people are you? Do you brave danger? Love your homes and friends?" M. N. Venkataswami relies on his unflagging memory: he names and honors his parents, wife, aunts, and siblings, and draws us into their vibrant everyday worlds through photographs and family stories. These worlds echo his admonition: "The Reader might think that we brood over our lot of being of low status, but he is mistaken. We are not brooding over our lot." He makes it clear that truths, both historical and fictional, can be approached only through the ethics and the art of acknowledgment, definitely not by evicting the subject as Europe's scientism fancied it could, nor by discriminating against a *particular* subject as casteism preferred to. Finally, S. M. Natesa Sastri demonstrates the resolve of a translator drawing on the strength of his lived experiences. It is his erudition and creativity that shatter the mold of the "native scholar." As he translates ancient inscriptions, recollects childhood tales, and invents new stories in Western genres, he shows not just a kaleidoscopic mastery over material but also a masterly overcoming of the material injustices built in to colonial employment.

So full of life are the voices of these raconteurs that the lack of biographical detail haunted me and sent me off on serendipitous ethnographic trails. Potholes, dead ends, and windfalls marked this journey. Years of search did not lead to Anna's grave, but the search connected me to her living quarters—Main Building on the Pune University campus, my own childhood haunt. And it also connected me to others, some old friends, some strangers, who became intrigued by my description of Anna's life. They shared with me the need to restore her person, however elusive the very idea of "restoration" might be. Perhaps here was my experience of Venkataswami's conviction that history is a "connected form." Stepping back, I find that the search for Anna has been an interrogation of the ends and means of historical narration; "just representation" *has* to be part of the answer. When Ramaswami Raju's great-grandson told me about his initiation into the Ramayana by the *bhikshu*, I began to sense the person in the poem. I was able to see how mystical experience formed the very breath of his final work. The ethnographic journey also gave me insight into a surprising mutuality that underlies research. My search for Natesa Sastri initiated a commitment among his family who had gathered in his grandson Gopalakrishnan's house in Chennai to discover and reclaim a fading legacy. How ironic yet fitting that this shared project of rediscovering Natesa Sastri was fulfilled through the coincidence of death: Gopalakrishnan passed away suddenly as I was writing the last few paragraphs of the chapter on Natesa Sastri. The ethnographic process of this book leads me to one final meditation: how extraordinary is the palpability of presence. I wonder whether we make too much of the distinction between non-things and things. Just as Gopalakrishnan saw his act of translating Natesa Sastri's novel as a palpable telling of his own life, so did Lakshman Rao believe that Venkataswami's old desk and almirah would help him tell his children who they are. This creative, generative threading of material and nonmaterial traces across symbiotic networks returns me to George Lamming, with whom I started this book. Lamming reflects:

> The question of sovereignty then, particularly in the light of the definition of nation as being a particular space defined in terms of politics and laws, that sovereignty is limited. The sovereignty which literally means your freedom from external influence, external interference in your domestic affairs, that is limited in the sense that you may not always have control to shield or protect yourself from interventions. But what I'm claiming that is *not* limited is another kind of sovereignty, and that is the capacity you have for *choosing* and making and remaking that self which you discover is *you*, is distinctly you. And which in a way

is always unfinished, but it has a very special essence that is you, and its power is that it allows you to create the meanings that are to be given to what happens to you.

Above all, Lamming reminds us that "that area" for choosing and remaking, that "acre of ground," should not be "abandoned, whatever the superiority of forces around you that call for its abandonment."[2]

I end with the story of Hanuman, whom I see as the most sovereign wielder of a tail in history. Hanuman, the son of Vayu, the god of wind, and Anjana, the beautiful monkey-princess, is an integral character in the ancient epic of the Ramayana, the story of how the god-prince Rama battles the demon-king Ravana, who has abducted his wife, Sita. We have already encountered Hanuman in M. N. Venkastaswami's folktale in chapter 3, where Hanuman strings a garland of golden flowers between two hilltops to mark a place for his beloved Rama and Sita to rest on their return to Ayodhya. Hanuman, paradigmatic devotee of Rama, leads the transoceanic quest to recover Sita, who is being held captive in the lavish gardens of Ravana's kingdom, Lanka, an island in the Indian Ocean. I see the story of his visit to Lanka as an allegory of audacious narration.[3] Indeed, I am one among the hundreds and thousands of storytellers across India and her diaspora who have for centuries recognized Hanuman as the archetype of a sovereign narrator. In his lively analysis of Hanuman's character, Philip Lutgendorf writes, "Gifted storyteller that he is, Hanuman, the original narrator of the tale of Rama, has something in common with historians, who construct narratives about the human past based on written records and surviving artifacts, albeit without, in most cases, the divine monkey's advantage of having been an eyewitness to the events they describe."[4]

When Rama and his brother Lakshmana, in search of Sita, find themselves in the forests of Kishkinda, the kingdom of monkey-humans, the troubled monkey-king Sugriva instructs Hanuman to disguise himself as a mendicant and assess both the strangers and their motives. Hanuman is more than adequate to the task. His eloquence and intelligence win Rama and Lakshmana's confidence. He reveals his identity, disclosing that he can change his form and his size at will. Also, like the wind, he can go wherever he pleases. It is small wonder then that Sugriva assigns to Hanuman the task of looking for Sita across the Indian Ocean in Lanka. "Not on earth or in the sky, not in the heavens or the abode of gods, nor in the waters," he proclaims, "is there anyone to rival your skills. . . . Mighty monkey, your speed, power, energy, and splendor can be compared only to your father's, the wind god's. . . .

I find strength and wisdom, courage, knowledge of place and time, as well as familiarity with modes of diplomacy and negotiation in you alone."[5]

Hanuman accepts the task but is unaware of his real powers. It takes the aging bear Jambavan to evoke self-recognition in Hanuman. Jambavan tells Hanuman the story of his birth and his childhood, of the gift of immortality bestowed on him, and of his deep, unmatched strengths. "You are the foremost among all those who can leap," Jambavan reminds him. Stirred by the stories and the encouragement, Hanuman becomes his full self in body and spirit. He exclaims: "I can go to where the sun rises with its garland of shining rays and return here without touching the ground. . . . My path shall be like that of the stars!"[6] As Hanuman flies over forests and mountains, through caves and oceans, overcoming hurdles and encountering mysterious and magical lands, his journey becomes more than a physical feat; it becomes a voyage of self-discovery.

Landing in Lanka, Hanuman looks for Sita in its palaces, in its tree-lined streets, in its gardens with gold-paved walkways, and in the clear lotus pools. His eye takes in everything, his descriptions making Lanka's wonders come alive for us. A first look does not locate Sita. Just when despair and doubt begin to dampen his determination, he sights a woman who fits Rama's description of Sita. And gradually, as he recalls each detail, with remembered images blending into the person before him, Hanuman is overcome with joy and also filled with an immense sadness at Sita's emaciated, forlorn state. He weighs how best to approach and talk to Sita. He considers the question of language. Should he speak to her in Sanskrit? Would that make him seem too much like Ravana, who also speaks in Sanskrit? If he uses a vernacular, which vernacular should he choose? He also struggles over the question of his own appearance. Should he appear as himself, a huge monkey, or should he change form? Would Sita mistake a talking monkey for Ravana in disguise? How could he persuade his precious listener of his mission and his person? Ultimately it is narrative that comes to the rescue.

Hanuman sits on a tree near Sita and sings in praise of Rama. "Once there was a king named Dasaratha," he begins, sweetly, gently. He narrates the episode of Sita's abduction in the forest. Sita listens, rapt. "Now I am sure I have found her," he concludes and falls silent.[7] But soon Sita retreats, terrified that it is yet another of Ravana's disguises. Then follows one of the most moving exchanges in the Ramayana. There, in the enchanted and lonely garden, Hanuman and Sita earn each other's trust by sharing stories. "Tell me the story of Rama," she pleads, doubting Hanuman yet longing for Rama and her home. Hanuman is wise; he understands. He relies on the power of words, and his story of Rama flows from empathy. He describes Rama's grief at being separated from Sita—how he does not eat meat or honey, how he eats the produce of the forest sparingly, and how, lost in grief, he does not even swat the mosquitoes that bite him. Sita believes him. Hanuman enthusiastically proposes that she ride back to Rama on his back, but she tells him that it would be more appropriate for Rama to come and kill Ravana, then take her home. With a jewel from her hair to show Rama as proof of their meeting, and a plan in place, Hanuman leaves her.

Sita is eventually rescued by Rama. But Hanuman is not done with Lanka. How can Lanka be beautiful if it abets a woman's abduction, and by its king? Furious with Ravana, he wrecks the garden, uprooting trees, upsetting animals and snakes, and destroying palaces and pavilion. Enraged, Ravana sends hordes of his demons and the best of his generals to fight Hanuman. Hanuman kills them all, making battle tools from Ravana's own garden and palace—an iron gate, the huge rocks, the uprooted trees, a golden pillar. Hanuman cannot be reined in. Ravana, now amazed by this powerful monkey, wants to have Hanuman seized, not killed. At last, Ravana's son Indrajit releases the powerful weapon of Brahma at Hanuman. The weapon traps him. As he submits to its power, he recalls what Jambavan has told him. "Even though I have been bound, I am not in danger, for I am protected by Vayu and Indra as well as by Brahma," he tells himself. He knows that he has been captured only because he has displayed his might; he looks forward to his face-to-face meeting with Ravana. The demons bind Hanuman in ropes then take him to Ravana's palace. There in the palace, Hanuman is struck by Ravana's splendor and thinks: "He has all the signs of a great king! Had he not been so unrighteous, he might well have been the protector of the world."[8] Self-infatuated Ravana, stung by the affront to his power by a "mere" monkey, subjects Hanuman to an interrogation.

Across India, oral tales of the Ramayana magnify this moment fittingly. They describe how Hanuman, demanding a stature equal to Ravana's, grows his tail—and grows it long enough to wind it and form a chair that is higher than Ravana's throne. Now, seated up high, he can look at Ravana eye to eye, or even cast a glance down on him, and speak as his peer or superior. In Hanuman's tail is his sovereignty. "I am Hanuman, the son of the Wind," he announces. Audaciously he begins to tell Ravana the story of Rama, and how immoral Ravana has been in stealing what was never his. Hanuman scolds Ravana for thinking that it was an act of magnanimity to grant Sita a year to consider being his consort and joining his harem as a prize jewel. It is instead nothing but a ruse, a self-serving rapaciousness disguised as righteousness. Hanuman lists the qualities that befit a true king but are lacking in Ravana.

Ravana is in no mood to listen. He orders that the monkey's tail—the tail that has given him his high position in the royal court—be set on fire. As the demons bind the tail in cloth and pour oil on it, Hanuman makes it grow longer and longer. The demons run out of cloth and oil, but they manage to set fire to the tail anyway. Sita, who learns about this, prays to Agni, the god of fire, to grant the burning tail a magical immunity. Hanuman breaks free from the ropes and starts to fly around, setting everything in the city ablaze. As Lanka burns all around him, Hanuman himself stays cool, and Sita's space in the garden is untouched by the fire.

Hanuman, the audacious raconteur, sovereign self, quenches his tail in the ocean, and flying through the sky high above the ocean, he returns to Rama, the source of his inspiration. His tail is intact.

NOTES

Introduction

1. Lamming, *The Pleasures of Exile*, 50.
2. Scott, "The Sovereignty of the Imagination," 162.
3. See Richards, "The Opium Industry"; and Frey, "The Indian Saltpeter Trade."
4. This amalgamated and simplified account of the British in India draws from various sources, such as Metcalf and Metcalf, *A Concise History of India*; and Asher and Talbot, *India before Europe*.
5. Edney, *Mapping India*.
6. Barrow, *Making History, Drawing Territory*.
7. For variations in colonial ethnographic practices, see Morrison, "Three Systems of Imperial Ethnography."
8. Frere, *Old Deccan Days*, xix. See Prasad, "The Authorial Other" for a contextualization of this period and an assessment of Frere's collection. To understand the history of Europe's interest in antiquarian subjects before Mary Frere's mid-nineteenth-century call, see Cocchiara, *History of Folklore in Europe*. For instance, William Camden's 1586 Latin work *Brittania* emerged from his "walking tours" through English counties to reconstruct traces of Britain's past; the natural philosopher John Aubrey's two-volume *Miscellanies* (1696) recorded English beliefs about the marvelous; the clergyman Henry Bourne defended "popular customs" in his *Antiquitates Vulgares* (1725); and Bishop Percy's *Reliques of Ancient English Poetry* (1765) celebrated oral ballads. Influenced by Giambattista Vico's *Scienza Nuova* (1744), English scholars turned away from Roman roots and looked to their Gaelic heritage to recover an English identity—for example, James MacPherson's *Works of Ossian* (1765) presented a Gaelic counterpart to Homer. Continental philosophers Jean-Jacques Rousseau and Johann Gottfried Herder bolstered interest in rustic cultures. See Bendix, *In Search for Authenticity*, for the emergence of folklore studies in Germany and North America.
9. For how institutional attempts were made to systematize this effort at mapping India, see Islam, *A History of Folklore Collections*; Datta, *Affinities between Folkloristics and Historiography*; Korom and Lowthorp, *South Asian Folklore in Translation*.
10. For instance, Sadhana Naithani in *In Quest of Indian Tales* shows how the administrator William Crooke appropriated tales that had actually been collected and translated by the scholar Ram Gharib Chaube of Uttar Pradesh; Gloria Raheja, in "The Illusion of Consent," studies the extensive collection of proverbs by British administrators across north India. She finds that British collectors severed proverbs from their vital lived contexts and expediently used them in administrative discourse to serve whatever administrative end they could be made to serve.

11. For an incisive analysis of Richard Carnac Temple's role in seeding the study of folklore in India, see Naithani, "The Colonizer-Folklorist."

12. Vatuk, "Shurreef, Herklots, Crooke, and *Qanoon-e-Islam.*"

13. Rouse, *The Talking Thrush and Other Tales from India,* viii.

14. There is a rich literature that traces the many careers of the term "folklore" in the Indian context. The term "folklore" had been coined as a "good Anglo-Saxon" word in 1846 by the antiquarian William Thoms. See Emrich, "Folk-Lore." Unsurprisingly, it developed in the background of Greco-Roman understandings of classicality; see Porter, *Classical Pasts.* For how the wide range of linguistic, cultural, and philosophical orientations in South Asian cultures made the term extremely imprecise, see Blackburn and Ramanujan, *Another Harmony.* For a further reassessment, see Korom and Lowthorp, *South Asian Folklore in Transition.*

15. Anaryan, *A Group of Hindoo Stories,* 26.

16. The Folklore Society (FLS) Archive, University College London (UCL) Special Collections. Later published as "A Folktale from Kumaon," *Folklore* 8, no. 2 (June 1897): 181–84.

17. Letters dated October 20, 1920, and January 22, 1922, University of Reading Publisher Archives, Records of Macmillan & Co., Ltd., 88/8.

18. Day, *Folk-Tales of Bengal,* ix. Gammer Grethel is the pseudonym of the famous narrator of the Grimms' tales. The Grimm brothers tell us that in real life she was a Frau Viehmännin, wife of a peasant from the state of Hesse-Cassel in western Germany.

19. For example, see Crooke, review of *Indian Folklore,* 368.

20. Ram Satya Mukharji, *Indian Folklore* (Calcutta: Sanyal Press, 1904).

21. Bhabha, "Of Mimicry and Man," 130.

22. Scott, *Domination and the Arts of Resistance,* xii.

23. Hatcher, *Vidyasagar,* 111.

24. Scott, "The Sovereignty of the Imagination," 122.

25. Foucault, *Power/Knowledge;* Agamben, *State of Exception.* See also Stoler, "On Degrees of Imperial Sovereignty."

26. Stein, *Vijayanagara.*

27. Talbot, *Precolonial India in Practice,* 147.

28. Singh, *Poverty and the Quest for Life,* esp. chap. 2, "The Headless Horseman," 33–58.

29. Jalal, *Self and Sovereignty;* Moin, *The Millennial Sovereign.*

30. Mayaram, *Against History, Against State.*

31. Banerjee, *The Mortal God,* 398.

32. Skaria, *Unconditional Equality,* 242.

33. Dirks, *Castes of Mind.*

34. Two analyses of Kantian moral vocabulary are especially useful; see essays by Thomas Hill and Andrews Reath in Sensen, *Kant on Moral Autonomy.*

35. Banerjee, *The Mortal God,* 24.

36. Newton, *Narrative Ethics,* 11.

1. The Ruse of Colonial Modernity

1. Steel and Gardiner, *The Complete Indian Housekeeper,* ix.

2. *Gazetteer of the Bombay Presidency: Poona,* 370.

3. *Lascar*, from a Persian word for soldier; a tent lascar was a native tent pitcher.

4. See Leela Prasad, "'Folk' and 'Classical'" in India: Conversations in Continuity" (MA thesis, Kansas State University, 1991); also Prasad, "Anklets on the Pyal," and the encyclopedia entries "Folklore about the British," "Mary Frere," and "Pandit S. M. Natesa Sastri."

5. Papers of Sir Bartle Frere, Oriental and India Office Collection (OIOC), MSS Eur. F81/51 (A-C): 1866–1881.

6. October 18, 1867, Frere letters, John Murray Archive.

7. The book was translated in Europe into German, Hungarian, and selectively into Danish, and in India into Marathi, Gujarati, and "Hindustani."

8. Frere, "The Collector's Apology," in *Old Deccan Days*, 4th ed. (1898), xix. All quotations from *Old Deccan Days* are from this edition unless I indicate otherwise.

9. Frere, "Preface," in *Old Deccan Days*, xi.

10. Narayan points out in her edition of *Old Deccan Days* that some reviewers of the book praised the reproduction of "broken English" while others disliked it.

11. The handwritten manuscript held in the OIOC of the British Library is closest to the third edition of 1881. It does not, however, contain Bartle Frere's introduction, the notes, and the glossary. In addition, the manuscript has accretions presumably from the original draft of 1868, such as blocks of text that did not make it into any edition.

12. In a delightful coincidence of interests, Kirin Narayan and I both found ourselves fascinated by this collection and referred to it in various publications. During the period 2001–2, when she was working toward a new introduction to an ABC Clio edition of *Old Deccan Days* and I was working on an article about the collection (Prasad, "The Authorial Other"), we shared our research stories with each other. She alerted me to the Frere papers in the OIOC in the British Library, and I drew her attention to Frere correspondence in the John Murray Archive. Much in agreement with each other, we discussed our findings and shared some notes that informed our individual publications.

13. North, *Recollections of a Happy Life*, 72–73.

14. August 14, 1872, Frere letters, John Murray Archive.

15. "The Collector's Apology," xviii.

16. "The Collector's Apology," xix.

17. "The Collector's Apology," xix.

18. Frere, "The Narrator's Narrative," in *Old Deccan Days*, xxix.

19. Bergson, *Creative Mind*, 109.

20. Bergson, *Creative Evolution*, 194.

21. Polanyi, "Sense-Giving and Sense-Reading," 306, 307.

22. See Bhabha, "The Other Question."

23. Kipling, *Something of Myself*, 4, emphasis added. I chased down Kipling's papers at his archives in Sussex in the UK to check whether Kipling's Portuguese Roman Catholic ayah was Anna Liberata. The physical description had matched, and the Freres' return to England in 1867 coincided with the hiring of Kipling's Goan ayah by his parents in Bombay. Further, the Kiplings and the Freres had known each other socially (See Lycett, *Rudyard Kipling*). But I discovered that Kipling saw his ayah again in 1891, by which time Anna had died, so Anna could not have been Kipling's ayah.

24. Colesworthey, *Anglo-Indian Domestic Life*. There is vast scholarship on various facets of the "domestic empire." On the status of the ayah per se in English homes,

see Chaudhuri, "Memsahibs and Their Servants in Nineteenth-Century India"; Conway, "*Ayah*, Caregiver to Anglo-Indian Children"; and Walsh, *Domesticity in Colonial India*. For examples from South Africa, see Comaroff and Comaroff, "Home-Made Hegemony." More broadly, for how the notion of the family came to be variably restructured in colonial domesticity, see the essays in Chatterjee, *Unfamiliar Relations*. For the impact of colonialism on employer-servant relationships in middle-class families in colonial Bengal, see Banerjee, *Men, Women, and Domestics*. The question of how conceptions and practices of empire were profoundly gendered has been studied considerably; see, for instance, Burton, *Dwelling in the Archive*; Chaudhuri and Strobel, *Western Women and Imperialism*; Grewal, *Home and Harem*; Procida, *Married to Empire*; Sangari and Vaid, *Recasting Women*; and Sen, *Gendered Transactions*.

25. Such as Paget, *Camp and Cantonment*.

26. Steel and Gardiner, *The Complete Indian Housekeeper*, 86.

27. Review in *Lippincott's Magazine of Literature, Science and Education*, December 1868, 678, 677–78.

28. *Bombay Saturday Review*, 241–45.

29. *Edinburgh Review*, October 1868, 352, emphasis added.

30. Letter dated October 21, 1879, in Long, *The Journals*, 305–6.

31. "Preface," Third edition, xi.

32. "The Narrator's Narrative," xxxi.

33. "The Narrator's Narrative," xxviii.

34. "The Narrator's Narrative," xxiii.

35. "The Narrator's Narrative," xxviii.

36. "The Narrator's Narrative," xxx.

37. Narayan estimated this time frame in 2002.

38. Mary Frere to John Murray, October 29, 1867, Frere letters, John Murray Archive. I could not locate the actual photograph referenced here.

39. North, *Recollections of a Happy Life*, 73.

40. "Preface," ix.

41. Frere, "Biographical Notice," in *Old Deccan Days*, v–vii.

42. The size of this contingent of helpers should not surprise us; after all, a married British couple, usually of lower- to middle-class status in Britain, without children in the Bombay Presidency would employ upwards of twenty servants. See Chaudhuri, "Memsahibs and Their Servants"; and Burton, *Dwelling in the Archive*.

43. Letter to Robert Napier, Acting Viceroy to India, December 19, 1865, Papers of Sir Bartle Frere, OIOC, MSS Eur. F 81/51A.

44. "Preface," x.

45. "Biographical Notice," v.

46. "Preface," x.

47. "Preface," Third edition.

48. Chatterjee, *Black Hole*, xi–xii.

49. Papers of Sir Bartle Frere, OIOC, MSS Eur. F 81/51A, emphasis added.

50. "A Mem Sahib in Plague-Stricken Bombay," *Temple Bar*, 120, no. 474 (May 1900): 64–92.

51. "The Narrator's Narrative," xxxi.

52. "The Narrator's Narrative," xxxi.

53. Frere, "Punchkin," in *Old Deccan Days*, 9.

54. "The Narrator's Narrative," xxxi.

55. Letter to John Murray, October 29, 1867, Frere letters, John Murray Archive.

56. "The Narrator's Narrative," xxix, xxxi.

57. Virginia Murray to Leela Prasad, February 7, 2001, London, in author's possession.

58. Mary Frere to John Murray, September 14, 1888, Frere letters, John Murray Archive.

59. In a letter from Mary Frere, September 22, 1896, Frere letters, John Murray Archive.

60. W. F. Littleton to Mother, October 21, 1879, William Francis Littleton Letters, 1877–1880, A721/I/6763, University of Witwatersrand Historical Papers Research Archive.

61. Edward Whymper, a well-known Victorian mountaineer and illustrator, was commissioned by John Murray to create the woodcuts for *Old Deccan Days*.

62. Mary Frere to John Murray, December 12, 1867, Frere letters, John Murray Archive.

63. Metcalf, *An Imperial Vision*, 14.

64. In 1862, after the dissolution of the East India Company, the college building and grounds were converted to a high school called Haileybury, which today has a residence hall named the Bartle Frere House after its imperial alum. https://www.haileybury.com/explore/boarding/boarding-houses/bartle-frere-boys.

65. Later Frere lost the affections of Parliament with his fiasco in Africa. In 1876, after Frere had worked to advise the Council of India and completed two foreign missions (first, to curb the Zanzibar slave trade, and second, to accompany the Prince of Wales on his tour of India), he was asked to become the governor of Cape Colony. In Frere's eyes, this was the compensatory equivalent of India's viceroyalty, which he had been tipped for but never given. Here he met his political downfall in attempting to create a confederation of the various states and colonies of southern Africa. The idea received stiff resistance from the independent African polities, and in a miscalculation, Frere issued a near impossible ultimatum to the Zulu king, Sekhukuni. The resulting Zulu-British war of 1879 resulted in heavy losses for the British, and soon afterwards, in 1880, Bartle Frere was recalled to England. A glorious career came to an ignominious end. See Benyon, "Frere." Also Ranade, *Sir Bartle Frere and His Times*; and Martineau, *Life and Correspondence of Sir Bartle Frere*.

66. George, "Homes in the Empire."

67. Kalamdani and Kalamdani, "Conservation of The Main Building," 88.

68. Russell, *The Prince of Wales' Tour*, 159–60.

69. Hull, *The European in India*, 112.

70. Lewis and Siemiatycki, "Building Urban Infrastructure."

71. From the diary of Joseph Fayrer, physician to Queen Victoria and the Prince of Wales, we know that the entourage stayed in the government houses that once had been home to the Frere family. While Fayrer met with his former domestic staff, there is no indication in either this memoir by Fayrer or the Frere correspondence that Bartle Frere looked up Anna or any of his old servants. Fayrer, *Notes of the Visits to India*, 73.

72. Russell, *The Prince of Wales' Tour*, 159.

73. *Gazetteer of the Bombay Presidency: Dharwar*, 539.

74. Tripathi, *The Oxford History of Indian Business*.

75. "The Narrator's Narrative," xxiv–xxv.

76. "The Narrator's Narrative," xxv.

77. Chatterjee, *The Black Hole of Empire*, 197.

78. Frere, "Note B," in *Old Deccan Days*, 217–18.

79. Duara, "The Discourse of Civilization and Pan-Asianism," 100.

80. Viswanathan, *Masks of Conquest*, 26.

81. "The Narrator's Narrative," xxvi.

82. "The Narrator's Narrative," xxvi.

83. Bloomer, *Possessed by the Virgin*, 10.

84. Dempsey, *Kerala Christian Sainthood*, 53.

85. Frere, "Introduction," in *Old Deccan Days*, xi.

86. Stokes, "Notes," in *Indian Fairy Tales*, 237.

87. Mill, *The History of British India*, 98.

88. In 1826 two vernacular schools were opened by the government. By 1865–66 there were ninety-six schools: eighty-three vernacular, eleven Anglo-vernacular, one high school, and one training college. *Gazetteer of the Bombay Presidency: Poona*, 52.

89. "The Narrator's Narrative," xxxi.

90. Nagarajan, "Children of Macaulay."

91. Elphinstone, *Report of the Territories*, 53. An earlier version of the report was circulated to Elphinstone's collectors in 1819.

92. "The Narrator's Narrative," xxix.

93. That policy on "education of India" remained a contentious issue throughout Company and Crown rule is evidenced by the observations of Arthur Mayhew, the director of public instruction, who said in 1926: "[British] education has done far less for Indian culture than for the material and political progress of India. She looks to our schools and colleges for equipment in the struggle for existence: for the secret of happy living, *vivendi causae*, she looks elsewhere." Mayhew, *The Education of India*, 4. One would, of course, want to debate whether "material and political progress" was such an assured achievement.

94. *Gazetteer of the Bombay Presidency: Poona*, 51.

95. Mary Frere to John Murray, October 20, 1870, Frere letters, John Murray Archive.

96. Prasad, "The Authorial Other," 24.

97. An ayah in Bombay in the 1870s was paid eighteen rupees per month (less than £2). See Hull, *The European in India*.

98. "The Narrator's Narrative," 23. For stories of ayahs who found themselves abandoned in England after being courted to accompany their English employers, see Visram, *Ayahs, Lascars and Princes*. Also see http://www.open.ac.uk/researchprojects/makingbritain/content/ayahs-home http://www.ourmigrationstory.org.uk/oms/a-home-for-the-ayahs-https://doi.org/10.1177/097152150901600301.

99. *The Little Papers*, 7.

100. *Report of the Administration of Bombay Presidency*, 299–300.

2. The History of the English Empire as a Fall

1. Email communication, July 17, 2013, reproduced with permission.
2. See Parthasarathy, "A Deceptively Naïve First Play in Tamil," 44.
3. Ramaswami Raju, "Stray Thoughts on the Religious Life of the Hindus," 304.
4. By this phrase, Dipesh Chakrabarty refers to the decentering of the imaginary but influential figure of Europe as the default referent and standard of modernity prevalent in scholarly discourses and everyday thought. See Chakrabarty, *Provincializing Europe*.
5. Ramaswami Raju, *The Tales of the Sixty Mandarins*, xi–xii.
6. For a list of South Asian members of the Inner Temple (one of the four Inns of Court) during 1864–1929, see https://hosted.law.wisc.edu/wordpress/sharafi/files/2010/07/Inner-Temple-List-25-Oct-2012.pdf.
7. Letter to the Secretary of University College London, December 9, 1882, UCL Special Collections, MS 1640/246/291.
8. Today the high school in Kanchipuram exists as a college. Pachiappah's has several branches in Tamil Nadu.
9. Although I have not been able to trace it, the search committee report (1883) mentions that Ramaswami Raju had written a Telugu play called *Subba Bhatlu, or the Village Poorohit* (priest), which, we learn from a testimonial, had been "performed with great success by the Sanskrit Dramatic Society." UCL Special Collections, MS 1640/246/291.
10. Report of the Committee on Lectureships in the Vernacular Languages of India, April 12, 1883, UCL Special Collections, MS 1640/246/291.
11. Letter dated March 5, 1883, UCL Special Collections, MS 1640/246/291.
12. The names Gog and Wire come from the world of towboats and steamships, apt for a seafaring country. Gogs, or chains and ropes, and wires are essential to the technology that brings ships into the harbor—implying the mechanics of a colonial enterprise that depended on its naval strength. House, *Marine Emergencies*.
13. Ramaswami Raju, *Lord Likely*. Unless otherwise noted, all quotations from the play are from act 3, scene 1, 22–23.
14. Ramaswami Raju, *Srīmat Rājāṅgala Mahodyānam;* henceforth *The Great Park*.
15. *Lord Likely,* act 2, scene 3, 13–16.
16. Alex Watson, "Phantom Museum," https://wsimag.com/art/20625-the-phantom-museum, accessed August 6, 2018.
17. See Shresth, "Sahibs and Shikar."
18. Davis, *Lives of Indian Images*; de Almeida and Gilpin, *Indian Renaissance*.
19. Chatterjee, *Black Hole of Empire*.
20. Dalyrmple and Anand, *Koh-i-Noor*.
21. Grewal, *Sikhs of the Punjab*.
22. Wahi, "Henry Miers Elliot."
23. H. T. W., "Flowers of Anglo-Indian Literature."
24. Bhabha, *The Location of Culture*, 88.
25. Houfe, *Dictionary of 19th Century British Book Illustrators*, 77.
26. *Sixty Mandarins*, xi, xiii–xiv, emphasis added.

27. *Sixty Mandarins*, xv. Maha Mondon, we will later see, is a sacred place in the imaginary cosmos of Ramaswami Raju's *The Great Park*—in which he tells us it is between Varanasi and Allahabad in north India. More on this later in the chapter.

28. Hui, "The Idea of Asia and Its Ambiguities," 986.

29. Duara, "Asia Redux," 983.

30. Alfred C. Lyall, home secretary to the government hencof of India, represents a fairly standard English view that England's occupation of Asia, and particularly of India, had brought a "flood of clear daylight in upon Asia at large." Lyall, *Asiatic Studies*, vi.

31. Azad, *Sacred Landscape in Medieval Afghanistan*, 4.

32. *Sixty Mandarins*, 84.

33. Qassem, "The Arab Story"; Lewis, " The Arab Destruction."

34. Gettleman and Schaar, "Abu Ali al-Husayn ibn Sina," 26–27.

35. *Sixty Mandarins*, xiii, 74.

36. Kramrisch, "Aditi-Uttānapad," 153.

37. Smith, "The Lotus as Tiger," 40.

38. These conversations took place in in English and Telugu between 2013 and 2018.

39. Email conversations over the summer of 2018.

40. Later collectively published as *Indian Fables* (1889).

41. Oral conversation, July 24, 2013. Interestingly, some of the testimonials in the P. V. Ramaswami Raju Correspondence, UCL Special Collections (MS 1640/246/291), mention this work, although I have been unable to find a copy. It is possible that Ramaswami Raju may have begun conceptualizing *Rajangala Mahodyanam* (*The Great Park*) and perhaps even composed small parts of it that colleagues and others learned about.

42. Oral conversation, April 2014.

43. *The Great Park*, 44.

44. Ramaswami Raju does not use diacritical marks. He makes his position on the subject clear: "The spelling of the English language has its own patent imperfections. They have been regretted from time to time by distinguished men, who have perceived the necessity for their mother tongue being represented by rational combinations of sounds. But *mamool* [habit] is all powerful. All the tyranny of the despots of the world, from the last day of the deluge to the minute that we pen these lines in, cannot compare with the tyranny of the custom which has been keeping the Queen's English in the condition in which it is in the manner of spelling. In spite of this, some *savants* in the west have nobly endeavoured to give to themselves a programme of phonetic representation anent Sanscrit names which has done more justice to their eagerness to sound Sanscrit reasonably than to the capacity of the people at large to utilize it. We need not trouble ourselves with these learned representations of Sanscrit sounds for the present." Ramaswami Raju, "Stray Thoughts on the Religious Life of the Hindus," 84.

45. *The Great Park*, unnumbered last page.

46. Page numbers in citations of *The Great Park* henceforth will refer to Ramaswami Raju's English translation, while verse numbers will refer to Giridhara Shastry's translation of the Sanskrit text.

47. The subject of self-translation, gawky as the term may be, in translation studies questions the vocabulary that has been standard in the field. Concepts such as

"original," "author," "translator," and "source text/target text" become unsettled in a literary practice in which the author and translator are the same individual, who explores and performs his or her many authorial selves, sometimes contrapuntally. For an overview, see Grutman, "Self-Translation." Self-translation draws attention to where the translational process occurs across the texts in question, amidst the movements of self across time and place, and across different language cultures and political circumstances. See Skaria, *Unconditional Equality*, for instance, for how Gandhi translates from Gujarati to English; Pannikar, "Self-Translation as Self-Righting," for translation practices across Malayalam and English in the works of Vijayan; and Asaduddin, "Lost/Found in Translation," on Qurratulain Hyder's translation of her Urdu and English-language novels.

48. Narayana Rao and Shulman, *Śrīnātha*, 72.

49. Narayana Rao, "Purana as Brahminic Ideology," 89. My all-too-brief summation of *purāṇa* scholarship draws on Narayana Rao, "Purāṇa" and Rocher, *The Purāṇas*.

50. Narayana Rao, Shulman, and Subrahmanyam, *Textures of Time*, 18.

51. Mandalas are prominent in Buddhist, Jain, and Hindu art, ritual, architecture, and individual spiritual practice. While the symbolism of the mandala varies widely across history and tradition, a core conceptualization is that it metaphorically reflects and reins in individual and cosmic energies. Bühnemann, *Mandalas and Yantras*.

52. "Three Maha Mondon Pur" we may remember is where Wazir Abdul Ali, whom Ramaswami Raju consulted for *Sixty Mandarins*, lived.

53. "Consciousness is infinite"; "I am that infinite"; "You are that [infinite]"; and "The self is infinite." Respectively, *prajñānam brahma, ayam ātmā brahma, tat tvam asi* and *aham brahmāsmi*.

54. Pollock, *The Language of the Gods*.

55. *The Great Park*, unnumbered last page.

56. Edgar, *The Royal Parks*.

57. *The Great Park*, unnumbered preface.

58. *The Great Park*, 2.

59. Shastry, trans., *The Great Park*, verses 43 and 45.

60. The mantra is part of the Rudram, which forms two chapters in the Taittiriya Samhita of the Krishna Yajurveda.

61. Rig Veda 3.62.10.

62. Prattis, "Mantra and Consciousness Expansion in India," 85.

63. For an excellent ethnographic study of mantra theory and practice in everyday life, see Rao, *Living Mantra*.

64. *The Great Park*, 5.

65. Pandey, "The Civilized and the Barbarian," 20.

66. *The Great Park*, 5–6.

67. *The Great Park*, 21, 29.

68. There is a great deal of scholarship on this subject, some of which I have summarized in *Poetics of Conduct*. For a focused treatment, see Elizabeth Kolsky, *Colonial Justice in British India: White Violence and the Rule of Law* (Cambridge: Cambridge University Press, 2010).

69. *The Great Park*, 7.

70. *The Great Park*, 21.

71. See, for example, Doty, *Mythography*.

72. Doniger, *The Implied Spider*, 3.

73. *The Great Park*, 43–44.

74. Partha Chatterjee points out that the term "the British Empire" first appeared in public discourse during the Seven Years' War (1756–1763), especially after Britain's gains over France in terms of overseas territory. Chatterjee, *Black Hole of Empire*, 49.

75. Childs, "1492–1494," 763–64. See also Scammel, "Essay and Reflection."

76. *The Great Park*, 57, 58.

77. *The Great Park*, 62, 65, 63.

78. Bleichmar, "The Geography of Observation," 378–80.

79. *The Great Park*, 65–66.

80. *The Great Park*, 67.

81. *The Great Park*, 72, 73.

82. *The Great Park*, 75.

83. *The Great Park*, 74.

84. *The Great Park*, 92.

85. Shastry, trans., *The Great Park*, verses 463–67.

86. I had known Dr. Shastry from my earlier fieldwork in Sringeri (Karnataka). See Prasad, *Poetics of Conduct*.

87. http://www.tnarchives.tn.gov.in/aboutus.html.

88. Ramaswami Raju, *Urjoon Sing*, 75, 81.

3. The Subjective Scientific Method

1. One version of this popular story can be read at https://www.thehindu.com/todays-paper/tp-features/tp-sundaymagazine/The-temple-of-Munroe/article15401887.ece.

2. Venkataswami, *Tulsemmah and Nagaya*, 86. Almost every region of India robustly told and performed stories about the colonial British, their policies, everyday interactions with them, and their cultural otherness and othering. See Prasad, "Folklore about the British."

3. *Gumasta* is a word of Persian origin for "clerk" or "accountant"—who could in fact oversee a broader range of tasks in an administration. *Mahanadu* in Telugu parlance means "great assembly."

4. Venkataswami, *Folk-Stories of the Land of Ind*, 1 (end of the book).

5. At the time when Venkataswami was studying at Hislop, it was an affiliated college of Calcutta University.

6. Venkataswami, *The Story of Bobbili*; *Tulsemmah and Nagaya*; *Heeramma and Venkataswami*; *Folk-Stories of the Land of Ind*; *Life of M. Nagloo*; and *101 Essays*.

7. Koilpillai, *The SPCK in India*.

8. Mantena, *The Origins of Modern Historiography*.

9. Burne, *The Handbook of Folklore*, 2.

10. Daston and Galison, *Objectivity*, 204. See also Pels, "After Objectivity."

11. Daston and Galison, *Objectivity*, 204.

12. See Narayan, "How Native Is a 'Native' Anthropologist?" Also Peacock, "Belief Beheld"; and Orsi, *Between Heaven and Earth*.

13. See, for example, Steel and Temple, *Wide-Awake Stories*, widely considered a model for folktale collection and presentation.

14. For instance, Johannes Fabian, *Time and the Other: How Anthropology Makes Its Object* (New York: Columbia University Press, 2014). Clifford and Marcus, *Writing Culture*; Clifford, *Predicament of Culture*. This turn, however, did not extend to recognizing the politics of gender, as was called out, for example, by Gordon, "Writing Culture, Writing Feminism"; Mills, "Feminist Theory and the Study of Folklore"; Visweswaran, *Fictions of Feminist Ethnography*; and Behar and Gordon's anthology *Women Writing Culture*.

15. Chakrabarty, *Provincializing Europe*, 239.

16. The Folk-Lore Society of London records that he was a member in 1898.

17. *Folk-Stories of the Land of Ind*, xxii–xxiii.

18. Other stories similarly puncture the power and superiority ascribed to the British. One, for example, ascribes the greater gifts of the English to the delay on the part of the Indian in reaching God, who was bestowing boons; the Indian and the Englishman were both answering the call of nature. The Indian had lost time washing himself thoroughly with water, while the Englishman quickly "made himself clean at once with a piece of paper that lay by, and running speedily presented himself [to God] first." *Heeramma*, 140.

19. *Tulsemmah*, 125.

20. *Tulsemmah*, 125.

21. Bergson, *Creative Evolution*.

22. *Tulsemmah*, viii–ix; *Nagloo*, vi.

23. *Nagloo*, vi.

24. Ngũgĩ, *Something Torn and New*, 28.

25. Nagloo was known as Maidara Nagaya or Nagannah in his community but among Europeans as Nagloo.

26. *Nagloo*, 39.

27. The summary becomes necessary because the book is not easily available to readers.

28. *Nagloo*, 13.

29. *Nagloo*, 24.

30. *Nagloo*, 22.

31. *Nagloo*, 36. "Palmer Sab" is the controversial financier William Palmer, who made large loans to the Hyderabad government and later fell out of favor with the East India Company. See Leonard, "Banking Firms."

32. *Nagloo*, 47. Bandar is the popular name of Machilipatnam (then Masulipatnam), a coastal town, then part of the Madras Presidency. *Basti* is the Urdu word for "settlement" or "neighborhood." In the context of the biography, Bandarbasti is the neighborhood in Kamptee where people from Bandar ("Bandarawandlu") lived.

33. *Nagloo*, 48.

34. Richard Temple's son was Richard Carnac Temple, author of the three-volume *Legends of the Punjab* (1884–1900) and *Wide-Awake Stories* with Flora Annie Steel (1884).

35. *Nagloo*, 90.

36. *Nagloo*, 109–10.

37. *Nagloo*, 171, 169.

38. *Bhonds* are people from the Kurmi caste, an agricultural community; Somasis are from the Mahar caste, generally weavers or laborers; the Pola bullock festival is celebrated by members of the Kunbi agricultural caste. Some glosses from R. V. Rus-

sell and Rai Bahadur Hira Lal, *The Castes and Tribes of the Central Provinces of India*, vol. 1 (London: Macmillan, 1916).

39. *Nagloo*, 145–46.

40. *Nagloo*, 146, 151–52.

41. *Nagloo*, 191.

42. *Nagloo*, 208.

43. *Nagloo*, 208. The verse translation is Venkataswami's.

44. See Chakrabarty, *The Calling of History* for an elaboration of Sarkar's opinion on the matter of historical truth.

45. Sarkar, "Life Story of a Great Pariah"; and Ali, "A Great South Indian Pariah."

46. *Nagloo*, i. The reference is to a story in the Chandogya Upanishad about a young boy, Satyakama, who, as was the custom, in order to be accepted as a student by his prospective teacher, was required to reveal his patrilineal lineage. When Satyakama asks this information of his mother, Jabala, she tells him that since she had moved among various men during her youth when she was working, she did not know who the father was. She suggests he identify himself as Satyakama ("one who loves the truth") and take on Jabala" as his lineal name. The sage who hears this from Satyakama admires him for this honesty, remarking that only a Brahmin could have spoken thus, and accepts him. The story has been variously interpreted to understand what the word "Brahmin" means. See Chandogya Upanishad 4.4.9, in O'Flaherty, *Textual Sources for the Study of Hinduism*, 32–33.

47. *Nagloo*, vi.

48. For an insightful and thorough assessment of the many entanglements around this issue in the public sphere, see Viswanath, *The Pariah Problem*.

49. Ali, "A Great South Indian Pariah," 439.

50. *Nagloo*, 234–35.

51. Venkataswami's ethnographic observations on caste are revealing. They expose the wooden understanding of caste in nationalist reform agendas. Lived realities, instead, show that caste designations are fluid, particular to region and to local conceptions of honor.

52. These exchanges are explored in Kumar, *Radical Inequality*; and in Skaria, "Gandhi's Politics," which work out the stakes involved in Gandhi's and Ambedkar's arguments over terminologies.

53. Gandhi correspondence, January 1929, Sabarmati Ashram Library, S.N. 16015.

54. *Nagloo*, 214.

55. *Nagloo*, 232–34.

56. Scott, "The Sovereignty of the Imagination," 75, 125.

57. Chakrabarty, *The Calling of History*, 26.

58. *Nagloo*, vi–viii, 159. The Greek biographer Plutarch (first to second century CE) influenced the evolution of the essay, biography, and historical writing. His *Parallel Lives* was especially influential in Europe between the sixteenth and nineteenth centuries. Duff, "General Introduction."

59. *Nagloo*, 59.

60. *Nagloo*, 108, my translation.

61. Here we must be careful to distinguish the concept of "ample history" from Robert Orsi's "abundant history." For Orsi, an abundant history is one that recog-

nizes the presence of the transcendent in a religious practitioner's life. A historian, Orsi urges, should construct abundant histories that engage interactions between transcendent time and worldly time. Such a representation would call for a rethinking of the analytical terms generally used by historians. Orsi, *History and Presence.*

62. Clough, *Social Christianity in the Orient.*

63. See especially White, *Metahistory*; and Carr, "Narrative and the Real World."

64. *Nagloo*, 50.

65. *Nagloo*, 56–57.

66. *Nagloo*, 57–59.

67. Two immensely popular Telugu films were based on it, *Bobbili Yuddham* (1964) and *Tandra Paparayudu* (1986).

68. Narayana Rao, Shulman, and Subrahmanyam, in their "On the Battle of Bobbili, January 1757," compare three prominent Telugu tellings of the Bobbili story: Peddada Mallesam's *Bobbili Yuddha Katha*, recorded in 1832; *Pedda Bobbili Raju Katha* (undated); and Dittakavi Narayanakavi's *Rangaraya Charitramu*, 1909. It is not my focus here to understand Venkataswami's version in light of the essay's insightful argument that each version presents a unique historical configuration with its own poetics, a "texture of time." According to the authors, C. P. Brown employed a minstrel by the name of Mallesam who recited the *Bobbili Yuddha Katha* in addition to two other oral epics in 1832. The Telugu scholar M. Somasekhara Sarma collected various manuscripts of the *Bobbili Yuddha Katha* and published an edited version (1956); he notes that many of these manuscript versions are attributed to Mallesam, who now appears as a bardic figure in them. The ways in which versions and variants crisscross with each other is fascinating to study. *Pedda Bobbili Raju Katha*, which Venkataswami disparages, and Mallesam's version both seem to have taken their material from some even earlier telling that would have been closer to the events of 1757. What is especially interesting for us is a detail that Somasekara Sarma provides—that among earlier versions of the Bobbili story is an ending in which the surviving son of Ranga Ravu meets the nizam of Hyderabad twelve years after the war. A reconciliation takes place in Venkataswami's version, making me wonder if Venkataswami's bards were telling a fairly early version of the story, or at least incorporating its elements.

69. Katten, *Colonial Lists / Indian Power*, provides a comparative reading of the *Bobbili* version, focusing on the caste identity and self-construction around it among the Velamas.

70. *Bobbili*, xii. I have not been able to trace the particular Telugu history of Bobbili that Venkataswami refers to. It is possible, however, that Venkataswami, who had been in touch with Venkata Swetachalapati Ranga Rao, the raja of Bobbili, for his photograph to include on the title page, was aware of the raja's book *A Revised and Enlarged Account of the Bobbili Zemindari* (Madras: Printed by Addison, 1900).

71. Robert Orme, *A History of the Military Transactions of the British Nation in Indostan—from the year MDCCXLV*, 3 vols. (London: Printed for J. Nourse, 1763–1778), 2:254–60.

72. The *Pedda Bobbili Raju Katha* is an oral epic that was most likely a performance transcript. For a translation of its telling of the story, see Narayana Rao, Shulman, and Subrahmanyam, "On the Battle of Bobbili, January 1757," 42–50.

73. *Bobbili*, xvii.

74. *Bobbili,* ix.

75. *Bobbili,* 72.

76. *Bobbili,* 68.

77. *Bobbili,* 65.

78. *Bobbili,* xvi.

79. In Dussen, *History as a Science,* 136.

80. *Bobbili,* viii–ix.

81. Chakrabarty, *The Calling of History,* 26.

82. Sarkar, "Foreword," c.

83. Sarkar, "Foreword," b-c.

84. *Tulsemmah,* xi.

85. For a history of this effort, see Falconer, "'A Pure Labor of Love.'"

86. See Mathur, *India by Design,* for an excellent study of how some Indians resisted being displayed.

87. Casey, *Remembering,* 218.

88. Ngũgĩ, *Something Torn and New,* 9.

89. *Nagloo,* 174, 175, 132.

90. Lakshmi Narayana is a form of Vishnu.

91. *Heeramma,* 181.

92. *Heeramma,* vi.

93. *Heeramma,* viii. James Lubbock was a nineteenth-century astronomer.

94. *Heeramma,* 181.

95. *Heeramma,* 83.

96. *Heeramma,* 192.

97. Pinney, *The Coming of Photography in India.*

98. Pinney, *Photography and Anthropology.*

99. Tylor, "Dammann's Race-Photographs," 184.

100. Gordon, "A City of Mourning."

101. Chaudhary provides an incisive analysis of this project in *Afterimage of Empire,* especially in chapter 1.

102. Desmond, "19th Century Indian Photographers in India," 315.

103. Gordon, "A City of Mourning."

104. Dewan and Hutton, *Raja Deen Dayal,* 27. For an interpretation of Deen Dayal's work through the lens of mimesis, see Chaudhary, *Afterimage of Empire,* 122–31.

105. Alkazi, "Foreword," 7.

106. *Nagloo,* 185.

107. *Heeramma,* 120–24.

108. *Heeramma,* 123.

109. *Heeramma,* 124.

110. I follow Venkataswami's use of "cenotaph" and "tomb" interchangeably—a usage that is in keeping with the family's practice of interment and memorialization.

111. *Heeramma,* 124.

112. *Nagloo,* 196.

113. *Heeramma,* x.

114. *Nagloo,* 193.

115. *Nagloo,* 244.

116. Preface to *Heeramma,* vii.

117. *Heeramma*, 96–98.

118. *Heeramma*, 96.

119. Benjamin, *The Work of Art in the Age of Its Technological Reproducibility*, 21.

120. Khanna, *Dark Continents*, 25.

121. Benjamin, *The Work of Art*, 27.

122. Email communication, March 24, 2004, reproduced with permission.

123. *101 Essays*.

124. Narendra Luther, *Lashkar: The Story of Secunderabad* (Hyderabad: Kalakriti Art Gallery, 2010).

125. *101 Essays*, 153–54.

126. Audio-recorded conversation, May 2010. Polygamy was legally outlawed in 1956. See Menski, *Modern Indian Family Law*, 194.

127. Audio-recorded conversation, August 20, 2013.

128. Audio-recorded conversation, June 14, 2014.

129. Audio-recorded conversation, June 14, 2014.

4. The Irony of the "Native Scholar"

1. As I describe in chapter 2, Mr. Muthaiah later helped me trace the descendants of Ramaswami Raju. Mr. Muthaiah passed away in April 2019.

2. The most detailed biographical sketch is an anonymously authored note in "Men and Women of India" (1908), included in the posthumously published *Indian Folk-Tales* by Natesa Sastri. R. E. Asher, in "Pandit S. M. Natesa Sastri (1859–1906): Pioneer Tamil Novelist," and Kamil Zvelebil, in *Tamil Literature* assess Natesa Sastri's impact on Tamil literature and also provide biographical details about Natesa Sastri. Stuart Blackburn considers Natesa Sastri's contribution to Tamil nationalism in *Print, Folklore, and Nationalism*.

3. Zvelebil, "The Amazing Natesa Sastri (1859–1906)," 204.

4. "Madras Miscellany," *The Hindu*, October 15, 2001.

5. Italics in this transcript indicate my observations and explanations. Text in brackets is also mine, mostly to provide detail.

6. Colonial monumentality became especially visible to me during the making of this book. I learned, without any manifest relevance to Natesa Sastri, that James Brodie, an officer in the East India Company, had drowned in the Adyar River in 1802. Harwood, *The Genealogist*, 53. A monument to Brodie commemorates him in Saint Mary's Cemetery, about five miles from Gopalakrishnan's house.

7. Ramanujan, *Folktales from India*, xxiii.

8. Prasad, "Pandit S. M. Natesa Sastri" and "The Authorial Other."

9. Narayan, *Everyday Creativity*, 225.

10. Rouse, "Power/Knowledge," 9.

11. Natesa Sastri, "Sanskrit vs. Vernaculars."

12. Cited in Singh, *The Discovery of Ancient India*, 316.

13. "Men and Women of India," 8–9.

14. *Illustrated Weekly* 93 (1972): 235.

15. J. Natarajan, *History of Indian Journalism* (New Delhi: Ministry of Information and Broadcasting, 1955), 135–36.

16. Ganesan, *The Press in Tamil Nadu*, 49.

17. For instance, in his article titled "Kalakshepas—Old and New," he decries what he regards as degradation in new-style puranic storytelling performances, arguing that storytellers had become flamboyant and possessed only a "smattering [of] knowledge of a few puranic tales." Natesa Sastri, *Hindu Feasts*, 55.

18. Govindarajan, *Builders of Modern India*.

19. It is no longer news that idiosyncratic remuneration, dis-acknowledgment, and seismic textual transformations characterized colonial knowledge projects. See Cohn, *Colonialism and Its Forms of Knowledge*; Dirks, *Castes of Mind*; Raheja, "Caste, Colonialism, and the Speech of the Colonized"; and Bayly, *Empire and Information*.

20. Guha-Thakurta, *Monuments, Objects, Histories*, 89.

21. Rocher, "British Orientalism in the Eighteenth Century."

22. Hatcher, "What's Become of the Pandit?" 693, 696. Wilson's remark was made in 1836, but the sentiment prevailed throughout the colonial era.

23. Personal conversation with Velcheru Narayana Rao, November 22, 2017.

24. Beauchamp, "Introduction," iii–iv.

25. Beauchamp, incidentally, was the editor of the second edition (1897) of J. A. Dubois's infamous *Hindu Manners, Customs and Ceremonies*, a work that the French scholar Sylvia Murr found was plagiarized.

26. Wilkins, *Modern Hinduism*.

27. This is an extremely rare use of the term. One other instance where it appears is in *Bengali Household Tales* (1912) by the missionary William McCullough, who describes the narrator this way: "[The young Bengali Brahman man] possessed fine gifts, both as a talker and a *raconteur*" (v).

28. Cardew, "Introduction," 4, 5.

29. Olcott, "South Indian Folklore," 319.

30. Natesa Sastri, *The Dravidian Nights Entertainments*, ii–iii.

31. Guha-Thakurta, *Monuments, Objects, Histories*, 3, 89.

32. Natesa Sastri, "Two Eastern Chalukya Copper Plates," 51, 53.

33. Natesa Sastri, "Notes on the Tiruvellarai Inscriptions," 264.

34. This detail is also mentioned by Stuart Blackburn, who cites the Tamil encyclopedia *Kalaikkaḷañciyam* (1959) published by the Tamil Propagation Society. Blackburn, *Print, Folklore, and Nationalism*, 167.

35. Sewell, *Lists of the Antiquarian Remains*. 5.

36. Robert Sewell, *Lists of Inscriptions and Sketch of the Dynasties of Southern India*, Archaeological Survey of Southern India, vol. 2 (Madras: E. Keys, 1884), 2.

37. Gopinatha Rao, "Ariyur Plates," 12.

38. *Hindu Feasts*, 40–41.

39. *Hindu Feasts*, 4. Sudras are broadly the labor caste in the traditional varna or caste system, and are not taught the Vedas and the Upanishads. Many Hindu *shastras* and the Brahmanical tradition prohibit Sudras from reciting Vedic texts.

40. For example, he translated and adapted into Tamil Sudraka's *Mrcchakatitika* and Vishakadatta's play *Mudraraksasa* on the Mauryan king Chandragupta's life, and also rendered into prose Kalidasa's celebrated epic *Raghuvamsa*.

41. Natesa Sastri, *Folklore in Southern India*, pt. 3, ix.

42. We might recall that Richard Carnac Temple's father was Richard Temple, who had been commissioner of the Central Provinces when Nagaya was setting

up his hotel (chapter 3), and had been the governor of Bombay in whose bungalow Marianne North ran into Anna de Souza (chapter 1).

43. *Folklore in Southern India*, pt. 3, vii–viii.

44. Natesa Sastri, "Origin of the Srivaishnavas," 255.

45. *Print, Folklore, and Nationalism*, 170.

46. Srinivas's fieldnotes and analytical materials were destroyed by an arsonist's fire while he was visiting Stanford University, and the richly detailed book is a testimony to the resilience and creativity of human memory and experience. M. N. Srinivas, *The Remembered Village* (Berkeley: University of California Press, 1976).

47. Mrs. Howard Kingscote [Adeline Georgiana Kingscote], *The English Baby in India*, 109–10, 116.

48. Natesa Sastri, *Tales of the Sun*, v–vi.

49. "The Conquest of Fate," tale 19, in *Tales of the Sun*, 237; and tale 26 in pt. 4 of *Folklore in Southern India*, 323.

50. Jacobs, *Indian Fairy Tales*, 232.

51. Hartland, "Report of Folk-Tale Research," 113.

52. https://doi.org/10.1093/ref:odnb/53497 (accessed January 6, 2019).

53. Chichester and Burges-Short, *Records and Badges of the British Army*.

54. http://www.headington.org.uk/history/famous_people/kingscote.htm. My thanks to Stephanie Jenkins, who maintains this website.

55. Fenby, *Other Oxford*, 81.

56. *Bournemouth Visitor's Directory*, September 19, 1908.

57. Raheja, "The Illusion of Consent," 122.

58. Raheja, "The Ajaib-Gher," 47.

59. Naithani, *Folktales from Northern India* and *In Quest of Indian Folktales*. Such appropriation of credit is a recurrent theme in colonial context. See Dirks, *Castes of Mind* for how the first surveyor general of India, Colin Mackenzie, passed off the findings of his brilliant polyglot "assistants," the scholar-brothers Kavelli Venkata Boria and Lakshmaiah, as his own.

60. Asher, "Pandit S. M. Natesa Sastri (1859–1906)," 109.

61. Natesa Sastri, *Tales of an Indian Detective* (1894).

62. See Asher's "Pandit S. M. Natesa Sastri (1859–1906)" and "The Tamil Renaissance" for a summary and analysis of Natesa Sastri's six novels. The other novels' translated titles are *The Rejuvenation of Komalam* (1902), *The Two Orphans* (1902), *A Wife Condoned* (1903), *The Mother-in-Law in Council* (1903), and *Curtain Lectures* (1907). For a review of the emergence of the Tamil novel in the nineteenth century, see Sundaram, "Pioneers of the Tamil Novel"; and Sundararajan, "The Tamil Novel as a Social Document."

63. Preface in Gopalakrishnan's translation, iii.

64. I use Gopalakrishnan's unpublished translation of *Dinadayalu*.

65. Chap. 10 of Gopalakrishnan's translation, 62, 65.

66. Personal email communication, February 21, 2002.

67. Narayan, *Everyday Creativity*, 225.

68. One is reminded of Jahan Ramazani's observations about A. K. Ramanujan's poetry: "With its multiple reflections and opacities, its sameness and difference, the family is frequently the locus of Ramanujan's poetic acts of self-definition. Across a

wide array of lyrics, the poet defines himself by sorting through his resemblances with his grandparents, parents, children, siblings, and wife." *The Hybrid Muse*, 97.

69. Personal email communication, February 21, 2002.

70. Oral conversation, July 8, 2016.

71. Chap. 10 of Gopalakrishnan's translation, 10. The Karna mantra is recited during the final moments of a departing person's life.

Conclusion

1. The spectacular complexity of this "empire" of Indian writing in English can be seen through many lenses: literary historiography, colonial education policy and institutions, and "world literature," for example. Illustrative studies, both monographs and edited anthologies, are Anjaria, *A History of the Indian Novel in English*; Joshi, *In Another Country*; Mehrotra, *A History of Indian Literature in English*; Mufti, *Forget English!*; Mukherjee, *The Perishable Empire*; Nagarajan, "Children of Macaulay"; and Viswanathan, *Masks of Conquest*.

2. Scott, "The Sovereignty of the Imagination," 147, 123.

3. The account I provide relies on Arshia Sattar's translation of the Valmiki Ramayana (2018), and on the oral tellings that I heard growing up in various parts of India. The Valmiki Ramayana has Hanuman narrating the story of Rama many times in the text, each intervention contributing to the mood and direction of the epic. See Sattar's dissertation "Hanuman in the Ramayana of Valmiki" (PhD diss., University of Chicago, 1990) for Hanuman's various roles as a narrator.

4. Lutgendorf, *Hanuman's Tale*, 35.

5. Sattar, *Vālmīki's Rāmāyaṇa*, 305.

6. Sattar, *Vālmīki's Rāmāyaṇa*, 321.

7. Sattar, *Vālmīki's Rāmāyaṇa*, 357.

8. Sattar, *Vālmīki's Rāmāyaṇa*, 377, 378.

BIBLIOGRAPHY

Special Collections Consulted

Archive of British Publishing and Printing, University of Reading
John Murray Archive, National Library of Scotland, Edinburgh
Oriental and India Office Collection, British Library, London
National Archives of India, New Delhi
Sabarmati Ashram Library, Ahmedabad, India
Tamil Nadu Archives, Chennai, India
University College London (UCL) Archives and Special Collections
University of Witwatersrand Historical Papers Research Archive, Johannesburg

References

Agamben, Giorgio. *State of Exception*. Translated by Kevin Attell. Chicago: University of Chicago Press, 2005.

Ali, Zahur S. "A Great South Indian Pariah." In *Life of M. Nagloo*, by M. N. Venkataswami, vii–xvi. Madras: Solden & Co., 1929.

Alkazi, Ebrahim. "Foreword: Photography: Art and Ritual." In *Painted Photographs: Coloured Portraiture in India*, edited by Ebrahim Alkazi, Rahab Allana, and Pramod Kumar, 7–9. Ahmedabad: Mapin Publishing, 2008.

Anaryan [F. F. Arbuthnot]. *A Group of Hindoo Stories*. London: W. H. Allen, 1881.

Anderson, Kristine J. "Self-Translators." In *Encyclopedia of Literary Translation into English*, edited by Olive Classe, 1250–52. Chicago: Fitzroy Dearborn, 2000.

Anjaria, Ulka, ed. *A History of the Indian Novel in English*. Cambridge: Cambridge University Press, 2015.

Asaduddin, M. "Lost/Found in Translation: Qurratulain Hyder as Self-Translator." *Annual Journal of Urdu Studies* 23 (2008): 234–49.

Asher, Catherine B., and Cynthia Talbot. *India before Europe*. Cambridge: Cambridge University Press, 2006.

Asher, R. E. "The Tamil Renaissance and the Beginnings of the Tamil Novel." *Journal of the Royal Anthropological Society* (1969): 13–28.

——. "Pandit S. M. Natesa Sastri (1859–1906): Pioneer Tamil Novelist." *Proceedings of the Second International Conference Seminar of Tamil Studies.* (1971): 107–15.

Azad, Arezou. *Sacred Landscape in Medieval Afghanistan: Revisiting the Fāḍ'il-i-Balkh*. London: Oxford University Press, 2013.

Banerjee, Milinda. *The Mortal God: Imagining the Sovereign in Colonial India*. Cambridge: Cambridge University Press, 2018.

Banerjee, Swapna. *Men, Women, and Domestics: Articulating Middle-Class Identity in Colonial Bengal*. New Delhi: Oxford University Press, 2004.

Barrow, Ian. *Making History, Drawing Territory: British Mapping in India, c. 1756–1905*. New Delhi: Oxford University Press, 2003.

Bayly, Christopher A. *Empire and Information: Intelligence Gathering and Social Communication in India, 1780–1870*. Cambridge: Cambridge University Press, 1996.

Beauchamp, Henry. Introduction. In *Hindu Feasts, Fasts and Ceremonies*, by Natesa Sastri, iii–vi. Madras: ME Publication House, 1903.

Behar, Ruth, and Deborah Gordon, eds. *Women Writing Culture*. Berkeley: University of California Press, 1995.

Bendix, Regina. *In Search of Authenticity: The Formation of Folklore Studies*. Madison: University of Wisconsin Press, 1997.

Benjamin, Walter. *The Work of Art in the Age of Its Technological Reproducibility and Other Writings on Media*. Edited by Michael W. Jennings, Brigid Doherty, and Thomas Y. Levin. Cambridge: Belknap Press of Harvard University Press, 2008.

Benyon, John. "Frere, Sir (Henry) Bartle Edward, First Baronet." In *Oxford Dictionary of National Biography*. Accessed March 2, 2018. https://doi.org/10.1093/ref:odnb/10171.

Bergson, Henri. *Creative Evolution*. Translated by Arthur Mitchell. New York: Random House, 1944.

———. *Creative Mind*. Translated by Mabelle Andison. New York: Philosophical Library, 1946.

Bhabha, Homi K. "Of Mimicry and Man: The Ambivalence of Colonial Discourse." *Discipleship: A Special Issue on Psychoanalysis* (1984): 125–33.

———. "The Other Question: Difference, Discrimination and the Discourse of Colonialism." In *Out There: Marginalization and Contemporary Cultures*, edited by Russell Ferguson, 71–87. New York: New Museum of Contemporary Art, 1990.

———. *The Location of Culture*. London: Routledge, 1994.

Blackburn, Stuart. *Print, Folklore, and Nationalism in Colonial India*. New Delhi: Permanent Black, 2003.

Blackburn, Stuart, and A. K. Ramanujan. Introduction. In *Another Harmony: New Essays on the Folklore of India*, edited by Stuart Blackburn and A. K. Ramanujan, 1–37. Berkeley: University of California Press, 1986.

Bleichmar, Daniela. "The Geography of Observation: Distance and Visibility in Eighteenth-Century Botanical Travel." In *Histories of Scientific Observation*, edited by Lorraine Daston and Elizabeth Lunbeck, 373–95. Chicago: University of Chicago Press, 2011.

Bloomer, Kristin. *Possessed by the Virgin: Hinduism, Roman Catholicism, and Marian Possession in South India*. New York: Oxford University Press, 2018.

Bombay Saturday Review of Politics, Literature and Commerce 10, no. 11 (March 1868): 241–45.

Bühnemann, Gudrun. *Mandalas and Yantras in the Hindu Traditions*. Boston: Brill, 2003.

Burne, Charlotte Sophia. *The Handbook of Folklore*. London: Folklore Society, 1913.

Burton, Antoinette M. *Dwelling in the Archive: Women Writing House, Home, and History in Late Colonial India*. New York: Oxford University Press, 2003.

Cardew, A.G. Introduction. In *Indian Folk-Tales*, by Natesa Sastri, 4–5. Madras: Guardian Press, 1908.

Carr, David. "Narrative and the Real World: An Argument for Continuity." *History and Theory* 25 (1986): 117–31.

Casey, Edward S. *Remembering: A Phenomenological Study*. Bloomington: Indiana University Press, 1987.

Chakrabarty, Dipesh. *Provincializing Europe: Postcolonial Thought and Historical Difference*. Princeton: Princeton University Press, 2000.

———. *The Calling of History: Sir Jadunath Sarkar and His Empire of Truth*. Chicago: University of Chicago Press, 2015.

Chatterjee, Indrani, ed. *Unfamiliar Relations: Family and History in South Asia*. Delhi: Permanent Black, 2004.

Chatterjee, Partha. *The Black Hole of Empire: History of a Global Practice of Power*. Princeton: Princeton University Press, 2012.

Chaudhary, Zahid R. *Afterimage of Empire: Photography in Nineteenth-Century India*. Minneapolis: University of Minnesota Press, 2012.

Chaudhuri, Nupur. "Memsahibs and Their Servants in Nineteenth-Century India." *Women's History Review* 3, no. 4 (1994): 549–62.

Chaudhuri, Nupur, and Margaret Strobel, eds. *Western Women and Imperialism: Complicity and Resistance*. Bloomington: Indiana University Press, 1992.

Chichester, Henry M., and George Burges-Short. *Records and Badges of the British Army*. 1900. 2nd ed. London: Frederick Muller, 1970.

Childs, Wendy R. "1492–1494: Columbus and the Discovery of America." *Economic History Review* 48, no. 4 (1995): 754–68.

Clifford, James. *The Predicament of Culture: Twentieth-Century Ethnography, Literature, and Art*. Cambridge: Harvard University Press, 1988.

Clifford, James, and George E. Marcus, eds. *Writing Culture: The Poetics and Politics of Ethnography*. Berkeley: University of California Press, 1986.

Clough, Emma. *Social Christianity in the Orient: The Story of a Man, a Mission, and a Movement*. New York: Macmillan, 1914.

Cocchiara, Guiseppe. *History of Folklore in Europe*. Philadelphia: Institute for the Study of Human Issues, 1981.

Cohn, Bernard. *Colonialism and Its Forms of Knowledge*. Princeton: Princeton University Press, 1996.

Colesworthey, Grant. *Anglo-Indian Domestic Life: A Letter from an Artist in India to His Mother in England*. Calcutta: Thacker, Spink, 1862.

Comaroff, Jean, and John L. Comaroff. "Home-Made Hegemony: Modernity, Domesticity and Colonialism in South Africa." In *African Encounters with Domesticity*, edited by Karen T. Hansen, 38–74. New Brunswick: Rutgers University Press, 1992.

Conway, Suzanne. "Ayah, Caregiver to Anglo-Indian Children, c. 1750–1947." In *Children, Childhood and Youth in the British World*, edited by Simon Sleight and Shirleene Robinson, 41–58. London: Palgrave Macmillan, 2016.

Crooke, William. Review of Ganeshji Jethabhai, *Indian Folklore. Folklore: A Quarterly Review* (1904): 368.

Dalrymple, William, and Anita Anand. *Koh-i-Noor: The History of the World's Most Infamous Diamond*. London: Bloomsbury, 2017.

Daston, Lorraine, and Peter Galison. *Objectivity*. New York: Zone Books, 2007.

Datta, Birendranath. *Affinities between Folkloristics and Historiography*. Chennai: National Folklore Support Centre, 2002.

Davis, Richard H. *Lives of Indian Images*. Princeton: Princeton University Press, 1997.

Day, Lal Behari. *Folk-Tales of Bengal*. London: Macmillan, 1883.

de Almeida, Hermione, and George L. Gilpin. *Indian Renaissance: British Romantic Art and the Prospect of India*. New York: Routledge, 2016.

Dempsey, Corinne. *Kerala Christian Sainthood: Collisions of Culture and Worldview in South India*. New York: Oxford University Press, 2001.

Desmond, R. "19th Century Indian Photographers in India." *History of Photography* 1, no.4 (1977): 313–17.

Dewan, Deepali and Deborah Hutton. *Raja Deen Dayal: Artist Photographer in 19th-Century India*. New Delhi: The Alkazi Collection of Photography, 2013.

Dirks, Nicholas. *Castes of Mind: Colonialism and the Making of Modern India*. Princeton: Princeton University Press, 2001.

Doniger, Wendy. *The Implied Spider: Politics and Theology in Myth*. New York: Columbia University Press, 2011.

Doty, William. *Mythography: The Study of Myths and Rituals*. Tuscaloosa: University of Alabama Press, 2000.

Duara, Prasenjit. "The Discourse of Civilization and Pan-Asianism." *Journal of World History* 12, no. 1 (Spring 2001): 99–130.

——. "Asia Redux: Conceptualizing a Region for Our Times." *Journal of Asian Studies* 69, no. 4 (November 2010): 963–83.

Duff, Timothy. General Introduction. In *The Age of Alexander*, by Plutarch, xv–xxix. Translated by Ian Scott-Kilvert and Timothy Duff. New York: Penguin, 2011.

Dussen, Jan Van Der. *History as a Science: The Philosophy of R. G. Collingwood*. Amsterdam: Springer, 2011.

Edgar, Donald. *The Royal Parks*. London: W. H. Allen, 1986.

Edney, Matthew H. *Mapping an Empire: The Geographic Construction of British India, 1765–1843*. Chicago: University of Chicago Press, 1997.

Elphinstone, Monstuart. *Report of the Territories Conquered from the Paishwa*. Calcutta: Government Gazette Press, 1821.

Emrich, Duncan. "'Folk-Lore': William John Thoms." *California Folklore Quarterly* 5 (1946): 355–74.

Falconer, John, "'A Pure Labor of Love': A Publishing History of *The People of India*." In *Colonialist Photography: Imag(in)ing Race and Place*, edited by E. Hight and G. Sampson, 51–83. London: Routledge, 2000.

Fayrer, Joseph. *Notes of the Visits to India of Their Royal Highnesses the Prince of Wales and Duke of Edinburgh, 1870–1875*. London: Kerry & Endean, 1879.

Fenby, Charles. *The Other Oxford: The Life and Times of Frank Gray and His Father*. London: Lund Humphries, 1970.

Foucault, Michel. *Power/Knowledge: Selected Interviews and Other Writings, 1972–1977*. Edited by Colin Gordon. New York: Pantheon, 1980.

——. *Technologies of the Self: A Seminar with Michel Foucault*. Edited by Luther H. Martin, Huck Gutman, and Patrick H. Hutton. Amherst: University of Massachusetts Press, 1988.

Frere, Georgina. "Biographical Notice." In *Catalogue of the Printed Books and of the Semitic and Jewish MSS in the Mary Frere Hebrew Library*, edited by Herbert Loewe, v–xii. Cambridge: Girton College, 1916.

Frere, Mary. *Old Deccan Days, or, Hindoo Fairy Legends Current in Southern India. Collected from Oral Tradition*. London: John Murray, 1868. Second edition, 1870; third edition, 1881; fourth edition, 1898.

Frey, James W. "The Indian Saltpeter Trade, the Military Revolution, and the Rise of Britain as a Global Superpower." *The Historian* 71, no. 3 (2009): 507–54.

Ganesan, A. *The Press in Tamil Nadu and the Struggle for Freedom, 1917–1937*. New Delhi: Mittal, 1988.

Gazetteer of the Bombay Presidency: Dharwar. Vol. 22, edited by James M. Campbell. Bombay: Government Central Press, 1884.

Gazetteer of the Bombay Presidency: Poona. Vol. 18, no. 3, edited by James M. Campbell. Bombay: Government Central Press, 1885.

George, Rosemary M. "Homes in the Empire, Empires in the Home." *Cultural Critique* 26 (Winter 1993–94): 95–127.

Gettleman, Marvin, and Stuart Schaar. "Abu Ali al-Husayn ibn Sina [Avicenna]: The Ideal Muslim Intellectual (11th Century)." In *The Middle East and Islamic World Reader*, 26–28. New York: Grove Press, 1997.

Gopalakrishnan, Chandrachudan, trans. *Dinadayalu*. Unpublished English translation, 2016.

Gopinatha Rao, A. "Ariyur Plates of Virupaksha, Saka Samvat 1312." *The Indian Antiquary* 38 (1909): 12–16.

Gordon, Deborah A. "Writing Culture, Writing Feminism: The Poetics and Politics of Experimental Ethnography." *Inscriptions* 3, no. 4 (1988): 6–24.

Gordon, Sophie. "A City of Mourning: The Representation of Lucknow, India in Nineteenth-Century Photography." *History of Photography* 30, no. 1 (2006): 80–91.

Gover, Charles E. *The Folk-songs of Southern India*. Higginbotham: Madras, 1871.

Govindarajan, S. A. *Builders of Modern India: G. Subramania Iyer*. New Delhi: Publications Division, Ministry of Information and Broadcasting, Government of India, 1969.

Grewal, Inderpal. *Home and Harem: Nation, Gender, Empire, and the Cultures of Travel*. Durham: Duke University Press, 1996.

Grewal, J. S. *The Sikhs of the Punjab*. New Cambridge History of India. Vol. 2, no. 3. Cambridge: Cambridge University Press, 1990.

Grutman, R. "Self-Translation." In *Routledge Encyclopedia of Translation Studies*, edited by M. Baker and G. Saldanha, 257–60. 2nd ed. London: Routledge, 2009.

Guha-Thakurta, Tapati. *Monuments, Objects, Histories: Institutions of Art in Colonial and Post-Colonial India*. Columbia University Press, 2004.

Hartland, Sidney. "Report on Folk-Tale Research." *Folk-Lore* 2 (1891): 99–122.

——. "Presidential Address." *Folk-Lore* 12 (1900): 15–40.

Harwood, Forsyth H. W., ed. *The Genealogist: A Quarterly Magazine of Genealogical, Antiquarian, Topographical and Heraldic Research* 21. London: George Bell & Sons, 1905.

Hatcher, Brian. "What's Become of the Pandit? Rethinking the History of Sanskrit Scholars in Colonial Bengal?" *Modern Asian Studies* 39, no. 3 (2005): 683–723.

———. *Vidyasagar: The Life and After-life of an Eminent Indian.* New York: Routledge, 2014.

Hokenson, J. W., and M. Marcella, eds. *The Bilingual Text: History and Theory of Literary Self-Translation.* London: Routledge, 2007.

Houfe, Simon. *The Dictionary of 19th Century British Book Illustrators and Caricaturists.* Woodbridge, UK: Antique Collectors' Club, 1996.

House, D. J. *Marine Emergencies: Ships and Mates.* Oxford: Routledge, 2014.

H. T. W. "Flowers of Anglo-Indian Literature." *Littel's Living Age* 137 (1878): 438–42.

Hui, Wang. "The Idea of Asia and Its Ambiguities." *Journal of Asian Studies* 69, no. 4 (November 2010): 985–89.

Hull, Edmund C. P. *The European in India or Anglo Indian's Vade Mecum.* London: Henry S. King & Co., 1871.

Islam, Mazharul. *A History of Folklore Collections in India, Bangladesh and Pakistan.* Calcutta: Panchal Prakasan, 1982.

Jacobs, Joseph. *Indian Fairy Tales.* London: D. Nutt, 1892.

Jalal, Ayesha. *Self and Sovereignty: Individual and Community in South Asian Islam since 1850.* London: Routledge, 2000.

James, Agatha. "Housekeeping and House Management in India." In *The Lady at Home and Abroad: Her Guide and Friend, Etc.* London: Abbott Jones and Co., 1898.

Joshi, Priya. *In Another Country: Colonialism, Culture, and the English Novel in India.* New York: Columbia University Press, 1995.

Kalamdani, Anjali and Kiran Kalamdani. *Conservation of the Main Building, University of Pune (Former Government House).* Unpublished report. Pune: Kimaya Architects, 2005.

Katten, Michael. *Colonial Lists/Indian Power: Identity Formations in Nineteenth-Century Telugu-Speaking India.* New York: Columbia University Press, 2005.

Khanna, Ranjana. *Dark Continents: Psychoanalysis and Colonialism.* Durham: Duke University Press, 2003.

Kingscote, Mrs. Howard. *The English Baby in India and How to Rear It.* London: J. & A. Churchill, 1893.

Kingscote, Mrs. Howard [Adeline Georgiana Kingscote] and Pandit S.M. Natesa Sastri. *Tales of the Sun: Or Folklore of Southern India.* London: W. H. Allen & Co., 1890.

Kipling, Rudyard. *Something of Myself.* London: Macmillan, 1937.

Koilpillai, Victor. *The SPCK in India:1710–1985.* Delhi: ISPCK, 1985.

Korom, Frank, and Leah Lowthorp, eds. *South Asian Folklore: A Handbook.* Westport, CT: Greenwood Press, 2006.

———. *South Asian Folklore in Transition: Crafting New Horizons.* New York: Routledge, 2018.

Kramrisch, Stella. "An Image of Aditi-Uttānapad." In *Exploring India's Sacred Art: Selected Writings of Stella Kramrisch*, edited by Barbara Stoler Miller, 148–58.

New Delhi: Indira Gandhi National Centre for the Arts & Motilal Banarsidass, 1983.

Kumar, Aishwary. *Radical Equality: Ambedkar, Gandhi, and the Risk of Democracy*. Stanford: Stanford University Press, 2015.

Lamming, George. *The Pleasures of Exile*. London: Michael Joseph, 1960.

Leonard, Karen. "Banking Firms in Nineteenth-Century Hyderabad Politics." *Modern Asian Studies* 15, no. 2 (1981): 177–201.

Lewis, Bernard. "The Arab Destruction of the Library of Alexandria: Anatomy of a Myth." In *What Happened to the Great Library of Alexandria*, edited by Mostafa el-Abbadi and Omnia Munir Fathallah, 213–17. Leiden: Brill, 2008.

Lewis, Robert, and Matti Siemiatycki. "Building Urban Infrastructure: The Case of Prince's Dock, Bombay." *Journal of Policy History* 27, no. 4 (2015): 722–45.

The Little Papers and the Monthly Papers of Mission News. London: J. Masters, 1881.

Long, Una, ed. *The Journals of Elizabeth Lees Price Written in Bechuanaland, Southern Africa, 1854–1883, with an Epilogue, 1889–1900*. London: Edward Arnold, 1956.

Lutgendorf, Philip. *Hanuman's Tale: The Messages of a Divine Monkey*. New York: Oxford University Press, 2007.

Lyall, Alfred, C. *Asiatic Studies: Religious and Social*. London: John Murray, 1884.

Lycett, Andrew. *Rudyard Kipling*. London: Orion Books, 2015.

Mantena, Rama. *The Origins of Modern Historiography in India: Antiquarianism and Philology*. New York: Palgrave Macmillan, 2012.

Martineau, John. *The Life and Correspondence of Sir Bartle Frere*. 2 vols. London: John Murray, 1895.

Mathur, Saloni. *India by Design: Colonial History and Cultural Display*. Berkeley: University of California Press, 2007.

Mayaram, Shail. *Against History, Against State: Counter-Perspectives from the Margins*. New York: Columbia University Press, 2003.

Mayhew, Arthur. *The Education of India*. London: Faber & Gwyer, 1926.

McCullough, William. *Bengali Household Tales*. London: Hodder and Stoughton, 1912.

McLaren, Martha. "From Analysis to Prescription: Scottish Concepts of Asian Despotism in Early Nineteenth-Century British India." *International History Review* 15, no. 3 (1993): 469–501.

Mehrotra, Arvind K, ed. *A History of Indian Literature in English*. New York: Columbia University Press, 2003.

"Men and Women of India." In *Indian Folk-Tales*, edited by Pandit S. M. Natesa Sastri, 7–11. Madras: Guardian Press, 1908.

Menski, Werner. *Modern Indian Family Law*. New York: Routledge, 2013.

Metcalf, Barbara D., and Thomas R. Metcalf. *A Concise History of India*. Cambridge: Cambridge University Press, 2002.

Metcalf, Thomas R. *An Imperial Vision: Indian Architecture and Britain's Raj*. Berkeley: University of California Press, 1989.

Mill, James. *The History of British India in Three Volumes*. Vol. 1. London: Baldwin Cradock and Joy, 1817.

Mills, Margaret. "Feminist Theory and the Study of Folklore: A Twenty-Year Trajectory toward Theory." *Western Folklore* 52, no. 2/4 (1993): 173–92.

Moin, A. Afzar. *The Millennial Sovereign: Sacred Kingship and Sainthood in Islam*. New York: Columbia University Press, 2014.

Morrison, Charles. "Three Systems of Imperial Ethnography: British Officials as Anthropologists in India." In *Knowledge and Society: Studies in the Sociology of Culture Past and Present*, edited by Henrika Kuklick and Elizabeth Long, 141–69. Greenwich, CT: JAI Press, 1984.

Mufti, Aamir R. *Forget English! Orientalisms and World Literatures*. Cambridge: Harvard University Press, 2016.

Mukherjee, Meenakshi. *The Perishable Empire: Essays on Indian Writing in English*. New Delhi: Oxford University Press, 2000.

Nagarajan, S. "Children of Macaulay." *New Quest* 46 (1984): 207–20.

Naithani, Sadhana. "The Colonizer-Folklorist." *Journal of Folklore Research* 34, no. 1 (1997): 1–14.

———, ed. *Folktales from Northern India by William Crooke and Pandit Ram Gharib Chaube*. Santa Barbara: ABC-CLIO, 2002.

———. *In Quest of Indian Folktales. Pandit Ram Gharib Chaube and William Crooke*. Bloomington: Indiana University Press, 2006.

Narayan, Kirin. "How Native Is a 'Native' Anthropologist?" *American Anthropologist* 95 (1993): 671–86.

———, ed. *Old Deccan Days by Mary Frere*. Santa Barbara: ABC-CLIO, 2002.

———. *Everyday Creativity: Singing Goddesses in the Himalayan Foothills*. Chicago: University of Chicago Press, 2016.

Narayana Rao, V. "Purāṇa." In *The Hindu World*, edited by S. Mittal and G. Thursby, 97–115. New York: Routledge, 2006.

Narayana Rao, V. "Purāṇa as Brahminic Ideology." In *Purana Perennis: Reciprocity and Transformation in Hindu and Jaina Texts*, edited by Wendy Doniger, 85–100. Albany: State University of New York Press, 1992.

———. *Text and Tradition in South India*. New Delhi: Permanent Black, 2016.

Narayana Rao, V., and David Shulman. *Śrīnātha: The Poet Who Made Gods and Kings*. Oxford: Oxford University Press, 2012.

Narayana Rao, Velcheru, David Shulman, and Sanjay Subrahmanyam. *Symbols of Substance: Court and State in Nayaka Period Tamilnadu*. Delhi: Oxford University Press, 1992.

———. "On the Battle of Bobbili, January 1757." In *Textures of Time: Writing History in South India, 1600–1800*, 25–92. New Delhi: Permanent Black, 2003.

———. *Textures of Time: Writing History in South India, 1600–1800*. New Delhi: Permanent Black, 2003.

Natesa Sastri, S. M. "Origin of the Srivaishnavas of Southern India." *Indian Antiquary* (1884): 252–55.

———. "Two Eastern Chalukya Copper Plates." *Indian Antiquary* (February 1884): 50–57.

———. *Folklore in Southern India*. 4 vols. Bombay: Education Society Press, 1884–1893.

———. *The Dravidian Nights Entertainments: Being a Translation of Madanakamarajankadai*. Madras: Excelsior Press, 1886.

———. *Tales of an Indian Detective*. Madras: Addison & Co., 1894.

———. *Medieval Tales of Southern India*. Madras: Madras School Book and Literature Society, 1897.

——. "Sanskrit vs. Vernaculars." *Madras Mail*, October 29, 1902.

——. *Hindu Feasts, Fasts and Ceremonies*. Madras: M. E. Publication House, 1903.

——. "Notes on the Tiruvellarai Inscriptions." *Indian Antiquary* (1905): 264–68.

——. *Indian Folk-Tales*. Madras: Guardian Press, 1908.

——. *Dinadayalu*. 1902. 2nd ed. Madras: Lawrence Asylum Steam Press, 2016.

Newton, Adam. *Narrative Ethics*. Cambridge: Harvard University Press, 1997.

Ngũgĩ wa Thiong'o. *Something Torn and New: An African Renaissance*. Philadelphia: BasicCivitas Books, 2009.

Nora, Pierre. "Between Memory and History: Les Lieux de Mémoire." *Representations* 26 (1989): 7–24.

North, Marianne. *Recollections of a Happy Life*. London: Macmillan, 1894.

O'Flaherty, Wendy D., ed., *Textual Sources for the Study of Hinduism*. Chicago: University of Chicago Press, 1990.

Olcott, Henry Steel. "South Indian Folklore." *The Theosophist* (February 1887): 319.

Orsi, Robert A. *Between Heaven and Earth: The Religious Worlds People Make and the Scholars Who Study Them*. Princeton: Princeton University Press, 2005.

——. *History and Presence*. Cambridge: Harvard University Press, 2018.

Paget, Georgiana T. *Camp and Cantonment: A Journal of Life in India in 1857–1859*. London: Longman Green Longman, Roberts & Green, 1865.

Pandey, Gyanendra. "The Civilized and the Barbarian." In *Hindus and the Others: The Question of Identity in India Today*, edited by Gyanendra Pandey, 10–34. New Delhi: Viking, 1993.

Pannikar, C. "Self-Translation as Self-Righting: O. V. Vijayan's *The Legends of Khasak*." In *Textual Travels: Theory and Practice of Translation in India*, edited by M. Chandran and S. Mathur, 21–34. Delhi: Routledge, 2015.

Parthasarathy, Indira. "A Deceptively Naïve First Play in Tamil." *Sruti* no. 350 (November 2013): 44.

Peacock, J. "Belief Beheld—Inside and Outside, Insider and Outsider in the Anthropology of Religion." In *Ecology and the Sacred: Engaging the Anthropology of Roy A. Rappaport*, edited by Ellen Messer and Michal Joshua Lambek, 207–26. Ann Arbor: University of Michigan Press, 2001.

Pels, Peter. "After Objectivity: An Historical Approach to the Intersubjective in Ethnography." *Hau: Journal of Ethnographic Theory* 4, no. 1 (2014): 211–36.

Pinney, Christopher. *The Coming of Photography in India*. London: British Library, 2008.

——. *Photography and Anthropology*. London: Reaktion Books, 2011.

Polanyi, Michael. "Sense-Giving and Sense-Reading." *Philosophy* 42 (1967): 301–25.

Pollock, Sheldon. *The Language of the Gods in the World of Men: Sanskrit, Culture, and Power in Premodern India*. Berkeley: University of California Press, 2006.

Porter, James, ed. *Classical Pasts: The Classical Traditions of Greece and Rome*. Princeton: Princeton University Press, 2006.

Prasad, Leela. "The Authorial Other in Folktales Collections in Colonial India: Tracing Narration and Its Dis/Continuities." *Cultural Dynamics* 15, no. 1 (2003): 5–44.

——. "Folklore about the British." In *South Asian Folklore: An Encyclopedia*, edited by Margaret Mills, Peter Claus, and Sarah Diamond, 77–79. New York: Routledge, 2003.

——. "Hospitality." In *South Asian Folklore: An Encyclopedia*, edited by Margaret Mills, Peter Claus, and Sarah Diamond, 287–89. New York: Routledge, 2003.

——. "Mary Frere." In *South Asian Folklore: An Encyclopedia*, edited by Margaret Mills, Peter Claus, and Sarah Diamond, 232–33. New York: Routledge, 2003.

——. "Pandit S. M. Natesa Sastri." In *South Asian Folklore: An Encyclopedia*, edited by Margaret Mills, Peter Claus, and Sarah Diamond, 436–38. New York: Routledge, 2003.

——. "Anklets on the Pyal: Women Present Women's Stories from South India." In *Gender and Story in South India*, edited by Leela Prasad, Ruth B. Bottigheimer, and Lalita Handoo, 1–33. Albany: State University of New York Press, 2006.

——. *Poetics of Conduct: Oral Narrative and Moral Being in a South Indian Town*. New York: Columbia University Press, 2007.

Prattis, Ian. "Mantra and Consciousness Expansion in India." *Journal of Ritual Studies* 16, no. 1 (2002): 78–96.

Procida, Mary A. *Married to the Empire: Gender, Politics, and Imperialism in India, 1883–1947*. Manchester: Manchester University Press, 2002.

Qassem, Abdou Qassem. "The Arab Story of the Destruction of the Ancient Library of Alexandria." In *What Happened to the Great Library of Alexandria*, edited by Mostafa el-Abbadi and Omnia Munir Fathallah, 207–12. Leiden: Brill, 2008.

Raheja, Gloria Goodwin. "Caste, Colonialism, and the Speech of the Colonized: Entextualization and Disciplinary Control in India." *American Ethnologist* 23, no. 3 (1996): 494–513.

——. "The Illusion of Consent: Language, Caste, and Colonial Rule in India." In *Colonial Subjects: Essays on the Practical History of Anthropology*, edited by Peter Pels and Oscar Salermink, 117–52. Ann Arbor: Michigan: University of Michigan Press, 1999.

——. "The Ajaib-Gher and the Gun Zam-Zammah: Colonial Ethnography and the Elusive Politics of 'Tradition' in the Literature of the Survey of India." *South Asia Research* 19, no. 1 (1999): 29–51.

Ramamurthi, K. S. "Drama (English)" In *Encyclopedia of Indian Literature*. Vol. 2, edited by A. Datta, 1069–71. New Delhi: Sahitya Akademi, 1988.

Ramanujan, A. K. *Folktales from India: A Selection of Oral Tales from Twenty-Two Languages*. New York: Pantheon Books, 1991.

Ramaswami Raju, P. V. *Lord Likely, A Drama*. Madras: Higginbotham, 1875.

——. *Urjoon Sing, or, The Princess Regained, An Indian Drama*. Madras: Christian Vernacular Education Society, 1876.

——. *Maid of the Mere, a Drama in Three Acts and Verse*. Madras: Higginbotham and Co, 1879.

——. *The Tales of the Sixty Mandarins*. London: Cassell and Co., 1886.

——. *Indian Fables*. London: Swan Sonnenschein, 1889.

——. *Srīmat Rājāṅgala Mahodyānam, or, The Great Park of Rajangala*. Kumbakonam: Sree Vidya Press, 1894.

——. "Stray Thoughts on the Religious Life of the Hindus." *Madras Review* 2 (1896): 73–304.

——. *Pratapa Chandra Vilasa, a prose drama in Tamil*. 1877. Chennai: Any Indian Pathippagam, 2006.

Ramazani, Jahan. *The Hybrid Muse: Postcolonial Poetry in English*. Chicago: University of Chicago Press, 2001.

Ranade, Rekha. *Sir Bartle Frere and His Times: A Study of his Bombay Years, 1862–1867*. New Delhi: Mittal Publications, 1990.

Rao, Mani. *Living Mantra: Mantra, Deity, and Visionary Experience Today*. Cham, Switzerland: Palgrave Macmillan, 2019.

Report of the Administration of Bombay Presidency. Bombay: Government Central Press, 1882.

Report of the Territories Conquered from the Paishwa. Calcutta: Government Gazette Press, 1821.

Richards, John F. "The Opium Industry in British India." *Indian Economic & Social History Review* 39 (2002): 375–430.

Rocher, Ludo. *The Purāṇas*. Weisbaden: Otto Harrassowitz, 1986.

Rocher, Rosane. "British Orientalism in the Eighteenth Century: The Dialectics of Knowledge and Government." In *Orientalism and Postcolonial Predicament: Perspectives on South Asia*, edited by Carol A. Brekenridge and Peter van der Veer, 215–49. Philadelphia: University of Pennsylvania Press, 1993.

Rouse, Joseph. "Power/Knowledge." *Division I Faculty Publications* 34 (2005): 1–20. https://wesscholar.wesleyan.edu/div1facpubs/34.

Rouse, W. H. D. *The Talking Thrush and Other Tales from India*. London: Dutton, 1922.

Russell, William Howard. *The Prince of Wales' Tour: A Diary in India*. New York: R. Worthington, 1878.

Sangari, Kumkum, and Sudesh Vaid, eds. *Recasting Women: Essays in Indian Colonial History*. New Brunswick: Rutgers University Press, 1990.

Sarkar, Jadunath. Foreword. In *The Story of Bobbili*, by M. N. Venkataswami, a–c. Hyderabad: Cheekoti Veerannah & Sons, 1912.

———. "Life Story of a Great Pariah." In *Life of M. Nagloo*, by M. N. Venkataswami, i–vi. Madras: Solden & Co., 1929.

Sattar, Arshia, trans. *Vālmīki's Rāmāyaṇa*. Lanham, MD: Rowman and Littlefield, 2018.

Scammell, G. V. "Essay and Reflection: On the Discovery of the Americas and the Spread of Intolerance, Absolutism, and Racism in Early Modern Europe." *International History Review* 13 (1991): 502–21.

Scott, David. "The Sovereignty of the Imagination: An Interview with George Lamming." *Small Axe* 12 (2002): 72–200.

Scott, James C. *Domination and the Arts of Resistance: Hidden Transcripts*. New Haven: Yale University Press, 1990.

Sen, Indrani. *Gendered Transactions: The White Woman in Colonial India, c. 1820–1930*. Manchester: Manchester University Press, 2017.

Sensen, Oliver. *Kant on Moral Autonomy*. New York: Cambridge University Press, 2013.

Sewell, Robert. *Lists of the Antiquarian Remains in the Presidency of Madras*. Archaeological Survey of Southern India. Madras: E. Keys, 1882.

Shastry, Giridhara. Unpublished translation of selected verses of P. V. Ramaswami Raju, *Srīmat Rājāṅgala Mahodyānam, or, The Great Park of Rajangala*. 2019.

Shresth, Swati. "Sahibs and Shikar: Colonial Hunting and Wildlife in British India, 1800–1935." PhD diss., Duke University, 2009.

Singh, Bhrigupati. *Poverty and the Quest for Life: Spiritual and Material Striving in Rural India*. Chicago: University of Chicago Press, 2015.

Singh, Upinder. *The Discovery of Ancient India: Early Archaeologists and the Beginnings of Archaeology*. New Delhi: Permanent Black, 2004.

Sivapathasundaram, S. "Rajangala Mahodyanam, a Rare Saga in Sanskrit." *Express Weekend,* December 9, 1989.

Skaria, Ajay. "Gandhi's Politics: Liberalism and the Question of the Ashram." *South Atlantic Quarterly* 101, no. 4 (2002): 955–86.

———. *Unconditional Equality: Gandhi's Religion of Resistance.* Minneapolis: University of Minnesota Press, 2016.

Smith, David. "The Lotus as Tiger: Aspects of the Symbolism of the Lotus in Kavya." *Quaderni del Dipartimento di Linguistica—Università di Firenze* 12 (2002): 27–45.

Spivak, Gayatri Chakravorty. "Can the Subaltern Speak?" In *Marxism and the Interpretation of Culture,* edited by Cathy Nelson and Lawrence Grossberg, 271–315. Urbana: University of Illinois Press, 1988.

Steel, Flora A. *Tales of the Punjab Told by the People.* London: Macmillan, 1894.

Steel, Flora A., and Grace Gardiner. *The Complete Indian Housekeeper and Cook.* London: Heinemann, 1888.

Steel, Flora A., and R. C. Temple. *Wide-Awake Stories.* Bombay: Education Society's Press, 1884.

Stein, Burton. *The New Cambridge History of India: Vijayanagara.* Cambridge: Cambridge University Press, 1989.

Stokes, Maive. *Indian Fairy Tales.* London: Ellis and White, 1880.

Stoler, Ann Laura. "On Degrees of Imperial Sovereignty." *Public Culture* 18, no. 1 (2006): 125–46.

Subrahmanyam, Sanjay. "Recovering Babel." In *Invoking the Past: The Uses of History in South Asia,* edited by Daud Ali, 280–321. Delhi: Oxford University Press, 1999.

Sundaram, Sivapatha S. "Pioneers of the Tamil Novel: New Discoveries." *Indian Literature* 21, no. 4 (July–August 1978): 25–39.

Sundararajan P. G. "The Tamil Novel as a Social Document." *Indian Literature* 21, no. 4 (July–August 1978): 10–24.

Swynnerton, Charles. *Indian Nights' Entertainment, or Folk-Tales from the Upper Indus.* London: Elliot Stock, 1892.

———. *Romantic Tales from the Panjab.* London: Archibald Constable and Company, 1903.

Talbot, Cynthia. *Precolonial India in Practice: Society, Region, and Identity in Medieval Andhra.* New York: Oxford University Press, 2001.

Temple, Richard Carnac. *Legends of the Panjab.* Vols. 1–3. Bombay: Educational Society's Press. 1884–1900.

Tripathi, Dwijendra. *The Oxford History of Indian Business.* Mumbai: Oxford University Press, 2004.

Tylor, Edward B. *Notes and Queries on Anthropology, For use of Travelers and Residents in Uncivilized Lands.* London: Edward Stanford, 1874.

———. "Dammann's Race-Photographs." *Nature* 13 (1876): 184–85.

Vatuk, Sylvia. "Shurreef, Herklots, Crooke, and *Qanoon-e-Islam:* Constructing an Ethnography of 'The Moosulmans of India.'" *South Asia Research* 19, no. 1 (1999): 5–28.

Venkataswami, M. N. *The Story of Bobbili.* Hyderabad: Cheekoti Veerannah & Sons, 1912.

——. *Tulsemmah and Nagaya, or, Folk-Stories from India*. Madras: Methodist Publishing House, 1918.

——. *Heeramma and Venkataswami; or Folktales from India*. Madras: SPCK, 1923.

——. *Folk-Stories of the Land of Ind*. Madras: Methodist Publishing House, 1927.

——. *Life of M. Nagloo (Maidara Nagaya)*. Madras: Solden & Co., 1929.

——. *101 Essays on Social and Literary Subjects*. Madras: Solden & Co., 1932.

Visram, Rozina. *Ayahs, Lascars and Princes: Indian in Britain, 1700–1947*. London: Pluto Press, 1986.

Viswanath, Rupa. *The Pariah Problem: Caste, Religion, and the Social in Modern India*. New York: Columbia University Press, 2014.

Viswanathan, Gauri. *Masks of Conquest: Literary Study and British Rule in India*. New York: Columbia University Press, 1989.

Visweswaran, Kamala. *Fictions of Feminist Ethnography*. Minneapolis: University of Minnesota Press, 1994.

Wahi, Tripta. "Henry Miers Elliot: A Reappraisal." *Journal of the Royal Asiatic Society of Great Britain and Ireland*, no. 1 (1990): 64–69.

Walsh, Judith. *Domesticity in Colonial India: What Women Learned When Men Gave Them Advice*. Lanham, MD: Rowman & Littlefield Publishers, 2004.

White, Hayden. *Metahistory: The Historical Imagination in Nineteenth-Century Europe*. Baltimore: Johns Hopkins University Press, 1973.

Wilkins, William J. *Modern Hinduism: Being an Account of the Religion and Life of the Hindus in Northern India*. London: T. Fisher Unwin, 1887.

Wilson. A. C. *Hints for the First Years of Residence in India*. Oxford: Clarendon Press, 1904.

Zvelebil, Kamil. *Tamil Literature: A History of Indian Literature*. Vol. 10, edited by Jan Gonda. Weisbaden: Otto Harrassowitz, 1974.

——. "The Amazing Natesa Sastri (1859–1906)." *Archiv Orientální* 63 (1995): 204–12.

INDEX

Page numbers in *italics* indicate illustrations. Titles of authored works will be found under the name of the author, unless otherwise indicated.

CPSIA information can be obtained
at www.ICGtesting.com
Printed in the USA
LVHW040100181120
671948LV00010B/1026